THE FEUD IN EARLY MODERN GERMANY

The practice of feuding amongst noblemen and princes represented a substantial threat to law and order, yet it was widely accepted and deeply
embedded in late medieval and early modern German society. Hillay
Zmora offers a new interpretation of this violent social practice, which
has long confounded historians and social scientists. His ground-breaking
study explains feud violence in its social context, demonstrating that, paradoxically, nobles feuded mostly not against strangers but with neighbours,
relatives and their feudal lords. Focusing on the ambivalent relationships
and symbolic communication between nobles, this study explores how
values, norms and moral sentiments linked to reciprocity provided the
most powerful incentives to engage in violent conflict. It will be essential
reading for historians, anthropologists, psychologists and anyone who
seeks to understand the link between culture, moral systems and endemic
violence.

HILLAY ZMORA is Professor of Early Modern History at Ben-Gurion University, Israel. His previous publications include *Monarchy, Aristocracy,
and the State in Europe, 1300–1800* (2001).

THE FEUD IN EARLY
MODERN GERMANY

HILLAY ZMORA

CAMBRIDGE
UNIVERSITY PRESS

CAMBRIDGE
UNIVERSITY PRESS

University Printing House, Cambridge CB2 8BS, United Kingdom

Cambridge University Press is part of the University of Cambridge.

It furthers the University's mission by disseminating knowledge in the pursuit of education, learning and research at the highest international levels of excellence.

www.cambridge.org
Information on this title: www.cambridge.org/9781107530430

© Hillay Zmora 2011

First published 2011
First paperback edition 2015

A catalogue record for this publication is available from the British Library

Library of Congress Cataloguing in Publication data
Zmora, Hillay, 1964–
The feud in early modern Germany / Hillay Zmora.
p.   cm.
Includes bibliographical references and index.
ISBN 978-0-521-11251-2
1. Dueling – Germany – History – 15th century.   2. Dueling – Germany – History – 16th century.   3. Vendetta – Germany – History – 15th century.   4. Vendetta – Germany – History – 16th century.   5. Vendetta – Social aspects – Germany – History – 15th century.   6. Vendetta – Social aspects – Germany – History – 16th century.   7. Nobility – Germany – History – 15th century.   8. Nobility – Germany – History – 16th century.   I. Title.
CR4595.G3Z66   2011
929.7'3 – dc23   2011017496

ISBN 978-0-521-11251-2 Hardback
ISBN 978-1-107-53043-0 Paperback

Contents

Illustrations

Map and figures

Tables

Preface

Can the minor brutalities of a small-time sixteenth-century squire give rise to a modern masterpiece? An author must be audacious to state that he stakes his entire genius on a feuding nobleman from Franconia. But that is precisely what Goethe claimed when he was writing *Götz von Berlichingen with the Iron Hand*, the play which established his reputation. Goethe, a lawyer by training, did not look down on the feuds of his hero as an expression of a barbarous age before the advance of the modern state guaranteed the civilising benefits of domestic peace and justice. For him the feud was not the law of the jungle, the quintessential image of haughty, aristocratic unruliness which it would become for later generations. On the contrary, perhaps: Goethe was evidently influenced by the view of Justus Möser, whom he read on Herder's advice, that the new world of centralised states robbed Germans of some natural rights and stifled the independent spirit which their forefathers had displayed in and through their feuds.

Every age creates its own vision of the feud – a window onto the past that doubles as a mirror in which it observes its own reflection(s). This is perhaps especially true of our age, even though the feud is now predominantly the subject of academic dissection rather than literary imagination. Since the 1930s the feud has become an ideologically contested theme, but the present struggle over its 'correct' understanding is probably fiercer than ever. Recent years have seen a succession of major studies and interpretations of the feud. Few of these works are not directly inspired by contemporary social and political concerns. Yet a second salient – and ostensibly conflicting – aspect of these works is that, whatever their underlying motivations, they have produced major gains in our factual knowledge of the feud as well as greater theoretical sophistication in its explication. The overall effect has been to change the study of feuds beyond recognition in a remarkably short time. Historians now understand the feud in wholly new ways.

It is this profound change in what has become an exceptionally fertile field of research which led me to revisit the subject, having already written one book about feuding in early modern Germany. This is not a revision of an earlier work, still less a defence of it against its critics. While the present book naturally builds on some parts of the previous one, it is based on a new set of empirical observations and offers a new interpretation.

The key finding of the previous book was that most feuding nobles were well-to-do men who held top positions in the territorial administration of the German principalities. This refuted the then prevalent assumption that the nobility was in the grips of an economic and social crisis and that nobles, under the legal cloak of the feud, took to banditry because they fell on hard times. Taking as a point of departure the intense rivalries set off by the process of territorial and juridical consolidation in late medieval Germany, my earlier book explained the feud as a practice manipulated by both princes and nobles, caught up in a competition for material resources and political power. It concluded that far from being a hindrance to princely state-building in Germany, the feud served as one of the chief strategies for furthering it. State-building was not simply a background against which to account for the noble feud. In fact, the overriding aim of that study was not so much to explain this kind of violent behaviour as to explore the process of state formation in the historiographically unfamiliar setting of a politically most incoherent zone: Franconia.

By contrast, the present volume aims primarily at explaining the feud per se, as a form of human behaviour. It follows necessarily that the questions it puts to the sources are fundamentally different, as are the methods it employs and the explanations it proposes. It seeks especially to explain why, in contradistinction to war and contrary to what one might expect, feud violence was eminently an in-group phenomenon; why nobles tended to feud against their neighbours, relatives and feudal lords, despite the ties that bound them and the obvious costs of attacking one's potentially closest allies. Thus, whereas my earlier book focused on the relationship between nobles and princes in the context of state formation, the present one centres on the social, institutional and economic constraints that shaped relationships and communication among nobles. It interprets the feud in terms of the preferences, norms and moral sentiments that shaped noble culture into an uncanny composite of conflict and cooperation.

Fortune is a woman, asserted Machiavelli, and I would certainly concur, without necessarily accepting the menacing connotation of his expression. Discussions with Sheilagh Ogilvie provided in large measure the initial impetus to revert to the subject of the feud. Sheilagh also read the chapters in different stages of their evolution and offered her keen criticisms in a marvellously gracious manner that made them not just invaluably helpful but positively pleasing to digest. Ilana Krausman Ben-Amos's wise counsel was instrumental in bringing me to embark on writing this book and equally important in bringing the writing to a conclusion. Yulia Ustinova showed sympathy for the travails of reconciling academic duties with preparing a manuscript, and her practical support facilitated the progress of my work.

One of the joys of writing the present book was the contact into which it brought me with other scholars. I can report with some astonishment that everywhere I turned I encountered kindness and a generous spirit of cooperation. Indispensable comments, reflections and help in other ways were offered by Kurt Andermann, Scott Dixon, Sven Rabeler, Ulinka Rublack, Joachim Schneider, Tom Scott and Thomas Winkelbauer. It is with pleasure that I record the assistance I received from the German archivists who gladly responded to my queries and searched for the documents I needed: Ingrid Heeg-Engelhart, Johann Pörnbacher, Gerhard Rechter, Klaus Rupprecht and Werner Wagenhöfer.

Some of the ideas contained in the book were tested on conference participants, whose questions and criticisms thankfully made me rethink my arguments. I am grateful to the organisers of these conferences for giving me the opportunity to present my research and for the warm welcome: Jeppe Büchert Netterstrøm and Bjørn Poulsen; Maria Pia Paoli and Paolo Broggio; Christine Reinle, Michael Rothmann and Julia Eulenstein; Jörn Leonhard and Christian Wieland; Antheun Janse and Peter Hoppenbrouwers; and Joachim Schneider.

Finally, my greatest debt is to my family. Yaël, my companion on a journey that began long ago, always kept me on the straight path. Her wisdom, integrity and vision of the good life served as a constant source of inspiration. I dedicate the book to the other woman in my life, my mother Zohara, in memory of my father.

Abbreviations

AO	*Archiv des Historischen Vereins für Oberfranken*
AU	*Archiv des Historischen Vereins von Unterfranken und Aschaffenburg*
Bb	Reichsstadt Nürnberg: Briefbücher des Inneren Rates
BPH	Brandenburg-Preußisches Hausarchiv
Fstm.Ansb.	Fürstentum Ansbach
GNM	Bibliothek des Germanischen Nationalmuseums, Nürnberg
GStAB	Geheimes Staatsarchiv Preußischer Kulturbesitz, Berlin
HZ	*Historische Zeitschrift*
JffL	*Jahrbuch für fränkische Landesforschung*
Ldf	Libri diversarum formarum
StAA	Staatsarchiv Amberg
StAB	Staatsarchiv Bamberg
StAN	Staatsarchiv Nürnberg
StAW	Staatsarchiv Würzburg
Stb	Standbücher
ZHF	*Zeitschrift für Historische Forschung*

CHAPTER ONE

Introduction

The struggle over the feud in early modern Germany

One of the striking features of late medieval and early modern Germany was the pervasiveness of feuds by noblemen. Foreign observers found it difficult to explain. A Roman cardinal, overcome with indignation, exclaimed 'all Germany is a gang of bandits and, among the nobles, the more grasping the more glorious'.[1] A similar point was made by Poggio Bracciolini in his treatise *On Nobility* (*c.* 1440). Pointing out the difficulty of defining what true nobility consisted in, he wrote that the Germans think 'that a noble lives in the mountains robbing those who pass through'.[2] Even as thoughtful a man of the world as Philippe de Commynes was perplexed by the custom of feuding in Germany. He noted that

> there are [in Germany] so many fortified places and so many people inclined to do evil and to plunder and rob, and who use force and violence against each other on the slightest pretence, that it is almost incredible. For a single man with only a valet to attend him will defy a whole city and even attack

[1] Johann Kamann, *Die Fehde des Götz von Berlichingen mit der Reichsstadt Nürnberg und dem Hochstifte Bamberg 1512–1514* (Nuremberg, 1893), 103 n. 2.

[2] Poggio Bracciolini, *On Nobility*, in *Knowledge, Goodness, and Power: the Debate over Nobility among Quattrocento Italian Humanists*, ed. Albert Rabil, Jr (Binghamton, NY, 1991), 63–89, at 74. See also p. 69: 'The Germans think that those are noble whose inherited property provides an adequate living, or who rule over fortresses and small towns far from the cities, even though most of this latter group engage in highway robbery.' On the treatise see Claudio Donati, *L'idea di nobiltà in Italia: secoli XIV–XVIII* (Bari, 1988), 11–12.

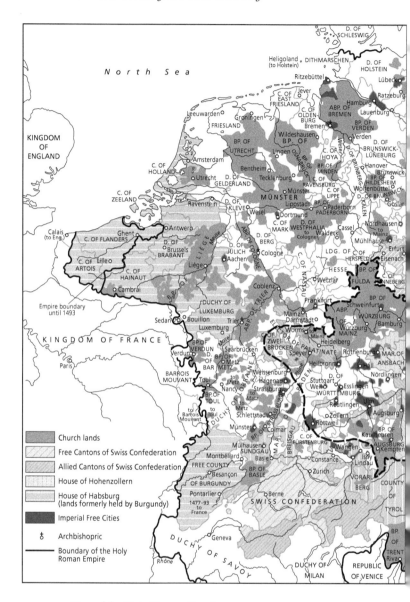

Map of the Holy Roman Empire, *c.* 1500

House of Wittelsbach (Palatine branch)
House of Wittelsbach (Bavarian branch)
House of Wettin (Albertine branch)
House of Wettin (Ernestine branch)
House of Habsburg (Austrian branch)

0   50   100   150   200   250 km

0   50   100   150 miles

a duke, so that he will have a better excuse to rob him, by using a small castle on a rock, where he can retire and where he has twenty or thirty horsemen.[3]

These observers were clearly struck by what they saw as the rule of lawlessness in Germany. Their reactions, allowing for misinformation about and misperception of the German reality, nevertheless encapsulate the deep significance of the phenomenon of the feud: it raises, in a fundamental way, the question of the nature of public order in Germany in the late Middle Ages.[4] Given their ubiquity and the power and prestige of the nobles who carried them out, feuds readily appear to have been antithetical to any public order worthy of the name, let alone to modern conceptions of state and law. By the same token, however, few historical phenomena are as fruitful for examining modern preconceptions about pre-modern polities.

Precisely this was the insight that stimulated the Austrian historian Otto Brunner, who effectively created the history of the feud as a research field with his publication, in 1939, of *'Land' and Lordship*. Its first chapter, devoted to the problem of the feud, has set the terms of debate up to the most recent scholarship.[5] Brunner began by criticising the widespread notion that the late medieval feud was merely banditry by another name. He contended that the language of the sources could not be taken at face value and that when 'an opponent is called a "brigand" (*Räuber*), this in principle means nothing more than that he is held to be acting unrightfully – something to

---

[3] Samuel Kinser (ed.), *The Memoirs of Philippe de Commynes*, 2 vols., trans. Isabelle Cazeaux (Columbia, SC, 1969–73), I, 354–5.

[4] This applies of course not only to Germany. A superb historiographical survey is Jeppe Büchert Netterstrøm, 'Introduction: The Study of Feud in Medieval and Early Modern History', in *Feud in Medieval and Early Modern Europe*, ed. Jeppe Büchert Netterstrøm and Bjørn Poulsen (Aarhus, 2007), 9–67.

[5] Otto Brunner, *'Land' and Lordship: Structures of Governance in Medieval Austria*, trans. Howard Kaminsky and James Van Horn Melton (Philadelphia, 1992), 1–94.

keep in mind in the countless cases where "brigand" appears in our sources'.[6]

Brunner thus shifted the basis of the discussion from the economic and social to the legal and political.[7] Indeed, Brunner's main argument was that the feud was not illegal, a criminal use of naked power, as historians had previously portrayed it. Quite the contrary – it was an eminently lawful means of conflict resolution, provided it was carried it out in accordance with the accepted rules of conduct. These ranged from a preliminary attempt to settle differences peacefully to a delivery of a cartel of defiance (*Absage* or *diffidatio*) well before opening hostilities.[8]

Brunner, however, sought to do a good deal more than explain the feud per se and rehabilitate it in historical judgment. His study of the feud served, among other things, the purpose of 'defamiliarising' the Middle Ages, of demonstrating its radical otherness, and thus exposing the inadequacies of explanations based on modern assumptions about the state and the law.[9] By viewing the feud with precisely these modern preconceptions in mind, historians did worse than doom themselves to misunderstanding the feud; they practically condemned themselves to misapprehending the world of the Middle Ages itself. For the feud, far from being an aberration, played a central role in shaping and sustaining the public order of this world. As Brunner put it, the feud was:

the juridical form of all medieval politics, in so far as it resorts, internally as well as externally, to the force of arms. Only from the perspective of the feud, which is simultaneously Right and Might, can one understand the relationship between these two factors in the Middle Ages. A world in which the feud is always a possibility, of necessity has a structure altogether

---

[6] Ibid., 7.

[7] Thomas Schweier, *Feudalismus in den Artusepopöen Hartmanns von Aue? Kritik der Schriften Otto Brunners im Rahmen sozialgeschichtlicher Interpretationen* (Würzburg, 2004), 304.

[8] For a more detailed discussion see Chapter 2.   [9] Brunner, *'Land' and Lordship*, 9.

Illustration 1. Gerhard von Valangin declares a feud on Bern, 1339. Diebold
Schilling, *Spiezer Chronik*, Burgerbibliothek Bern, Mss.h.h.I.16, p. 248

completely different from the civil world of an absolute state which claims
the monopoly of the legitimate use of force.[10]

In *'Land' and Lordship*, this crucial point is demonstrated by four
examples of noblemen's feuds against kings and emperors.[11] That

---

[10] Otto Brunner, 'Moderner Verfassungsbegriff und mittelalterliche Verfassungsgeschichte',
Mitteilungen des österreichischen Instituts für Geschichtsforschung. Erg.-Band 14 (1939), 513–
28, at 527. See also Brunner, *'Land' and Lordship*, 9.
[11] Brunner, *'Land' and Lordship*, 9–14.

these could be considered lawful and not high treason reveals 'pre-conditions for political action radically different from those we take for granted in the modern state . . . these nobles believed that their actions were entirely legitimate'. A dramatically alien practice from a state-centred perspective, the feud represents a historical problem which is impervious to modern preconceptions. 'In the Middle Ages . . . we see rulers and subjects declare war and conclude peace with each other "as if" each were subject to international law. Were such actions merely an abuse of power based on "the law of the fist?" To the contrary: they were the expression of a legal consciousness.'[12] Legitimacy and justice were not defined by sovereignty, which had no place in this world. Rather, they were embodied in the 'good old law' or 'good custom' – a shorthand for a system of moral and religious norms and sensibilities.'[13] This legal order provided the framework of a general consensus within which conflicts between the various power-holders were carried out and settled. The feud was essentially a legal mechanism for the maintenance of order in a commonwealth of aristocratic lordships.

Brunner's achievement is perhaps best appreciated by comparing his break with the historiography of his day with the research on the feud in England and, especially, France. The contrast could hardly be sharper: Brunner discarded the anachronistic contradiction between noble violence and viable public order. Inevitably, his study of the feud 'has had far-reaching implications for a re-evaluation of the place of the nobility in the body politic, helping to overcome the view that it was the Antistate incarnate. French historiography, on the other hand, has largely remained 'monarchist'. Whereas

---

[12] Ibid., 13–14.

[13] Brunner, *'Land' and Lordship*, xix, 192, 195–6. See also, for instance, O. Brunner, 'Die Freiheitsrechte in der altständischen Gesellschaft', in his *Neue Wege der Verfassungs- und Sozialgeschichte*, 3rd edn (Göttingen, 1980), 187–98, at 194: 'Denn Recht ist hier eine über den Menschen stehende Ordnung.'

Brunner argued that it was impossible to write medieval political and constitutional history without giving the feud pride of place,[14] French historians have mostly gone about this task as if it were impossible to accomplish without banishing the ghost of feuding to the limbo of recalcitrant facts. It is not that feuds did not occur in France. As Howard Kaminsky has observed, 'The remarkable thing is not the ubiquity and legitimacy of the noble feud but the failure of French historians to come to grips with it.'[15] A historiographical tradition dominated by the grand narratives of the monarchically directed state formation and the emergence of the nation could find no useful role for feuding nobles:

historians who identify the interest of the nation with the rise of the state are not moved to focus on mentalities and practices whose prima facie import was to interfere with that rise, as well as to destroy the civil peace whose enforcement would be the main business of the post-medieval state. From their point of view the noble feud can only appear as disruption, anarchy, and might-makes-right, a view taken as confirmed by medieval testimony in the same sense by non-nobles who suffered from the warfare – burghers, clerics, intellectuals.[16]

While Brunner's *'Land' and Lordship* has generally been passed over in France and, to a lesser extent, in the Anglo-Saxon world,[17] in Germany it has had an immense and lasting impact. Greeted with

---

[14] *'Land' and Lordship*, 14.

[15] Howard Kaminsky, 'The Noble Feud in the Later Middle Ages', *Past and Present* 177 (2002), 55–83, at 66.

[16] Ibid., 67. See also Stuart Carroll, *Blood and Violence in Early Modern France* (Oxford, 2006), 4, 6, who doubts, however, the applicability to France of Brunner's interpretation of the feud. For 'feud' in England see Christine Reinle, '"Fehde" und gewaltsame Selbsthilfe in England und im römisch-deutschen Reich', in *Akten des 36. Deutschen Rechtshistorikertages*, ed. Rolf Lieberwirth and Heiner Lück (Zurich, 2008), 99–132; Kaminsky, 'The Noble Feud in the Later Middle Ages', 74–9.

[17] The translation of Brunner into English in 1992 perhaps signalled a change. In Italy Brunner's works enjoyed earlier and greater acceptance: *'Land' and Lordship* was translated in 1983 and *Adeliges Landleben und europäischer Geist: Leben und Werk Wolf Helmhards von Hohberg 1612–1688* (Salzburg, 1949) in 1972.

What is the Anglo-Saxon world?

admiration and disapproval in equal measures, ever since Brunner put forward his interpretation the feud has become a veritable battleground – ideological as well as historiographical. None of the numerous critical appraisals of Brunner's work, however, has been as sustained and systematic as Gadi Algazi's *Herrengewalt und Gewalt der Herren*.[18] Algazi's study is divided into two main parts. The first challenges Brunner's understanding of 'protection and safeguard' (*Schutz und Schirm*) in the Middle Ages.[19] According to this teaching, the relationship between peasants and lords was contractual: the lords defended the peasants, the peasants rendered submission, services and payments to the lords. Algazi argued that the protection extended by the lords to the peasants was actually of the kind offered by Mafia bosses to their 'customers': it was 'protection' from the threat of violence which they themselves posed to the peasants. When the lords undertook to 'protect and safeguard' peasants they committed themselves to nothing beyond refraining from further violating the rights of their peasants.

The second part of Algazi's critique of Brunner focuses on the feud. The argument here aims to provide an alternative account of the foundations of lordship over peasants. Rather than reciprocity, argues Algazi, lordship rested on violence – not in the form of direct coercion, but in the diffuse form of regularly recurring feuds between noblemen: whilst the rivals were exclusively lords, the actual victims of the hostilities were, almost as exclusively, the rival lords' subject peasants. Precisely this form of violence, as the consequence of the struggles between individual lords, made it difficult for its victims to perceive the feud as a means of their subjection. As Algazi puts it:

[18] Gadi Algazi, *Herrengewalt und Gewalt der Herren im späten Mittelalter: Herrschaft, Gegenseitigkeit und Sprachgebrauch* (Frankfurt am Main, 1996).
[19] Brunner, *'Land' and Lordship*, 280–7.

the feud, as an expression of a noble unorganised monopoly of the means of violence, had a concealed sharp edge, which was directed at those who were prevented from possessing these means. The individual warring lords appear as 'private entrepreneurs of extra-economic coercion', whereby precisely the fact that they acted as 'private entrepreneurs' and not as an organised group, was constitutive of the presumed social effect of this form of violence.[20]

Yet considered as a social category, the lords were the perpetrators of the violence from which protection was needed. Even if feuds were a menace to the economic and social position of individual lords, the feud legitimated their protective function and hence bolstered their collective prominence as lords. The violent dispossession of the peasants by feuding nobles can therefore be construed as a political means to the periodic re-establishment of the 'social order', to the keeping of the peasants in their place. Viewed from this perspective, the feud was in effect a *Kleinkrieg* against the peasants and the feuding nobles were racketeers, forming an uncoordinated cartel of unorganised 'crime'. If for Brunner the feud was a privilege of the lords, for Algazi it was what constituted and reconstituted the lords qua lords in the first place. The indirect consequence – if not necessarily the intention – of feuds was to reproduce the peasants' need for protection and the lords' power over them.

Historians of late medieval Germany were not slow to gainsay Algazi.[21] Praising the theoretical sophistication of his model of the relationship between lords and peasants, they have exposed some serious problems in it. The contradiction between the two parts of his

---

[20] Algazi, *Herrengewalt und Gewalt der Herren*, 157–8.

[21] Some were too quick. It is not correct to criticise Algazi's interpretation as a functional explanation of the feud (see Klaus Graf, 'Gewalt und Adel in Südwestdeutschland: Überlegungen zur spätmittelalterlichen Fehde', *Online-Reprint eines Beitrags auf dem Bielefelder Kolloquium 'Gewalt' am 29.11.1998*; www.histsem.uni-freiburg.de/mertens/graf/gewalt.htm (2000)).

Illustration 2. A raid on a village, *Wolfegg Housebook*, scene entitled
Mars and his children

study is perhaps not the most unfortunate of them.[22] More disturbing
is the narrow factual basis on which the entire construct rests. Thus,
evidence for the use of the term 'protection' in the crucial sense of
lordly forbearance from further curtailing the peasants' rights has

[22] As Howard Kaminsky noted, 'Algazi's analysis of the feud undermines his argument
about *Schirm*; insofar as we imagine peasants generally subject to the violence of feuding
lords, we must also imagine them needing their own lords' protection against external
attack': Howard Kaminsky, review of Gadi Algazi, *Herrengewalt und Gewalt der Herren
im späten Mittelalter: Herrschaft, Gegenseitigkeit und Sprachgebrauch, Speculum* 73, no. 3
(1998), 799–802, at 800.

not been found in more than a single source, from 1435.[23] Moreover, in a document from the same collection, and dating from 1437, 'protection' is used in the very contractual sense which Algazi set out to refute.[24]

A similar economical approach to the sources mars Algazi's treatment of the feud. It is not based on sources for actual feuds at all, but on a set of assumptions on how feuds were conducted and by whom. The sources, however, tell a story which is a good deal more complex than Algazi's model of the peasant–lord relationship can accommodate. This is nowhere more evident than in the role which the model assigns to central governments: they appear in it as little more than foci of expectations – expectations of noblemen that their feuds be regulated, expectations of non-nobles that feuds be eradicated.[25] However, as a later chapter will show,[26] central governments in Germany, in the form of princely rule, were in various ways not only, and perhaps not primarily, regulators of feuds, but rather their chief agents. An analysis of feuds in Franconia between 1440 and 1570 shows, first, that the number of feuds between princes and nobles was nearly as high as the number of feuds among nobles (103 and 111, respectively);[27] and secondly, that the most violent periods in terms of the incidence of feuds in general also saw the three highest peaks in the number of feuds between princes and nobles. Moreover, a large number of feuds – both among nobles and between nobles and princes – were carried out by noblemen who held high office in princely administrations; and quite a few of these feuds were in

---

[23] Algazi, *Herrengewalt und Gewalt der Herren*, 236.

[24] This source is not mentioned by Algazi. See Sigrid Schmitt, 'Schutz und Schirm oder Gewalt und Unterdrückung? Überlegungen zu Gadi Algazis Dissertation "Herrengewalt und Gewalt der Herren in späten Mittelalter"', *Vierteljahrschrift für Sozial- und Wirtschaftsgeschichte* 89 (2002), 72–8, at 77.

[25] Algazi, *Herrengewalt und Gewalt der Herren*, 162–3.   [26] Chapter 5.

[27] See Appendix for a chronological list of feuds.

one way or another conducted in the service of competing princes.[28]
It was arguably the princes and their 'central governments' which,
more than the nobles themselves, were responsible for the violence
from which peasants needed and sought protection. Not for nothing
has the modern scholarship on the emergence of states equated the
process to a 'protection racket'.[29]

By shifting the ground of the discussion to the social effects
of feuding, Algazi's model provided an important corrective to
Brunner's emphasis on the legal aspect of the feud.[30] However,
as Algazi himself recognised, his model of the lord–peasants relationship does not furnish an explanation of the feud.[31] By the very
nature of its avowed aim, which is to conceptualise the 'unintended
systematic' consequences of feuds, it cannot account for the reasons
and motives of the feuders. Its aim, rather, is to identify the place
which the feud occupied in the medieval society.[32] Yet its failure to
feature the major part which the princes played in feuding vitiates this
project. While the nobles were those who did the actual fighting, they
were often players – sometimes mere pawns – in a game over which
they had only partial control. This is not to deny that feuds could and
sometimes did have the effects that Algazi attributed to them. But it

---

[28] See below nn. 49–50. It is remarkable in this respect that Regina Görner, *Raubritter: Untersuchungen zur Lage des spätmittelalterlichen Niederadels, besonders im südlichen Westfalen*
(Münster in Westfalen, 1987) is mentioned only once in Algazi, *Herrengewalt und Gewalt
der Herren* (142 n. 31), and her findings regarding the true nature of many feuds are not
reported at all.

[29] Charles Tilly, 'War Making and State Making as Organized Crime', in *Bringing the State
Back In*, ed. Peter B. Evans, Dietrich Rueschemeyer and Theda Skocpol (Cambridge,
1985), 169–91. See also Kurt Andermann, 'Raubritter – Raubfürsten – Raubbürger? Zur
Kritik eines untauglichen Begriffs', in *'Raubritter' oder 'Rechtsschaffene vom Adel'? Aspekte
von Politik, Friede und Recht im späten Mittelalter*, ed. Kurt Andermann (Sigmaringen,
1997), 9–29, at 12, for a suggestion that the term 'robber-prince' might not be less justified
than 'robber-knight'.

[30] For Algazi's argument that Brunner failed to distinguish between norms and social reality,
and that this failure was the result of his Nazi sympathies, see Algazi, *Herrengewalt und
Gewalt der Herren*, 110–12. See also Schweier, *Feudalismus*, 304–5.

[31] Algazi, *Herrengewalt und Gewalt der Herren*, 151.   [32] Cf. ibid., 142, 153 and n. 51.

does qualify the claim that feuds had the effect of forcibly 'typecasting' lords and peasant and reproducing a social order favourable to the former. For the predominant role of the princes in feuding means that, in the terms of Algazi's model, feuds would necessarily have increased the dependence of the nobles on the princes, and would in time have made noble local authority redundant. And in fact, feuds did create a need for protection not only in peasants but also in the feuding nobles themselves, who frequently turned to the princes and asked for 'protection and safeguard'.[33]

One could of course argue that this observation supports rather than controverts Algazi's interpretation, in that the nobles' feuds unwittingly produced the power differential not only between themselves and peasants, but also between themselves and princes, thus reproducing the entire social hierarchy from top to bottom. This would be a grossly reductive misjudgment. For feuds were sometimes also acts of resistance to princely power. As one noble stated in an open letter to his fellow nobles, the unjust actions of the prince left him no alternative but to wage a feud on the prince. 'The Law of Nature', he added, 'permits self-defence.'[34] Secondly, princes often depended on nobles to pursue feuds that were in their, the princes', interests.[35] In other words, feuds were a complex social phenomenon that did not necessarily have only one final outcome, favouring the initially stronger party. The feud could shape social relationship in a variety of ways, binding *and* separating, strengthening *and* limiting power.

---

[33] Hillay Zmora, *State and Nobility in Early Modern Germany: The Knightly Feud in Franconia, 1440–1567* (Cambridge, 1997), 127–8.

[34] Klaus Rupprecht, *Ritterschaftliche Herrschaftswahrung in Franken: Die Geschichte der von Guttenberg im Spätmittelalter und zu Beginn der Frühen Neuzeit* (Neustadt a.d. Aisch, 1994), 499. Further on this feud in Chapter 5.

[35] Cf. Zmora, *State and Nobility*, passim.

A second and germane implication of acknowledging the influence of the princes on feuding is that it puts paid to the contention that feuds were 'private wars',[36] and instead lends support to Brunner's notion of the eminently 'public' and political character of the feud. The significance of this implication is this: if one considers the feud as 'private war', this facilitates its historiographical 'criminalisation' as a socially repressive protection racket; but if one considers the feud as a public institution, this inevitably places it well within the bounds of the legal. It is one thing to describe the noblemen as acting violently in their private interests, it is quite another to ascribe similar motives to the princes, the putative guardians of law and order. One can collapse this distinction into an undifferentiated mass of 'lords' only at the cost of picturing the entire medieval social and political order as perverse.

It is not only a historical view from above, from the perspective of the princes, that shows Algazi's identification of the place of the feud in the medieval society to be partial. A look at feuding from below is equally, or even more, revealing. This has been the accomplishment of Christine Reinle's pioneering study on peasant feuds. Whereas Algazi, following Brunner, assumed the feud to have been the preserve of nobles, Reinle demonstrated that it was a popular means of conflict resolution also among peasants and other commoners. It is hard to miss a certain irony here: whilst Reinle does not share Algazi's ideological convictions and does not speak in the name of the downtrodden, it is she who has turned the peasants from essentially passive

[36] For the use of the term 'private war' see Gadi Algazi, 'The Social Use of Private War: Some Late Medieval Views Reviewed', *Tel Aviver Jahrbuch für deutsche Geschichte* 22 (1993), 253–73; Gadi Algazi, '"Sie würden hinten nach so gail": Vom sozialen Gebrauch der Fehde im späten Mittelalter', in *Physische Gewalt: Studien zur Geschichte der Neuzeit*, ed. Thomas Lindenberger and Alf Lüdtke (Frankfurt am Main, 1995), 39–77, at 52, 53.

objects into flesh-and-blood historical actors. Focusing on Bavaria between the middle of the fifteenth century and the beginning of the sixteenth, she has found evidence of 258 feuds by non-nobles.[37] They pursued feuds not only against other commoners but also against lords; and they carried them out in a manner closely akin to that of nobles. It has thus emerged that the alleged victims of an assumed lordly monopoly of violence employed the very same means that according to Algazi were used to oppress and subjugate them. Now if peasants resorted to feuds as readily as did the nobles, it follows that Otto Brunner cannot be faulted primarily on the ground that he ignored the multiplicity of late medieval legal perspectives, and that he accorded the noblemen's self-serving perception of the feud as a legitimate practice the undeserved status of the prevalent view in the late medieval society.[38] A similar objection applies to contemporary condemnations of the feud: given that peasants and other commoners waged feuds and considered them as a legitimate means of pursuing their claims,[39] late medieval denunciations of the noble feud do not necessarily offer a perspective on lordly violence that balances out that of the nobles.[40] The nobles and the peasants clearly shared some important ideas about feuding. The 'dynamic heterogeneity'

---

[37] Christine Reinle, *Bauernfehden: Studien zur Fehdeführung Nichtadliger im spätmittelalterlichen römisch-deutschen Reich, besonders in den bayerischen Herzogtümern* (Stuttgart, 2003), 254. For the question of social status see ibid., 294–5. Reinle found that damage was actually inflicted in only 13.56 per cent of the feuds: ibid., 259. For a similar finding concerning feuds against Nuremberg see Thomas Vogel, *Fehderecht und Fehdepraxis im Spätmittelalter am Beispiel der Reichsstadt Nürnberg (1404–1438)* (Frankfurt am Main, 1998), 209–10. That the feud was a privilege of the nobility was refuted already by Vogel, *Fehderecht und Fehdepraxis*, 118.

[38] Gadi Algazi, 'Otto Brunner – "Konkrete Ordnung" und Sprache der Zeit', in *Geschichte als Legitimationswissenschaft, 1918–1945*, ed. Peter Schöttler, 2nd edn (Frankfurt am Main, 1998), 166–203, at 169, 170.

[39] See Christine Reinle, 'Bauerngewalt und Macht der Herren: Bauernfehden zwischen Gewohnheitsrecht und Verbot', in *Gewalt im Mittelalter: Realitäten-Imaginationen*, ed. Manuel Braun (Munich, 2005), 105–22, at 114.

[40] Cf. Algazi, *Herrengewalt und Gewalt der Herren*, 220–3.

that Algazi detected in medieval literary texts appears to have been considerably more pronounced in letters than in life.[41]

Much the same can be said even of the anti-noble criticisms of the feud that originated from the cities. The cities were arguably the politically and ideologically staunchest enemies of the feud, in part no doubt because as hubs of trade they were particularly vulnerable to this form of fighting, and usually had much to lose from it.[42] And yet, their fundamental rejection of it was not so fundamental as to blind them to the advantages of political reason. Thomas Vogel has shown that even as prosperous and powerful a metropolis as Nuremberg, determined as it was to see feuding brought under control, adopted a pragmatic approach and was by and large indifferent to the question of whether a feud declared on it had a valid reason or not.[43] Nor did the cities wholly avoid succumbing to the temptation of waging a feud when this opened up an opportunity for political gains.[44]

Lastly, it can be shown that ruling princes also saw no intractable contradiction between feuding and their duty to provide good government. They shared with their nobles and humbler subjects the view that the feud was a legitimate practice, and defended this position even when they had no immediate territorial or political axe to

---

[41] Ibid., 223. For criticisms of Algazi's use of literary texts see André Holenstein, review of Gadi Algazi, *Herrengewalt und Gewalt der Herren im späten Mittelalter: Herrschaft, Gegenseitigkeit und Sprachgebrauch*, ZHF 25, no. 4 (1998), 592–7, at 595–6; Reinle, 'Bauerngewalt und Macht der Herren', 108–9; Reinle, *Bauernfehden*, 39.

[42] See Ulrich Andermann, *Ritterliche Gewalt und bürgerliche Selbsbehauptung: Untersuchungen zur Kriminalisierung und Bekämpfung des spätmittelalterlichen Raubrittertums am Beispiel norddeutscher Hansestädte* (Frankfurt am Main, 1991), esp. 120–2, who emphasises the differences in ways of life and mentalities between burghers and nobles. See also Thomas A. Brady, Jr, *Turning Swiss: Cities and Empire, 1450–1550* (Cambridge, 1985), 242–5.

[43] Vogel, *Fehderecht und Fehdepraxis*, 161–6.

[44] Horst Carl, *Der Schwäbische Bund, 1488–1534: Landfrieden und Genossenschaft im Übergang vom Spätmittelalter zur Reformation* (Leinfelden-Echterdingen, 2000), 480–1; Christine Reinle, 'Fehden und Fehdebekämpfung am Ende des Mittelalters: Überlegungen zum Auseinandertreten von "Frieden" und "Recht" in der politischen Praxis zu Beginn des 16. Jahrhunderts am Beispiel der Absberg-Fehde', ZHF 30 (2003), 355–88. For more on this point see Chapter 6.

avoid the peasants & nobles

grind. A case in point is Margrave Albrecht 'Achilles' of Brandenburg (1440–86). The margrave was truly concerned about feuding
and often urged his office-holders to do their utmost to curb 'robbery
and brigandage'. In a letter to one of his top officials he enjoined

Not allowing any one involved

him to see to it that no one was harmed in the area under his com-
mand, and that no one who was involved in a feud was allowed to
operate from there. He did not want to hear people say, he stressed,
that he was permitting such deeds to originate from his castles and
towns.[45] Yet when in 1482 Archduke Sigmund of Austria asked
for his help in bringing to book one of his, the margrave's, noble
vassals who had feuded against him and had been placed under an
imperial ban, Albrecht declined. He was only prepared to commit
himself not to assist the nobleman. He pointed out that it would
be inappropriate for him to have the nobleman arrested since the
latter was not his enemy.[46] Margrave Albrecht and other princes did
often argue against the legality of this feud or that, especially when
it happened to be against them; but they did not make the crucial
step towards considering the practice of feuding itself as illegal by
definition.

These observations demonstrate that the feud was neither a defining prerogative of the nobility nor its distinctive vice. It was not a
mark of its status and identity and, as Reinle has pointed up, did not
lend itself to the construction of social types.[47] Rather, the feud was
widely accepted and deeply embedded in the German society of the
late Middle Ages. Customary law both reflected and sustained this
state of affairs.[48]

---

[45] StAN, Fstm.Ansb., Differenzen mit Benachbarten, Bayerische Bücher, no. 8, fol. 225r.
[46] Ibid., Fstm.Ansb., Fehdeakten, no. 176.   [47] Reinle, *Bauernfehden*, 340.
[48] Ibid., 46–61, 343–4; cf. Christine Reinle, 'Umkämpfter Friede: Politischer Gestaltungswille und geistlicher Normenhorizont bei der Fehdebekämpfung im deutschen
Spätmittelalter', in *Rechtsveränderung im politischen und sozialen Kontext mittelalterlicher
Rechtsvielfalt*, ed. Stefan Esders and Christine Reinle (Münster, 2005), 147–74.

The findings about the pervasiveness of peasants' feuds pose a challenge also to the view that the feud was part and parcel of the process of princely territorialisation. This interpretation has been put forward for both Westphalia and Franconia. In her study on Westphalia, Regina Görner has shown that large segments of the lesser nobility coped successfully with economic and social change. Juxtaposing noblemen vilified as robber knights with the economic conditions of their families, she has established that an alleged penury had nothing to do with their violence. On the contrary, it was the most affluent families which were mostly responsible for feuds. Moreover, many of the feuding nobles were district governors. Görner therefore sees the roots of violence in the gestation of the state: the nobles involved in feuds were, on the one hand, executing their overlord's policies, many of which were perceived as iniquitous novelties. Meting out punishments and imposing fines on behalf of the territorial lord were seen by the 'victims' as nothing better than robbery. And since no clear distinction existed between the private and the public spheres, these nobles' actions met with poor understanding from the population. Trying to enforce order, they were seen as its very breakers. On the other hand, because these nobles held their district governorships in contractual lien, they tended to treat them not simply as collateral for the money they had invested in them but rather as a 'private' source of income and sometimes as a resource for local empire-building. So long as the process of state-building was underway, they were bound to be looked upon not as obedient public servants but rather as rapacious privateers. Only when the state reached maturity and stability, accompanied by a new mentality of its subjects, did such misdemeanours cease – or cease to be regarded as such.[49]

---

[49] Görner, *Raubritter*, esp. 209–10, 220–3.

A comparable picture has emerged from the study of feuds in Franconia in the fifteenth and sixteenth centuries. Here, too, the majority of the feuding nobles were closely associated with princes. Most of them were either prominent office-holders or creditors of princes, or both. However, the pattern of their involvement in feuds was different from that which has been described for Westphalia. The formative context of feuds in Franconia was the political fragmentation of the region and the struggle between its three major princes: the bishop of Würzburg, the bishop of Bamberg, and the margrave of Brandenburg-Ansbach-Kulmbach. For the princes, the feuds of nobles were often a useful means of pursuing interests against rival princes or other nobles. Feuds were in many cases small-scale 'proxy wars' led by loyal nobles; this was one reason for the prominence of office-holders among the feuders. For nobles, feuds were often a means of making themselves useful to princes and hence of gaining proximity to them – an essential ingredient of success in the aristocratic world. Franconia was thus the scene of three interlocking competitions: one among the princes, who vied also for the loyalty, the military expertise and the financial wherewithal of the nobles. Another competition was among the nobles themselves, who fought both over the resources at the disposal of the princes and over the resources which could be put at the disposal of the princes in order to gain political proximity to them. The third competition was between princes and nobles. The feud, the study concluded, arose from the interplay between the ongoing conflict among the Franconian princes over geopolitical advantage and the contest among nobles over the elements and benefits of status.[50]

It is striking that the studies of the feud in Westphalia and Franconia, despite significant differences both in their approach and in the territories on which they focus, have reached remarkably

---

[50] Zmora, *State and Nobility*.

similar conclusions. This convergence clearly lends some support to the interpretation of the feud as an integral part of the process of princely state-building. However, as has been said, this interpretation is now confronted by the evidence that peasants and other commoners resorted to feuds much like the nobles. For peasants were not involved in the process of state formation in the same ways and to the same degree that nobles were, and the pressures that this process placed on them were different from those to which the nobles were exposed. If peasants feuded all the same, and in a manner reminiscent of the nobles, then this necessarily qualifies the force of the territorialisation thesis. It does not invalidate the argument that the relationship between princes and nobles, in the context of state formation, was a powerful factor in feuds.[51] But it does mean that princely state formation cannot be made the basis of a general theory of the feud in late medieval and early modern Germany.

Christine Reinle's book represents not only a significant advance in the research on the phenomenon of the feud, but also a major intervention in the historiographical and ideological struggle over its interpretation which goes back to Otto Brunner. That such a struggle has been taking place is scarcely surprising: at stake are opposing visions of pre-modern society, and of the status of law and force, conflict and peace in German and European history.[52] As Reinle suggested, quoting another scholar, the reason why Brunner's analysis of the feud has not truly gained acceptance is in large part because it portrays a society in which violent conflict is not

---

[51] See Chapters 4 and 5 below.
[52] A recent trend in the research on feuding is indeed comparative studies, intended, among other things, as a method of examining whether the widespread feuding characteristic of late medieval Germany was unique and therefore attributable to an undeveloped state structure and weak central government. See Reinle, '"Fehde" und gewaltsame Selbsthilfe'; Reinle, 'Bauerngewalt und Macht der Herren', 106; Kaminsky, 'The Noble Feud in the Later Middle Ages'.

dysfunctional and peace is not by definition the foundation of human progress.[53] The Nazi ideology which Brunner espoused,[54] and its horrific effects, made such thoughts all but anathema in polite society. Ironically, however, the ideologically motivated criticism of Brunner risks validating his point of departure, namely that modern political concepts pervert the historical understanding of the feud.[55] Thus Reinle, albeit critically transcending Brunner in important respects, vindicates and actually reinforces Brunner's fundamental position on the primacy of the legal dimension of feuding. Hence her criticism, while directed chiefly at Algazi's interpretation, actually targets – and to an extent hits – all explanations of the feud that emphasise its social functions at the expense of its legal character.

That the feud was deeply entrenched and widely accepted as legitimate, however, still does not explain why people, and nobles in particular, chose to feud. Indeed, in this respect, the legal-historical approach to the feud shares a limitation with the state-formation thesis. Both describe necessary conditions that together constituted an environment susceptible or even conducive to feuding: without the widely held belief that feuding was legitimate many feuds would surely not have broken out, in the same way that many would not have come to pass without the pressures and opportunities created by the state-building activities of the princes. But these conditions were not sufficient. They do not in themselves explain the individual motivations that induced nobles to resort to this particular form

---

[53] Reinle, *Bauernfehden*, 21, quoting Alexander Patschovsky, 'Fehde im Recht: Eine Problemskizze', in *Recht und Reich im Zeitalter der Reformation*, ed. Christine Roll (Frankfurt, 1996), 145–78, at 147.

[54] For the 'elective affinity between Brunner's chief work and the thought patterns, perspectives and linguistic usage of National Socialism', see Algazi, 'Otto Brunner – "Konkrete Ordnung" und Sprache der Zeit' (quotation at p. 183). See also Peter N. Miller, 'Nazis and Neo-Stoics: Otto Brunner and Gerhard Oestreich before and after the Second World War', *Past and Present* 176 (2002), 144–86, esp. 152–8.

[55] Reinle, *Bauernfehden*, 21.

of violence in a particular instance.[56] A crucial link is missing that connected the political and legal conditions to the preferences of nobles, and to the choices they made whether to feud or not.

An attempt to formulate a new general, or quasi-general, interpretation of the feud will have to supply this missing link. It will centre on a crucial empirical observation whose self-evidence has obscured its vital importance: in most feuds, the rival parties usually knew each other all too well already before they came to blows; indeed, they were regularly linked to each other by a web of ties – generating what modern social scientists might call 'social capital'. The relationship between feuders was thus essentially one of familiarity.[57] This fact has not gone entirely unnoticed by historians.[58] It is telling, however, that it took an economist, Oliver Volckart, to make conceptually creative use of that fact.

Volckart has interpreted the feud as an economic response to an environment lacking in efficient state institutions. In his view the feud was an instrument used to enforce commercial contracts between strangers. People who sought redress for a broken contract could entrust their cause to an entrepreneur of violence, usually a nobleman, who would pursue a feud on their behalf as a

---

[56] Cf. the criticism of the works of Algazi (*Herrengewalt und Gewalt der Herren*), Joseph Morsel ('"Das sy sich mitt der besstenn gewarsamig schicken, das sy durch die widerwertigenn Franckenn nit nidergeworffen werdenn"': Überlegungen zum sozialen Sinn der Fehdepraxis am Beispiel des spätmittelalterlichen Franken', in *Strukturen der Gesellschaft im Mittelalter: Interdisziplinäre Mediävistik in Würzburg*, ed. Dieter Rödel and Joachim Schneider (Wiesbaden, 1996), 140–67) and Zmora (*State and Nobility*) in Graf, 'Gewalt und Adel in Südwestdeutschland'.

[57] This observation is especially pertinent to the two kinds of feuds that between them make up the majority of cases: feuds among nobles and feuds between nobles and princes. Feuds against cities and/or commoners are not inconsistent with this approach but are not captured by it as immediately as feuds within the aristocracy.

[58] Algazi seems to have had this in mind when he suggested that a mixture of 'hostility and solidarity' is a hallmark of the noble feud: Algazi, *Herrengewalt und Gewalt der Herren*, 144–5.

means of exerting punishing pressure on the other side to honour the agreement.[59] Feuds converted one-shot encounters into iterated games, so that claimants had the chance to penalise defectors. In this way feuds helped to solve the problem of transacting over time and space and stabilise exchange.[60] Rather than wanton anarchy and wasteful destruction, feuds functioned to protect property rights. Not only were feuds more profitable than is generally assumed,[61] but they 'allowed an increase in exchange and overall prosperity, even though many people suffered'.[62]

Original though it is, Volckart's theory led him to marginalise what was central to feuding and focus on what was marginal. For feuds between strangers, where the legal claim was pressed by a 'patron', constituted a relatively minor aspect of feuding, both in terms of numbers and in terms of aggregate consequences.[63] The majority of feuds were between people who were familiar with each other. Feuds did not normally turn one-shot encounters into iterated games; they were typically violent breaks in an otherwise continuous social intercourse. What enabled Volckart to discount this salient fact is that his interpretation assigns to the observed familiarity between feuders the role of a mere regulating mechanism: it simply was one of the reasons for compliance with the rules of conduct which controlled feuding and which the rival parties generally respected despite the absence of any authority able to enforce them.[64] But this only raises the truly central question about feuding: if the familiarity between

---

[59] For 'patron' feuds see Brunner, *'Land' and Lordship*, 49–50; Vogel, *Fehderecht und Fehdepraxis*, 123–34.

[60] Oliver Volckart, 'The Economics of Feuding in Late Medieval Germany', *Explorations in Economic History* 41 (2004), 282–99, at 295, 296.

[61] Ibid., 294–5.   [62] Ibid., 296.

[63] Even in the case of feuds against cities, 'patron' feuds constituted a minority. Of 145 identified feuders against Nuremberg in 1404–38, 15 (10.3 per cent) were 'patrons' of a claimant: cf. Vogel, *Fehderecht und Fehdepraxis*, 125–6 n. 332 and ibid., 262–300.

[64] Volckart, 'The Economics of Feuding', 290–1.

Illustration 3. Cattle rustling as a means of feuding. *Soester Nequambuch*, Stadtarchiv Soest, A No. 2771*

nobles was a sufficiently strong constraint on behaviour during a feud, why was it not strong enough to prevent the feud in the first place? If familiarity provided the mutual trust needed for the rivals to be willing to play by the rules and accept limits on the violent pursuit of self-interest, why did this familiarity not provide the mutual trust needed for cooperation to outweigh conflict altogether?

The broader theoretical implications of these questions underscore their import. Steven Pinker remarked that in today's intellectual climate, the banal observation that blood is thicker than water is shocking to many people: 'A Martian who wanted to learn about human interactions from a textbook in social psychology would have no inkling that humans behave any differently to their relatives than to strangers.' Hence, for example, the assumption that one is more likely to be killed by a relative in the home than by a mugger in the street could gain wide currency. This assumption, Pinker pointed out, is suspicious to anyone familiar with evolutionary theory, and is indeed unfounded. The risk of being killed by a blood relative is at least eleven times smaller than the risk of being killed by a nonrelative.[65] This simply reflects the fact that our mind was designed by natural selection, and that those who in the so-called environment of evolutionary adaptedness were kinder to strangers than to kin were less likely to pass their genes on to the next generation. It is with this ancestral environment in mind that economist Paul Seabright stressed how unlikely an achievement a modern society is. Given our evolutionary past, 'it is astonishing that systematic exchange among nonrelatives should have evolved at all, let alone that it should have become the foundation of the fantastically complex social and economic life we know today'. Modern life has come about through 'the gradual integration of local cultures of trust into larger regional, national, or even global cultures of trust'.[66] These reflections, which incidentally suggest one reason for the modern denial of kin solidarity, throw the problem of the feud into relief: a local or regional nobility in late medieval Germany was precisely such a culture of trust, yet it was also a culture of feuding. Feuds against 'strangers' were relatively rare; nobles feuded mostly against those in whom they would normally be expected to trust.

---

[65] Steven Pinker, *How the Mind Works* (New York, 1997), 431, 434–5.
[66] Paul Seabright, *The Company of Strangers: A Natural History of Economic Life* (Princeton, 2004), 53, 63–4.

The present book addresses this puzzling problem and some of its implications. The explanatory model it offers is based on relationships within the aristocracy: among nobles and between nobles and princes. It argues that these relationships, involving both cooperation and conflict, provided a set of powerful incentives to engage in feuding. They informed a set of beliefs, preferences and motivations that, in many cases, drove nobles to feud as the best available strategy for protecting and promoting their interests. And even though – indeed probably because – feuds were remarkably costly, the nobles apparently believed that the payoffs were high enough to render it a rational strategy to pursue.

The explanatory model that is offered, while claiming wide applicability, does not pretend to exhaustiveness. In the first place, the focus on the relationships among nobles requires a reconstruction of the genealogical, social and economic ties that made up their community. Such a reconstruction is research-intensive to the point of forcing concentration on one regional community and precluding a systematic comparative analysis. In the context of the geopolitical fragmentation and diversity characteristic of late medieval and early modern Germany, this methodological limitation must be accepted with due humility. Secondly, it is in the nature of history that no explanatory model can account for all the variations. Hence, following Chapter 3, which elaborates the general theory of the feud, two chapters deal with significant historical variations whose explanation requires the formulation of specific propositions. Chapter 4 seeks to make sense of the upsurge in feuding among nobles in the 1470s, while Chapter 5 accounts for the proliferation of feuds by nobles against princes between 1490 and 1510. After that date the feud began to decline. The reasons for this are explicated in Chapter 6: drawing on the conceptual resources of the model, it also tests the model's ability to explain historical change.

The plausibility of the theory is put to the test also in Chapter 2. Its first objective is to describe a feud in some detail in order to give a sense of what it was like. But the feud chosen for the task – Georg von Puchheim vs Emperor Friedrich III in 1453 – enjoys a special status in the literature: it was Brunner's paradigmatic example for his interpretation. Brunner's analysis of this feud and his reading of the sources are therefore still debated and impugned. The choice of this feud here, however, is not intended primarily as an exercise in refutation. Drawing in large part on the Austrian material adduced by Brunner himself, the chapter's second objective is to examine whether the explanatory model proposed in this book can account for the available evidence better than – or at least equally well as – other theories, even when applied to a social and political setting altogether different from that which has supplied its empirical foundation.

CHAPTER TWO

The rules of the game

Jakob Protzer, emissary of the city of Nördlingen, arrived in Vienna on 28 May 1453. Entrusted with some legal business, he quickly realised that his mission could not have been more ill-timed. Violence was rampant, royal authority defunct, chaos reigned supreme. His dispatches reveal a man concerned for his personal safety. A provost travelling with Emperor Friedrich III, he reported, had been attacked and robbed, even though he was bringing up the rear of the entourage. Protzer was uncertain whether he would fare better and come through the next leg of his journey, from Wiener Neustadt to Graz, in one piece. But Wiener Neustadt was not much more hospitable than its surroundings. The inhabitants lived in fear and allowed no one in without recommendation. The gallows erected for the execution of some captured highway robbers was hacked down and set on fire overnight. Law and order had for all practical purposes collapsed. Protzer knew who or what to blame. The cause of the trouble was the many feuds, but especially that of Georg von Puchheim, against the emperor. Puchheim and others presented the emperor with claims for large sums of money, and feuded against him when their demands were not satisfied.[1]

---

[1] Christine Reinle, *Ulrich Riederer (ca. 1406–1462): Gelehrter Rat im Dienste Kaiser Friedrichs III.* (Mannheim, 1993), 336–7.

Bad as the feuds were, they were not the cause of the political crisis in Austria, but rather its result. They broke out in the wake of a conflict between Emperor Friedrich III and the Estates. This crisis had its origins in a mix of financial difficulties and biological vicissitudes of the Habsburg dynasty. Since early in the century, the growing debts of the rulers had increased their financial dependence on the Estates and weakened their political position. When Duke Albrecht V (aka King Albrecht II of Germany) died in 1439, members of the Estates formed an interim government. They then recognised Duke Friedrich of the Styrian branch of the Habsburgs as regent. In early 1440 he also became the guardian of Ladislaus, the posthumously born son of Albrecht and therefore the nominal duke of Austria and heir to the thrones of Hungary and Bohemia. Friedrich, who was elected king of Germany that same year, encountered strong opposition in the Austrian lands. Having grandly jotted down 'AEIOU' in his notebook, he was hardly able to exert effective control at home.[2] Prominent among his problems was Ladislaus Posthumus. The nobility and the Estates demanded an end to Friedrich's guardianship over his ward.

The conflict came to a head shortly before Friedrich's planned departure for his imperial coronation in Rome. Thirty-nine nobles, under the leadership of Ulrich von Eytzing, a massively disgruntled former chief of government finances,[3] assembled in Mailberg in October 1451 and concluded a union. Slightly later, a further 250 representatives of the Estates added their signatures to the charter of the union. They announced that they were taking over the administration of the land until such time as Ladislaus was emancipated. The

[2] AEIOU meant 'all the world is subject to Austria' in both Latin ('Austrie est imperare orbi universo') and German ('als erdreich ist Osterreich underthan').

[3] See Aeneas Silvius de Piccolomini, *Österreichische Geschichte*, trans. Jürgen Sarnowsky (Darmstadt, 2005), 213–17.

king decided to proceed with his journey to Rome nevertheless. He appointed a regency council and set out on his way. On his return from Italy, Emperor Friedrich III found the Estates under arms. At the end of August 1452 the army of the Estates laid siege to Wiener Neustadt. The emperor had to give in and hand Ladislaus over.[4]

The defeat of the emperor did not bring peace. It led straight to another round of violence. The enemies this time were former friends. Foremost among them, as Protzer pointed out, was Baron Georg von Puchheim. Puchheim had been in Friedrich's service since the early 1440s. In 1442 he recruited several hundred soldiers for a campaign against the Moravian mercenary leaders Bítovsky of Lichtenburk, who conducted a feud against Friedrich for arrears of payments.[5] In the same year, as Friedrich travelled to Germany, he named Puchheim as one of the regents.[6] In 1445 Puchheim was one of Friedrich's envoys to negotiations in Moravia.[7] He was a member of the regency council during Friedrich's coronation in Rome.[8] He belonged to a minority among the barons who did not take the Estates' side in 1451. When the emperor arrived in Wiener Neustadt, 'he was welcomed joyfully by the Austrians who remained loyal, Georg von Puchheim, Rüdiger von Starhemberg, Sigismund von Eberstorff and numerous other barons, who considered as unworthy what von Eytzing and the count of Cilli did. And it was with them

---

[4] For a detailed discussion of the conflict between emperor and Estates see Reinle, *Ulrich Riederer*, 312–41. See also Karl Gutkas, *Geschichte Niederösterreichs* (Vienna, 1984), 80–3.

[5] Uwe Tresp, *Söldner aus Böhmen. Im Dienst deutscher Fürsten: Kriegsgeschäft und Heeresorganisation im 15. Jahrhundert* (Paderborn, 2004), 50.

[6] Eduard Marie Lichnowsky, *Geschichte des Hauses Habsburg*, part 6, *Von Herzogs Friedrichs Wahl zum römischen König bis zu König Ladislaus Tode* (Vienna, 1842), 31–2; Paul-Joachim Heinig, *Kaiser Friedrich III. (1440–1493): Hof, Regierung und Politik*, 3 vols. (Cologne, 1997), I, 257.

[7] Joseph Chmel (ed.), *Regesta Chronologico-Diplomatica Friderici IV. Romanorum Regis (Imperatoris III.)*, part 1, *Vom Jahre 1440 bis März 1452* (Vienna, 1838), 192, no. 1908.

[8] Piccolomini, *Österreichische Geschichte*, 216–17; Thomas Ebendorfer, *Chronica Austriae*, ed. Alphons Lhotsky (Berlin and Zurich, 1967), 413.

that the war plans were discussed.'[9] Puchheim was assigned to hiring Bohemian soldiers and was one of the leading commanders in the field.[10]

When the hostilities ended with the emperor's capitulation, Puchheim embarked on recouping his damages. The obvious place to begin was the emperor. Puchheim kept a letter from 11 July 1452 in which the emperor promised him that 'if he or his servitors sustained damages to their persons, their castles, people or property, through dispossession, devastation, capture or ransom, we would compensate the said von Puchheim or his heirs . . . We also undertake to pay regularly, as long as we are at war, the soldiers we have placed under him, so that he might last out and not come to damages.'[11] Taking the emperor at his word, Puchheim now presented him with a gigantic bill. Puchheim made two kinds of financial demands. In the first category were payments owed to him for twelve years of political and military service. In the second and more expensive category were the losses visited on him in the recent conflict with the Austrian Estates. Puchheim's was an unabashedly pedantic, peasant-by-peasant inventory of everything that had been taken from his landed estates.[12] The total amount came to 28,000 pounds. This was the equivalent of more than one-third of the yearly income of the duke of Austria.[13]

On 12 December 1452 Puchheim wrote to the emperor that he had been waiting in vain for a reply to his financial demands. 'I have for a long time been in Your Grace's service and served faithfully, paid heed to neither lords nor relatives nor anyone else . . . and did

---

[9] Piccolomini, *Österreichische Geschichte*, 448–9.

[10] Ibid., 458–9, 508–9; Victor Bayer, *Die Historia Friderici III. Imperatoris des Enea Silvio de' Piccolomini: Eine kritische Studie zur Geschichte Kaiser Friedrichs III.* (Prague, 1872), 172; Tresp, *Söldner aus Böhmen*, 50.

[11] Otto Brunner, 'Beiträge zur Geschichte des Fehdewesens im spätmittelalterlichen Oesterreich', *Jahrbuch für Landeskunde von Niederösterreich* 22 (1929), 431–507, at 438.

[12] Ibid., 439–47 and appendices 1–3.   [13] Ibid., 448.

not spare my body and property, and paid no heed to my ruin.' The emperor, he concluded, no longer required his service and he must therefore ask for a settlement of his claims.[14] It took another letter to bring the emperor to respond by inviting Puchheim to appear before his councillors in Vienna. The meeting yielded no results.[15] Puchheim wrote again on 31 January 1453, but not only to the emperor. He also complained to Archduke Albrecht VI and to the burgomaster and community of Wiener Neustadt that he gained no hearing from the emperor. 'Should His Grace not reimburse me, He would bring me into greater damages, which I hope He would not, and which I do not deserve. God knows that if I were to have to act differently, then I would have been compelled to do so by His Grace; and I would do so only unwillingly and would rather become reconciled.'[16] The threat worked, Archduke Albrecht did intervene, and the emperor offered to pay Puchheim 3,000 Gulden of debt over the next two years, and to negotiate over the rest and over Puchheim's reparations claims. Puchheim replied that he could not wait for so long. He demanded that the 3,000 Gulden be reimbursed by 10 March, and the rest within a year. Puchheim then wrote to the Styrian and Carinthian Estates, which were assembled in Graz, and urged them to intercede with the emperor on his behalf. He wrote two more letters to the emperor. For whatever reason, his tone now was supplicatory: 'I do not wish that Your Grace should let me go, to the pleasure of others and to my disgrace, for I and my family have never demonstrated towards the House of Austria anything other than loyalty and justice.'[17]

---

[14] Ibid., 449. Even as late as 6 January 1453, Puchheim was one of the witnesses of the confirmation of crucial Habsburg privileges, including the so-called *Privilegium maius*: Joseph Chmel (ed.), *Materialien zur österreichischen Geschichte*, vol. II (Vienna, 1838), 38, no. 34.

[15] Brunner, 'Beiträge zur Geschichte des Fehdewesens', 449.   [16] Ibid., 449–50.

[17] Ibid., 451.

His next letter to the emperor, dated 17 April 1453, was the cartel of defiance, without which a feud could not be considered legal. As Article 17 of the Golden Bull of Emperor Karl IV enjoined in 1356: 'It is not allowed to attack someone, under the pretext of a feud, with arson, robbery or plunder, unless the feud has been announced publicly to the one against whom one feuds, in person or at the place where he habitually resides, three days in advance, and this announcement can be attested to by reliable witnesses.'[18] Conforming to the formal requirement, Puchheim announced:

I am letting Your Grace know that I want to be enemy of Your Grace's land and people, and wherever I encounter your servitors and subjects, I will cause them damage, whenever I can, excluding however all of the princes over whom Your Imperial Grace has authority derived from the Holy Empire; I do not intend to become enemy either of them or of their men, but rather to ask them to have Your Grace make up for my damages. Towards Your Imperial Grace's person I am always humbly inclined to ask for the grace of paying me and making up for my damages, so that further claims, war and damages will be unnecessary. With this letter I wish, for honour's sake, to have preserved my honour and name in relation to Your Grace, and also that of my servitors, helpers and helpers' helpers.[19]

---

[18] Karl Zeumer, *Die Goldene Bulle Kaiser Karls IV.*, part 2, *Text der Goldenen Bulle und Urkunden zu ihrer Geschichte und Erläuterung* (Weimar, 1908), 33. This ruling was widely known and frequently referred to by feuding parties, especially with a view to questioning the legality of the actions of opponents. An example is the correspondence of Nuremberg concerning its feud with Heinz Rüdt von Collenberg in 1459–62. The last piece is a German translation of Article 17 of the Golden Bull ('Articulus in der guldein von der entsagnuß wegen'). It was prefaced 'Zum ersten, daz nyemant dem andern schaden tun oder zufugen sol, Er hab in dann zuvor zu gleichen pillichen lantleufftigen rechten ervordert, und ob im sollich recht villeicht so palde als er wolt oder begert gedeyhen und widerfaren möchte, so sol er dennoch den nit angreiffen noch beschedigen Er hab denn vor alles das völliclich und gantz getan und vollpracht das keyser karls des vierden seliger gedechtnuß unsers vorfarn am reiche guldein Bulle in dem Capitel von dem widersagen eygentlich ynnhellt und ausweiset': StAN, Reichsstadt Nürnberg, Akten des siebenfarbigen Alphabets, no. 32, doc. 17. For an explication of the passage on feuding see Mattias G. Fischer, *Reichsreform und 'Ewiger Landfrieden': Über die Entwicklung des Fehderechts im 15. Jahrhundert bis zum absoluten Fehdeverbot von 1495* (Aalen, 2007), 43–58.

[19] Brunner, 'Beiträge zur Geschichte des Fehdewesens', 452.

guttern die fie alzo verlaffen pren vntertane alweg bebal-
ten fem| vnd die·die alzo die offt genäte burger vnd frembe
and leut vntertane alzo neme wid ditz gefecz vnfers rechte
od fie genüme haben · vnd die mit gäczer weife m eine mo
nat mit laffen noch dem vnd m ditz gegewurtig bot vkündet
wirt·die fülle vmb filch vberfarn· als offt vnd das geldi-
cht hündert marck lauters golbes verfallen fem·vnd die fül-
len halp gefallen m die keiferlichekamern vnd d aud halb
teyl dem herzen der vutertan fie fem·
Eos qui decetero aduerfus aliquos iuftam diffidacioms ꝛc

< Das fibenzehendt Capitel ift vo der entfagnuß.
Je die furbaß wid etlich·m dichte em rechte vr
fach einer entfagtnuß vnd entfagen m an fulch
en fteten vmzeitlich·do fie bawfüg noch wonung
nicht halten · noch do fie nicht gewölich ficzel mi
wol wir welcherley fchaden · es fey mit brant od mit raub
od wie d fchabe genant fey·das das kemerley den|den al-
zo entfagt wirt mit kemen eren nicht zu zihen mag|vñ wa
nyemant freuel vnd vntrew zu hilff küme fol Darumb ge
biet wir mit gegewurtikeit dytz gefecz ewiglich zu halten
das fulch entfagnuß welcherley herzen ober perfonen myt
den etlich m gefelfchafft ober heimlikeit ober m welcher an
der freütfchafft die mit em ander we ñ| fulch entfagnuß ge
fcheben ober gefcheben werñ|das die mit krafft hab noch
entugen fol Vnd wollen auch dz niemant zimlich fey noch
enfulle vo fulcher entfagnuß niemant angreiffen wider myt
brene noch mit rauben· es fey den das dye felb entfagnuß
drey naturlich tag dem felben dem entfagt ift felber vñ an
d ftat·da er gewonlich pflygt zu wonen·offenlich fey ver
kundet·Vnd das man dye felben egenanten verkuntnuß
myt frummen· Erbern Redlichen zewgen beweyfen muge

Illustration 4. The Golden Bull of Emperor Karl IV, chapter 17. Bayerische
Staatsbibliothek, Munich, 2 Inc. s.a. 251 (Nuremberg: Friedrich Creussner, *c.* 1474)

By now Puchheim had recruited dozens of helpers, foremost among
them the all too aptly named mercenary captain Nabuchodonosor
Nankenreuter.[20] He had also tried to enlist the assistance of the
Bohemian lords whom he had recently worked to win over for the

---

[20] Ibid., 452–3 and nn. 2–3.

emperor during the conflict with the Estates.[21] Alongside these military preparations, Puchheim made an attempt to secure his political flank. He wrote to some German princes, attached a copy of his cartel of defiance, and asked for their help in persuading the emperor to pay him. Even two months after he had issued his cartel of defiance, Puchheim still did not make good his threat, preferring to write yet more letters to the emperor.[22] It was when these too got him nowhere, that he changed tack and began to bring force to bear on the government. The little concrete evidence there is for his actions suggests that he drew on the more or less fixed repertoire of sanctioned methods of feud making. Thus, on 5 July 1453 he abducted several people and burghers of Wiener Neustadt.[23] But nothing else is known beyond the general impression that he made the whole region around the town unsafe.

As has been indicated in the preceding chapter, the reason why the feud of Puchheim in particular has been described here is the special role it plays in Otto Brunner's interpretation of the feud in general. In 1929 Brunner subjected this feud to an extended analysis, complete with an edited selection of the relevant documents.[24] Ten years later, the Puchheim feud became the paradigmatic example of a feud in Brunner's book, *'Land' and Lordship*. Brunner stressed that the sources concerning the feud of Puchheim originated, 'rather exceptionally', not from the chancellery of the ruler or of the city of Vienna. They came from the Puchheim family archive.[25] This provenance allowed Brunner to look at the feud not through the eyes of the rivals of the nobleman and thus, by extension, to escape

---

[21] Ibid., 453.   [22] Ibid., 454–5.   [23] Ibid., 457.   [24] Ibid., 435–83.
[25] Otto Brunner, *'Land' and Lordship: Structures of Governance in Medieval Austria*, trans. Howard Kaminsky and James Van Horn Melton (Philadelphia, 1992), 10 n. 34; Brunner, 'Beiträge zur Geschichte des Fehdewesens', 431, 434.

the biased perspective through which historians normally viewed the noble feuds of the late Middle Ages. Brunner was aware that the feud would have looked very differently from the vantage point of the emperor and his councillors.[26] But his point was that Puchheim regarded his feud, and the violence it involved, as self-evidently legitimate. One indication is that 'the content as well as the form of his [declaration of feud] strictly conformed to formal procedures. Puchheim had given careful consideration to existing law.' Another indication is the wide publicity which Puchheim sought to give to his feud by writing about it to various electors and princes of the Holy Roman Empire. This, Brunner noted, 'was not the behaviour of a "robber knight" or a wanton violator of the peace'.[27] Like other nobles who took to feuding, Puchheim was acting out the legal consciousness of the time and 'behaved in strict accordance with legal procedure'.[28] 'That this right of feud (*Fehderecht*) could also be used against a ruling prince can only be grasped on the basis of the medieval right of resistance, which granted the right of self-help against an unjustly acting authority.'[29]

It is not surprising that given the paradigmatic value for Brunner of Puchheim's feud, his reconstruction of it has been contested with a view to challenging his overall interpretation of feuding. This has been done by reviewing the feud from the perspective of the emperor and his councillors. A week before Puchheim's declaration of feud, one of the emperor's advisers, Bishop Aeneas Sylvius Piccolomini, the future Pope Pius II (1458–64; b. 1405), reported on the conflict in a letter to Cardinal Nicholas of Cusa:

When the lord of Puchheim, who in the previous war defended lands of the emperor, saw that [his offer of] peace had been disregarded, he went to see

---

[26] Brunner, 'Beiträge zur Geschichte des Fehdewesens', 456.
[27] Brunner, *'Land' and Lordship*, 11–12.   [28] Ibid., 14.
[29] Brunner, 'Beiträge zur Geschichte des Fehdewesens', 456.

King Ladislaus. He then sent a letter to the emperor, requesting a large sum of money in compensation for the losses he had sustained fighting for his cause. The emperor replied that he would give him what he was entitled to. [Puchheim] was not content, complained at the royal council, and demanded aid against the king, but obtained none. To the speakers who presided over the council he said that he would be satisfied with an offer by the emperor to do justice by him. He nevertheless recruited soldiers as if he intended to make war with private forces. Harmful though this may be, albeit not more, one could say, than banditry, it will not affect us and will be more harmful to the perpetrator than to the victim.[30]

One historian has argued that Brunner suppressed this letter, which he must have known about, because it contradicted his interpretation and proved that Puchheim was acting unjustly: Emperor Friedrich acknowledged his liability to pay Puchheim and did not deny him his rights. The dispute, rather, turned on the amount to be paid. Moreover, by his address to the royal council, Puchheim effectively recognised the council as the proper legal instance to deal with the matter. Hence his military campaign was a 'private war'. According to this argument, Piccolomini realised that Puchheim's were economic motives, and therefore refrained from dignifying them with the term 'war', calling them what they really were: banditry.[31]

---

[30] 'dominus de Puchaim, qui bello superiori cesaris partes defendit, ut vidit pacem spretam, ad regem Ladislaum se contulit; deinde litteras ad cesarem misit, magnam pecuniam petens loco dampnorum, que sui causa tulerat. Cesar ei, quod justum esset, daturum se respondit. Ille non contentus in consilio regis questus, auxilia contra regem efflagitavit nihilque obtinuit, dicentibus qui consilium regunt, satis esse cesarem sibi jus offerre. Ille tamen militem conducit quasi privatis viribus bellum gesturus. id quamvis nocivum sit nihil tamen amplius quam latrocinium dici poterit neque nos afficiet et gerenti quam ferenti noxium erit': Bishop Aeneas Sylvius Piccolomini to Nicholas of Cusa, 10 April 1453: Rudolf Wolkan (ed.), *Der Briefwechsel des Eneas Silvius Piccolomini*, part 3, *Briefe als Bischof von Siena*, vol. 1 (Vienna, 1918), 135, no. 64.

[31] Hans-Henning Kortüm, '"Wissenschaft im Doppelpaß"? Carl Schmitt, Otto Brunner und die Konstruktion der Fehde', *HZ* 282 (2006), 585–617, at 614–15. See also Heinig, *Kaiser Friedrich III.*, 1, 257 n. 472.

Whether Piccolomini's brief statement can carry the weight of this construct is doubtful. First, Piccolomini did not have to be particularly clever to note that Puchheim's motives were economic – Puchheim never attempted to put a different gloss on them. Whether this is ground enough to brand Puchheim's actions as 'banditry' is questionable. Secondly, there is no compelling reason for according an account by a councillor to the emperor a degree of credence one normally reserves for objective, uninvolved observers. The same applies to the reported refusal of the royal council to recognise Puchheim's claim against the emperor. The council could not convincingly be described as a disinterested body. To judge Puchheim's feud from the perspective of Piccolomini and the royal council is no less one-sided than to judge it from the perspective of Puchheim. Brunner surely erred on the side of the noble, but his was a conscious effort to look at feuding from a different point of view than that of the eventual victors, namely the modern state. Indeed, there are few better examples of the latter's advantage in shaping the later view of historical events than its ability to secure the services of eloquent humanists such as Piccolomini. His analysis of the conflict between Emperor Friedrich III and the Estates, which led to the feud with Puchheim, is equally partisan. And so long as Puchheim served the emperor loyally against the rebellious Estates, he was for Piccolomini 'a dignified Austrian baron'.[32]

These different contemporary takes on the feud are important not because they may be considered as yet another proof of the postmodern truism that 'truth' in human affairs is often a matter of perspectives and constructed, self-serving 'narratives'. Rather they are significant because they point to some of the inherent problems which generated feuding in late medieval Germany and Austria.

[32] Piccolomini, *Österreichische Geschichte*, 458–9.

Criticisms such as those Piccolomini levelled at Puchheim were utterly commonplace in the blame game which accompanied every feud, but which was played without an authoritative referee. As Janine Fehn-Claus has pointed out, armed conflict occurred also because each party to a dispute always claimed to have justice on its side, whereas no single supreme institution existed which bindingly defined the law.[33] Indeed, such was the uncertainty about legal procedures in the fifteenth century that disputes often could not be taken to court before an agreement was reached as to which court of law had jurisdiction. Law often fell prey to politics as a result.[34] The highest judge himself, the Holy Roman Emperor, was not consistently above the factional fray. In fact, disputes were sometimes brought before emperors precisely because they were recognised to have vested political interests in the matters at issue.[35] To expect Georg von Puchheim to accept the opinion of the royal council as the final verdict in his quarrel with the emperor is to ascribe to him a naivety he most evidently lacked. For historians to assume the role of a judge over contested issues over which contemporary opinions – feeding on self-interest, self-righteousness and downright hypocrisy – widely diverged, is to disregard the limits of their métier. It is a fundamentally hopeless ambition. The same of course also applies to Brunner's explication of Puchheim's feud. While he freely admitted, at least in his 1929 article, that his study was biased by the sources,

[33] Janine Fehn-Claus, 'Erste Ansätze einer Typologie der Fehdegründe', in *Der Krieg im Mittelalter und in der Frühen Neuzeit: Gründe, Begründungen, Bilder, Bräuche, Recht*, ed. Horst Brunner (Wiesbaden, 1999), 93–138, at 98–9. See also Regina Görner, *Raubritter: Untersuchungen zur Lage des spätmittelalterlichen Niederadels, besonders im südlichen Westfalen* (Münster in Westfalen, 1987), 166.

[34] Ingeborg Most, 'Schiedsgericht, rechtliches Rechtsgebot, ordentliches Gericht, Kammergericht: Zur Technik fürstlicher Politik im 15. Jahrhundert', in *Aus Reichstagen des 15. und 16. Jahrhunderts* (Göttingen, 1958), 116–53, at 153. See also Rolf Sprandel, 'Das Raubrittertum und die Entstehung des öffentlichen Strafrechts', *Saeculum* 57 (2006), 61–76, at 66 7.

[35] Most, 'Schiedsgericht, rechtliches Rechtsgebot, ordentliches Gericht, Kammergericht', 152.

his conclusions were nevertheless too categorical, certainly in the version incorporated into *'Land' and Lordship* ten years later.[36] For in the final analysis, the relation between feuding and the law was, until late in the fifteenth century, indeterminate. Side by side with the nascent positive legal order, which fundamentally rejected the feud, there existed another, traditional conception of legality which accepted the feud. This means that the late medieval feud was neither a generally undisputed legal institution, nor a legally prohibited practice.[37] To pronounce unanimous verdicts on the legality of individual feuds was therefore a difficult task even for contemporary legal instances.[38]

While neither the historical circumstances nor the extant evidence permit a clear-cut judgment over the legality of Puchheim's feud, an analysis of the forces, considerations and motives that shaped Puchheim's decision to take on the emperor is feasible. Indeed, the sources on this feud published by Brunner warrant an interpretation of the feud that is somewhat different from the one he offered. That the military service which Puchheim rendered to the emperor in the

[36] In 1929 Brunner wrote that the view of the emperor and his councillor required a further investigation. In 1939 he threw this caution to the wind. On the difference between the 1929 article and *'Land' and Lordship* see also Gadi Algazi, 'Otto Brunner – "Konkrete Ordnung" und Sprache der Zeit', in *Geschichte als Legitimationswissenschaft, 1918–1945*, ed. Peter Schöttler, 2nd edn (Frankfurt am Main, 1998), 166–203, at 170.

[37] Fischer, *Reichsreform und 'Ewiger Landfrieden'*, 58–63, 201; Herbert Obenaus, *Recht und Verfassung der Gesellschaft mit St Jörgenschild in Schwaben: Untersuchungen über Adel, Einung, Schiedsgericht und Fehde im fünfzehnten Jahrhundert* (Göttingen, 1961), 65–6.

[38] An example is the diverging legal opinions of the Magdeburg and Leipzig jury benches concerning the case of Kunz von Kaufungen (1454). The Magdeburg jury bench indirectly recognised the legality of feuding; the Leipzig jury bench maintained that a feud could be waged only with permission of imperial or princely authority. See Uwe Schirmer, 'Kunz von Kaufungen und der Prinzenraub zu Altenburg (1455): Strukturen eines mittelalterlichen Konflikts', *ZHF* 32 (2005), 369–405, at 391–3; Christine Reinle, 'Fehdefürung und Fehdebekämpfung am Ende des Mittelalters', in *Der Altenburger Prinzenraub 1455: Strukturen und Mentalitäten eines spätmittelalterlichen Konflikts*, ed. Joachim Emig, Wolfgang Enke, Guntram Martin, Uwe Schirmer and Andre Thieme (Beucha, 2007), 83–124, at 113–14 n. 123.

war with the Estates plunged him into deep financial difficulties is not in doubt. Even if his claims were inflated, and even if he did not face as total a ruin as Brunner thought,[39] his losses could not but grievously impinge on his economic situation. The immediate material elements of his claims, however, can hardly be disentangled from the social and symbolic ones. It is noteworthy that in his letters to the emperor Puchheim stressed his need to settle his own debts to third parties. In rejecting the emperor's offer to pay him 3,000 Gulden over two years he explained that he himself was deeply in debt to the von Neitperg and von Starhemberg families, and that the settlement dates were imminent.[40] In his cartel of defiance he presented this as an important reason for his declaration of feud on the emperor: he wished 'that those to whom I gave my oath will also take note of my willingness to repay the debt into which I had got and into which I am still getting every day because of that matter'.[41] The creditors are not identified. Yet it is most likely that Puchheim was referring not (or not only) to the mercenary soldiers whom he had hired for the emperor but (especially) to the nobles whom just a few weeks earlier he named as his debtors. His debts to them might well have been incurred precisely in order to hire the mercenaries.[42] Thus it was not merely — and perhaps not even primarily — because of the financial loss he had suffered that he declared a feud on the emperor as a last resort to obtain his money. What he emphasised in his cartel of defiance was not so much the emperor's debt to him as his own debts to others.

As Brunner himself noted, Puchheim 'viewed his feud as not only a right but an obligation' towards his debtors. 'Not to have done so

---

[39] Brunner, 'Beiträge zur Geschichte des Fehdewesens', 448 and Brunner, *'Land' and Lordship*, 10, argued that the fate of the house of Puchheim depended on collecting the debt.
[40] Brunner, 'Beiträge zur Geschichte des Fehdewesens', 450.
[41] 'Das auch die schen, den ich gelobt hab umb schuld, da ich von der sachen wegen in komen pin noch tegleich mer kum, das ich gern zaln wolt': ibid., 451–2.
[42] Cf. Brunner, *'Land' and Lordship*, 42.

would have put him in default and would even have compromised the noble honour that often served as a pledge in the promissory notes of the period.'[43] But Brunner did not work out the implications of his own insight. He subsumed Puchheim's declared motive for feuding under a legalistic concept of honour and did not seek to place it within the context of the relationship and communication among the Austrian nobles. For him the Puchheim case was chiefly a substantiation of his argument for the lawfulness of feuding: if a feud against the emperor could be regarded as legal, then surely any properly conducted feud was legal. But the Puchheim case is also a typical example of the central role which the tight relationships among nobles played in motivating feuds. For Puchheim, as for most other nobles, the main concern was his reputation – and reputation was inescapably informed by the structure of relationships among nobles who were familiar with each other. That Puchheim, being at once creditor and debtor, felt constrained by this kind of relationship was far from incidental. It was an inherent and constitutive feature of the social life of the nobles of that period.[44] The feud of Puchheim was thus determined not solely by his relationship with the emperor, but also – and perhaps predominantly – by his place in the community of nobles. The obligation he had towards his debtors was a great deal more than a matter of conscience – it was a vital self-interest. If reputation for honesty and trustworthiness was so critical as to drive a nobleman to feud against an emperor, how much more likely was such a concern to drive nobles to feud against mere princes and fellow nobles.

The feud of Georg von Puchheim against Emperor Friedrich III was not atypical. Although waged against an emperor, which was on the whole uncommon, in most other respects it did not differ

---

[43] Ibid., 11. See also ibid., 42.   [44] See Chapter 3.

from countless other feuds in Austria and Germany. A first salient feature of many feuds was that they were preceded by efforts to reach a peaceful solution which continued even while the feud was well underway. The opposing parties normally set much store by 'public opinion' and legitimacy: they wielded the pen as well as the sword and torch. Violence was only one of the strategies employed in a feud, and feuders who exercised it to the exclusion of other available instruments of conflict resolution were actually doing disservice to their cause and narrowing their own room for manoeuvre.[45] This suggests a second observable prominent feature of most feuds: the violent attacks that did occur were by and large limited. They were regulated by accepted rules of conduct and by a more or less fixed repertoire of sanctioned methods: sporadic yet organised, usually small-scale raids involving burning, looting, abductions, and causing all sorts of material damage to the rival and his interests. Brutality *à l'outrance* was on the whole exceptional.[46] Killings were rare, and usually not premeditated. Although the actions of Puchheim in actually carrying out his feud are poorly recorded, it seems safe to assume that they did not include homicides. Shortly before the feud was settled in the autumn of 1453,[47] he is mentioned as having kidnapped some people.[48] Fatalities would not have been passed over and would probably have changed the course and nature of the feud.

---

[45] This emerges clearly from another feud which Brunner studied closely in 1929, that of Kaspar von Jedenspeigen against Kunigunde von Pottendorff (1440–1). See Alexander Jendorff and Steffen Krieb, 'Adel im Konflikt: Beobachtungen zu den Austragungsformen der Fehde im Spätmittelalter', *ZHF* 30 (2003), 179–206, esp. 197–8, 204.

[46] See Chapter 3.

[47] Ernst Birk, *Urkunden-Auszüge zur Geschichte Kaiser Friedrich des III. in den Jahren 1452–1467 aus bisher unbenützten Quellen* (Vienna, 1853), 6, no. 37; Wolkan (ed.), *Der Briefwechsel des Eneas Silvius Piccolomini*, 242, 264, nos. 134, 141.

[48] See n. 23 above.

Illustration 5. The abduction of Johann von Dietzelau, 1482. Lorenz Fries, *Chronik der Bischöfe von Würzburg 742–1495*, Stadtarchiv Würzburg, Ratsbuch, 412, fol. 347v

A third common and decisive characteristic of feuds was the crucial role played by the social networks of the rivals. Feuds were not carried out by kin groups, but rather by two principal feuders and their followers. Yet, as Jendorff and Krieb pointed out, feuds quickly drew in other people who had or could have a stake in the conflict and its outcome: from the ruler through fellow nobles to family, friends and neighbours. Some acted as helpers, others as mediators. Feuds could be neither conducted nor resolved without these networks.[49] The Puchheim feud, however, suggests that the role of the social networks of the rivals could be even more fundamental: they could actually give rise to feuds. In this respect, too, Puchheim's feud was part of a larger pattern. As Brunner stressed, unsettled debts arising from war-related financial transactions were the cause of nearly all of the noble feuds against Emperor Friedrich III, and in fact became a major problem of his reign.[50] The other nobles who feuded against

---

[49] Jendorff and Krieb, 'Adel im Konflikt', esp. 204.
[50] Brunner, 'Beiträge zur Geschichte des Fehdewesens', 455–7; Brunner, *'Land' and Lordship*, 12, 42.

the emperor argued in the same vein as Puchheim: they had financial commitments to meet; the emperor defaulting on his obligations towards them was bringing them into disrepute. Debts may have been the proximate cause of the feuds, but the ultimate cause was the feuders' relationships with other members of the aristocratic community. That their insolvency was the result of loyal service to the preeminent ruler of Christendom was remarkably not perceived by their creditors or guarantors as an extenuating circumstance. The relationships among the aristocracy seem to have had an iron logic of their own. They were compelling enough to turn a dependable noble councillor into an enemy of his lord, and generally, 'friends' into 'foes'.

The Puchheim feud thus supports the preliminary observation made in the preceding chapter, namely that it was the relationships among nobles familiar with each other which in themselves provided the most powerful incentives to feuding. The next chapter explains why.

CHAPTER THREE

Values and violence

The morals of feuding

The feud of Georg von Puchheim against Emperor Friedrich III indicates that a close connection existed between feuds and wars. Wars could easily touch off feuds. Conversely, feuds could lead to wars.[1] The intimate relationships between war and feud, and the absence of clear criteria for distinguishing between them, is reflected in the contemporary terminology. The sources sometimes apply the term 'feud' even to what were major wars in all but name.[2]

The question of the difference between war and feud has long been an important aspect of the debate over the nature of the feud and what it reveals about the social and political world in which it existed. Otto Brunner contended that 'all wars within Christendom must be understood as feuds, in a legal sense'.[3] But his is too sweeping a statement. For it might be argued that, even though it is indeed quite difficult to tell feud from war with regard to earlier times, the

---

[1] See Chapter 5.

[2] Friedrich von Weech (ed.), 'Das Reissbuch anno 1504: Die Vorbereitungen der Kurpfalz zum bairischen Erbfolgekriege', *Zeitschrift für die Geschichte des Oberrheins* 26 (1874), 137–264, at 143; Friedrich Stein (ed.), *Monumenta Suinfurtensia historica inde ab anno DCCXCI usque ad annum MDC: Denkmäler der Schweinfurter Geschichte bis zum Ende des 16. Jahrhundert* (Schweinfurt, 1875), 357. Cf. Mattias G. Fischer, *Reichsreform und 'Ewiger Landfrieden': Über die Entwicklung des Fehderechts im 15. Jahrhundert bis zum absoluten Fehdeverbot von 1495* (Aalen, 2007), 20.

[3] Otto Brunner, *'Land' and Lordship: Structures of Governance in Medieval Austria*, trans. Howard Kaminsky and James Van Horn Melton (Philadelphia, 1992), 35.

military renaissance of the late medieval and early modern period had rendered the contrast between war and lower forms of violence unmistakable.[4] The emergence, or resurgence, of a military culture which can be characterised as Western (re)introduced massed, well-drilled armies arrayed in close-ordered ranks and fighting shock combats to the bitter end.[5] This approach to war making – which the Marshal de Saxe was later to describe generically as 'l'ordre, et la discipline, et la manière de combattre'[6] – was a far cry from the 'typical' feud.

Yet, as far as the Old *Reich* is concerned, these military-historical arguments overshoot the mark. The Holy Roman Empire was not one of the crucibles of furious, interminable and devastatingly expensive wars in which modern states were forged in Western Europe in the late Middle Ages. It matters little in this respect that the Swiss style of warfare was well known in Germany and that experiments with comparable, innovative formations and tactics were made in the late fifteenth century.[7] No great battles were fought on German soil in this period. In terms of intensity, magnitude, organisation, mobilisation of resources, or historical importance, there were no Ravennas, Marignanos, or Pavias in German-speaking central Europe before the seventeenth century. And military conflicts within Germany, between its multiple constituent powers, remained modest. On the

---

[4] Brunner was of course aware that armed conflicts were of different scope. But such dissimilarities do not necessarily vitiate his point: wars were great feuds, feuds small wars. He did point out that by the end of the Middle Ages war and feud could practically be distinguished: ibid., 34. See also Christine Reinle, *Bauernfehden: Studien zur Fehdeführung Nichtadliger im spätmittelalterlichen römisch-deutschen Reich, besonders in den bayerischen Herzogtümern* (Stuttgart, 2003), 36–7.

[5] See Thomas Arnold, *The Renaissance at War* (London, 2001), esp. 69–100. On the peculiar military culture of the West see Victor Davis Hanson, *Why the West Has Won: Carnage and Culture from Salamis to Vietnam* (London, 2001).

[6] Quoted by John Keegan, *A History of Warfare* (London, 1993), 11.

[7] Harald Kleinschmidt, 'Disziplinierung zum Kampf: Neue Forschungen zum Wandel militärischer Verhaltensweisen im 15. und 16. Jahrhundert', *Blätter für deutsche Landesgeschichte* 132 (1996), 173–200, at 175–82; Arnold, *The Renaissance at War*, 82–3.

other hand, it was precisely in such a 'provincial' atmosphere, in the small landscapes disturbed but not transformed by the violent movements of modern state formation, that feuds proliferated. It must then be conceded in advance of any analysis of the causes and aims of feuds, that if Brunner's claim is grotesque with regard to Christendom at large, it does make fairly good sense with regard to the south and south-west of Germany. In this geopolitically highly fragmented area, with its puny territorial states, its kaleidoscopic jumble of ill-defined, intermingled and competing jurisdictions, wars and feuds had more resemblances and links than elsewhere. Moreover, given the nature of territorial contests in these politically incoherent zones, wars sometimes appear as little more than concatenations of feuds, feuds as integral parts of – or apologies for – war.[8]

German realities, then, make it difficult to demarcate the feud, and hence to define and explain it. However, one hallmark of a great many feuds, which, as has been indicated, has not hitherto received attention commensurate with its significance, was not a characteristic of wars: the rivals were more often than not part of the same local or regional social setting, and were regularly linked to each other by multi-stranded social and economic ties. They frequently knew each other all too well already before they came to blows.[9] Their feuds punctuated what was an ongoing relationship. This simple and ubiquitous fact was a crucial factor: it did a good deal to shape the methods employed in feuds as well as to inform their causes and motives. It may thus serve not simply to differentiate feuds from

---

[8] Hillay Zmora, *State and Nobility in Early Modern Germany: The Knightly Feud in Franconia, 1440–1567* (Cambridge, 1997), 96–100.

[9] Cf. the analysis of the relationship between the von Thüngen and the von Hutten families in Joseph Morsel, *La noblesse contre le prince: L'espace sociale des Thüngen à la fin du Moyen Âge (Franconie, vers 1250–1525)* (Sigmaringen, 2000), 403–423, 621. The Huttens, who were among the most sought-after matrimonial allies of the Thüngens, were also the Thüngens' leading adversary in terms of the number of conflicts in 1300–1525.

wars, but also as an interpretative key.[10] Feuds, it will be argued, were rooted in a type of reciprocal relationship which might be termed 'inimical intimacy'.

Several telling examples are contained in the *Geschichten und Taten* of the Franconian nobleman Wilwolt von Schaumberg (*c.* 1450–1510).[11] Written in the early years of the sixteenth century by his relative Ludwig von Eyb the Younger, the 'biography' of Wilwolt was conceived with a view to educating the young in the values and ideals of the nobility.[12] Given its expressly didactic purpose on the one hand, and its protagonist's evident taste for feuding on the other, the *Geschichten und Taten* is rich in information on the expectations and attitudes associated with, and expressed in, noblemen's aggressive conduct towards each other. Thus, at a tournament in Mainz in 1480, this paragon of nobiliary virtues accused one Martin Zollner von Rothenstein of dispossessing a mutual female relative of her inheritance. At first Wilwolt and Zollner only exchanged harsh words. Then Wilwolt became concerned that if he left it at that he would be held in contempt. He spent the rest of the day recruiting followers, and the night working out his tactics. When the games opened the next day he managed to corner Zollner and gave him a thrashing. This was not the end of the matter, for now Zollner

---

[10]   The feuds at issue here are primarily those between nobles and between nobles and princes. The interpretation suggested below does, however, apply also to some feuds against cities, though in a modified form that takes account of the different kind of relationship between the parties.

[11]   Adalbert von Keller (ed.), *Die Geschichten und Taten Wilwolts von Schaumburg* (Stuttgart, 1859).

[12]   Ibid., 5. For Wilwolt von Schaumberg, Ludwig von Eyb and the work see the remarkable study by Sven Rabeler, *Niederadlige Lebensformen im späten Mittelalter: Wilwolt von Schaumberg (um 1450–1510) und Ludwig von Eyb d.J. (1450–1521)* (Würzburg, 2006). See also Hartmut Boockmann, 'Ritterliche Abenteuer – adlige Erziehung', in his *Fürsten, Bürger, Edelleute: Lebensbilder aus dem späten Mittelalter* (Munich, 1994), 105–27, at 107–9. An abridged English rendering is in Nina Cust, *Gentlemen Errant, Being the Journeys and Adventures of Four Noblemen in Europe during the Fifteenth and Sixteenth Centuries* (London, 1909), 123–240.

in turn became concerned about his honour and felt that he had to do something to redress the balance. So when Wilwolt made his way home, Zollner confronted him brandishing a spear, shouting and taunting. Wilwolt feared indignity if he put up with such an affront, and reached for his own spear. Only the intervention of their companions prevented a bloody conclusion there and then.[13]

This episode suggests the difficulty of disentangling the material and symbolic motives for feuding and ranking them in order of importance. Indeed, in none of the 278 feuds carried out by Franconian nobles between 1440 and 1570 was honour the immediate cause of the conflict.[14] Rather, the immediate causes for feuds were more often than not disputes over material resources, rights and entitlements. Once the dispute was underway, honour was then invoked and suffused the conflict. The clash between Wilwolt von Schaumberg and Martin Zollner, though it did not become a full-blown feud,[15] illustrates the normal progression: what began as a conflict over the property rights of a woman to whom both parties were related mutated into a violent confrontation between men in which honour and reputation were at stake. Wilwolt and Zollner evidently took their honour and reputation very seriously. And both felt they were under pressure from a certain public to pick up the gauntlet or lose face. The sequence of events brings out the crucial importance of the symbolic, non-instrumental dimension of feuding.

---

[13] Keller (ed.), *Geschichten und Taten*, 48–51. For Martin Zollner and the dispute over inheritance see Rabeler, *Niederadlige Lebensformen*, 135–8; Werner Spielberg, 'Martin Zollner von Rothenstein und seine Sippe', parts 1 and 2, *Familiengeschichtliche Blätter* 15 (1917), 129–36; 167–80. Zollner was district governor in Wallburg: StAW, Ldf, no. 15, fols. 82–3.

[14] See also Rolf Sprandel, 'Das Raubrittertum und die Entstehung des öffentlichen Strafrechts', *Saeculum* 57 (2006), 61–76, at 65–6. Sprandel has pointed out that chronicles virtually never adduce 'honour' as an explanation for violent actions.

[15] A younger relation of Wilwolt, Adam von Schaumberg, is said to have taken up the claim upon coming of age and to have bullied Zollner into accepting a settlement on his terms: Keller (ed.), *Geschichten und Taten*, 51.

These aspects of feuding predominate and animate the various writings which feuders produced for public consumption and which remain a staple documentary source. An integral part of the feuding process, these self-justifying accounts evince the same anxiety about the opinion of others that weighed so heavily on Wilwolt and Zollner. Baron Friedrich von Schwarzenberg, who had a feud with Ludwig von Hutten about lordship over peasants, betrayed evident signs of distress in his pamphlet of 1533.[16] He began by trying to explain why it had taken him more than two years to respond to an earlier pamphlet disseminated by Hutten (1531).[17] In principle, he says, it would have been unnecessary to answer Hutten, since Hutten is a dishonourable person whereas he is an honourable nobleman.[18] Hutten is not in a position to revile or accuse him. He has waited for Hutten to become more upright so that he, Schwarzenberg, would have cause to reply. But in practice he is compelled to respond now, 'because it has come to us from trustworthy people that a rumour has been spread in Saxony, Hesse and other places' to the effect that he had been defeated and taken captive by Hutten. Schwarzenberg must set the record straight, for otherwise Hutten might hold himself to be in the right and believe that Schwarzenberg is afraid of him. Moreover, Hutten might even convince others to this effect. Hence

---

[16] *Unser Friderichen Freyherren von Schwartzenberg und zu Hohenlandsperg diser zeit Wirtembergischen Obervogts zu Schorndorf / warhafftiger bericht und gegenschrifft / auff Ludwigs der sich von Hutten und einen ritter nennt ausschreiben zum andern mal im druck ausgangen / im angang / mittel / ende / und durchaus erlogen (sovil er des wider und zusein vermeint) dann er sich auch sonst abermals in vil stucken selbst zum höchsten und mer verletzt / dann verantwort hat.* I have used the copy GStAB, XX.HA: Hist. Staatsarchiv Königsberg, Herzogliches Briefarchiv, A 4, 1534 January 29 (K. 191).

[17] I have used the copy British Library, C.38.k.16.

[18] 'Das dieser Hutten, bey allen die ine und sein wesen kennen, für kein sollichen man geacht würdet, der uns als einen, der sein tage (Gott lob) mit eren herbracht hat, im wenigsten zuschmehen, oder unpillichs zubeschuldigen tüglich. [Schwarzenberg had waited to see whether Hutten] redlicher worden, und sein angemaste eere, daran er angetast zusein vermeynt, baß dann bißhere verantworten wolt, damit wir mer ursach hetten, auff sein schreyben und klagen antwort oder ferner bericht zugeben.'

Schwarzenberg must provide his own version of the 'real' truth. Schwarzenberg's rhetoric was the stock-in-trade of pamphlet wars between nobles. He and other feuding nobles used a passionate moral language of right and wrong, of norms and their infringement. They explained and defended their actions in terms of justice, probity and honour, and denounced their opponents as acting out the opposite set of qualities and motives.

It would be incorrect to dismiss this rhetorical strategy as nothing more than deliberate dissimulation on the part of feuders. The very fact that they regularly justified themselves by invoking a uniform set of notions of right conduct suggests that these notions represented moral standards by which their behaviour was evaluated and judged. Feuders clearly felt compelled to conform, or to appear to conform, to a pattern of behaviour which these standards publicly circumscribed and sanctioned. That feuding nobles are certain to have internalised these moral standards to unequal degrees is immaterial. What mattered were the external constraints imposed by the social setting of feuds, and these ensured that the room for individual simulation and deception was limited. This was so because the public to whom the feuders appealed and whose opinion significantly affected the outcome consisted of people whom it was not easy to mislead over the motives and the details of a local conflict.

The point here is not the veracity of the feuders' accounts of their feuds. It certainly was not beneath them to bend the facts. The point is that the majority of feuds between Franconian nobles occurred within the boundaries of a moral community. This is a fact which poses a fundamental problem of interpretation. Nobles engaging in feuds were not simply people who typically knew each other, nor merely people who shared values and norms. They were people who often depended on each other in a whole variety of ways. Local nobles were each other's main marriage partners, and so had to keep their relationship with neighbouring families in good repair; they were each other's main suppliers of credit and loan guarantees; they relied on each other to provide patronage in princely courts and in cathedral chapters; they needed each other as witnesses and advocates in legal proceedings or infrajudicial dispute settlements; and, not least, they turned to each other as allies and helpers in feuds. When Wilwolt von Schaumberg became embroiled in a feud, he asked Otto von Aufseß for permission to use his castle as refuge. Aufseß agreed and said 'whoever flees to me on trust, will also find trust'.[19] The truth of the anecdote is less important than the subjective significance it had come to possess in Wilwolt's mind: it was recalled some twenty years after the event. An even more famous feuder, Götz von Berlichingen, recorded in his autobiography how Veit von Vestenberg lent him his best horse when Götz badly needed one. People at the princely court were astonished and said that even if Veit's feudal lord, the margrave of Brandenburg, had asked him for this horse, Veit would have refused. The event had carved itself on Götz's memory: he wrote the autobiography more than fifty years after the gesture had been made.[20] For the nobles these episodes were clearly anything but trivial. They show how profoundly concerned nobles were with cooperation and trust. And yet it is precisely with the people with whom they cultivated such vital ties that nobles tended to have feuds.

This mutual dependence and the need to think about tomorrow explain the relative mildness with which noblemen acted against each other in feuds. The violence they exercised was directed mostly

[19] Keller (ed.), *Geschichten und Taten*, 58.
[20] Helgard Ulmschneider (ed.), *Götz von Berlichingen. Mein Fehd und Handlung* (Sigmaringen, 1981), 69.

against property and the tenants of the rival noble, much less often against his person. For one thing, killing a rival noble in feud was counterproductive: it defeated the immediate objective of forcing a claim on him, and in addition entailed risks of revenge or punishment. For another, it was normatively beyond the pale.[21] But if shared values and mutual dependence help account for the relative restraint which noblemen exhibited in feuds against fellow nobles, they seem by the same token to make it difficult to explain why noblemen waged such feuds in the first place. The question, to put it simply, is why noblemen would tend to feud against the very people from whose goodwill they had so much to gain and from whose enmity so much to lose. Feuds were not isolated, one-shot encounters between strangers but normally part of a continual interaction between neighbours, relatives and acquaintances. In other words, they occurred in a social environment which on the face of it could be expected to discourage feuds: first, geographical proximity made retaliation easy and must have constituted something of a deterrent. Secondly, availability of mutual friends and kin could serve to facilitate mediation and accommodation. Thirdly, and for the same reasons, feuds involved the peril of estranging quite a few people with whom one had or could have multiple ties – economic, social, cultural – whose severance would have dire consequences. In addition, feuds were expensive;[22] there are strong indications that they were, in economic terms, loss-making business, a fact of which nobles were unlikely to be

---

[21] Brunner, *'Land' and Lordship*, 68; Thomas Vogel, *Fehderecht und Fehdepraxis im Spätmittelalter am Beispiel der Reichsstadt Nürnberg (1404–1438)* (Frankfurt am Main, 1998), 227–9. Count Froben Christoph of Zimmern alleged in his chronicle that Margrave Friedrich of Brandenburg 'many times addressed his nobles, saying: "it is all right to shake the wallets of merchants so long as you do not endanger their lives"': Hansmartin Decker-Hauff (ed.), *Die Chronik der Grafen von Zimmern*, vol. II (Sigmaringen, 1967), 185.

[22] Some nobles even complained of the expenses involved in the correspondence that was an integral part of the feuding process. StAB, Hofrat Ansbach-Bayreuth, no. 565, doc. 2; Rabeler, *Niederadlige Lebensformen*, 142.

oblivious.[23] The costs of feuds were thus considerable in several crucial respects.

Given these costs and their specific sources, the fact that a large number of feuds occurred between people inhabiting the same social and moral universe must serve as a point of departure for any attempt to understand the feud in terms of the morals, norms and beliefs that informed them. To wit, one has to seek an explanation in terms of ethical principles and perceptions precisely because the material bonds of interdependence between nobles not only often failed to mitigate against feuds, but, on the contrary, actually motivated and precipitated them. A case in point is unpaid debts, a prevalent cause of feuds.[24] The incentive behind such feuds might superficially seem quite clear: to coerce the debtor to repay the sum outstanding, an undertaking rendered all the more justified by the absence or weakness of institutions capable of enforcing contracts. However, the social context of credit transactions between nobles suggests that things were not that simple. The first thing to note is that nobles did not lend money to just anyone. They typically lent to those they knew or to those their kin and friends knew. Of the 24,584 Gulden of debts owed by Hans-Georg von Absberg in 1523, slightly more than 15,000 Gulden were owed to fellow nobles. And looming large among the latter were his son (5,000 Gulden), his son-in-law (1,500 Gulden), and the margraves of Brandenburg-Ansbach (2,000 Gulden).[25] These mountainous debts impelled the Absbergs to sell their castle Vorderfrankenberg. One of the buyers was the prominent *financier gentilhomme* Ludwig von Hutten. A list of his

---

[23] Markus Bittmann, *Kreditwirtschaft und Finanzierungsmethoden: Studien zu den Verhältnissen des Adels im westlichen Bodenseeraum* (Stuttgart, 1991), esp. 109–10.

[24] Janine Fehn-Claus, 'Erste Ansätze einer Typologie der Fehdegründe', in *Der Krieg im Mittelalter und in der Frühen Neuzeit: Gründe, Begründungen, Bilder, Bräuche, Recht*, ed. Horst Brunner (Wiesbaden, 1999), 93–138, at 115–16. See also Chapter 2 n. 50.

[25] StAN, Fstm.Ansb., AA-Akten, no. 1402, fols. 126r–129r.

debtors drawn up in 1548 names, apart from Margrave Kasimir (for 4,000 Gulden), Bernhard von Hutten (for 2,000), Lorenz von Hutten (for 1,000), and several other local nobles for smaller but not trivial sums.[26] Not only borrowers, but also guarantors were chosen on the basis of some personal acquaintance. When Count Wilhelm of Henneberg suggested to Wilwolt von Schaumberg some Thuringian counts as guarantors for his loan, Wilwolt refused on the grounds that he would have no leverage over them in the event of default. 'But I would be happy', he added, 'to accept Franconian counts or barons as guarantors whom I can better admonish than [I can the Thuringians].'[27]

Loans were not unalloyed financial transactions. They were multi-stranded, mixing political, social and economic considerations – often in that very order.[28] And they linked nobles to each other and to princes in a dense web of reciprocal relations. A register of debtors drawn up after his death in 1516 reveals that Philipp von Seckendorff-Gutend was not only a chief creditor of the margraves of Brandenburg (for 7,000 Gulden), but also a creditor of their creditors. He loaned, for example, 900 Gulden to his brother-in-law Wolf von Crailsheim, who at that time was creditor of the margraves for 2,000 Gulden.[29] Another margravial creditor, Moritz

[26] Richard Schmitt, *Frankenberg: Besitz- und Wirtschaftsgeschichte einer reichsritterschaftlichen Herrschaft in Franken, 1528–1806 (1848)* (Ansbach, 1986), 386 n. 1.

[27] Rabeler, *Niederadlige Lebensformen*, 361.

[28] Ludwig von Hutten (father of the above-mentioned Ludwig) pointed out in a pamphlet against Duke Ulrich of Württemberg, who killed his son Hans von Hutten, that he had lent the duke 10,000 Gulden free of interest, although he could have invested them elsewhere with profit: Eduard Böcking (ed.), *Ulrichi Hutteni, equitis Germani, Opera quae reperiri potuerent omnia*, 5 vols. (Leipzig, 1859–61), I, 77.

[29] Cf. Alfred Wendehorst and Gerhard Rechter, 'Ein Geldverleiher im spätmittelalterlichen Franken: Philipp von Seckendorff-Gutend', in *Hochfinanz, Wirtschaftsräume, Innovationen: Festschrift für Wolfgang von Stromer*, ed. Uwe Bestmann, Franz Irsigler and Jürgen Schneider, 3 vols. (Trier, 1987), I, 487–529, at 509, and StAN, Fstm.Ansb., Brandenburger Literalien, no. 643. Wolf von Crailsheim went on to become one of the margraves' major creditors: StAN, Ansbacher Landtagsakten 8, no. 36, fol. 148r (14,000 Gulden).

von Seckendorff (at 700 Gulden), owed his kinsman Philipp 150 Gulden.[30] The correspondence among nobles and between nobles and princes also reveals how financially interdependent they were. When in 1524 Albrecht von Vestenberg asked for a repayment of 2,000 Gulden he had lent to the margrave of Brandenburg, he explained that he himself owed 2,000 Gulden to Count Wilhelm of Henneberg who now wanted his money back in order to pay off his own debt of 2,000 Gulden to another nobleman.[31] In 1507, the count asked Wilwolt von Schaumberg for a loan of 2,300 Gulden, which he needed in order to pay the von Hutten. In 1510 Wilwolt reminded Count Wilhelm of an interest payment due on 22 February; he, Wilwolt, had to pay his brother and another noble on that same date.[32] Christoph-Philipp von Sparneck insisted that another nobleman, who stood surety for a defaulting prince, would now settle the debt as the contract required. Sparneck explained that he had to satisfy his own creditors and warned the guarantor that he would have to make this breach of faith public. [33]

Nobles were thus simultaneously creditors and debtors. The consequences of any default were bound to have a ripple effect. If a nobleman was not repaid or reimbursed in time, that could make it difficult for him to repay his own debts. And this in turn could bring about two unpleasant outcomes: one was damage to his creditworthiness; the other was the likelihood that he too would become a target of other noblemen seeking to enforce their contractual claims.[34] In

---

[30] Cf. Wendehorst and Rechter, 'Ein Geldverleiher im spätmittelalterlichen Franken', 510, and StAN, Fstm.Ansb., Brandenburger Literalien, no. 643. Philipp von Seckendorff was also a creditor of the above-mentioned Hans-Georg von Absberg: ibid.

[31] StAN, Fstm.Ansb., AA-Akten, no. 728, doc. of Donnerstag nach Matthei [22 September] 1524.

[32] Rabeler, *Niederadlige Lebensformen*, 356, 357 n. 1755.

[33] Alban von Dobeneck, 'Geschichte des ausgestorbenen Geschlechtes der von Sparneck', part 1, *AO* 22, no. 3 (1905), 1–65, at 37–8.

[34] Brunner, *'Land' and Lordship*, 11; Fehn-Claus, 'Erste Ansätze einer Typologie der Fehdegründe', 118; Alexander Patschovsky, 'Fehde im Recht: Eine Problemskizze', in

such circumstances, the decision to wage a feud was not senseless. Alternative avenues for seeking redress were often less effective. When the failure of Archbishop Dietrich of Mainz to pay the interest on a loan he had taken in 1455 from the Hessian nobles Hermann and Georg Riedesel exposed them to pressure from their own creditors, they demanded from the guarantors that they fulfil their obligations. They reproached one of the guarantors, Count Sigmund of Gleichen, saying they did not believe he was of an honourable lineage and bloodline, for otherwise he would have respected his sealed pledge. And they threatened him with the dissemination of defamatory letters that would bring his 'forgetfulness' to public attention. The threat was either futile or else too forceful, for the dispute escalated into a feud.[35] Moreover, such alternatives to feud, if they did not generate one, risked being taken for cowardice or weakness or indeed for downright dereliction of duty. Baron Friedrich von Schwarzenberg sneered that Ludwig von Hutten recoiled from fighting and instead took the case to the Imperial Chamber Court (*Reichskammergericht*) requesting that Schwarzenberg be enjoined to refrain from violence. These, Schwarzenberg added, were Hutten's knightly deeds.[36] The same idea was enunciated more directly by Count Erasmus of Wertheim during his conflict with Georg von Rosenberg: 'The nobles (*Rittermessigen*) of past time', he wrote, 'used to say that any nobleman has to maintain his honour with his hand; but when one doubts the justice of one's cause, one goes

Recht und Reich im Zeitalter der Reformation. Festschrift für Horst Rabe, ed. Christine Roll (Frankfurt am Main, 1996), 145–78, at 177.
[35] Eduard Edwin Becker, *Die Riedesel zu Eisenbach: Geschichte des Geschlechts der Riedesel Freiherrn zu Eisenbach*, vol. 1, *Vom ersten Auftreten des Namens bis zum Tod Hermanns III. Riedesel 1500* (Offenbach, 1923), 262–4; Matthias Lentz, *Konflikt, Ehre, Ordnung: Untersuchungen zu den Schmähbriefen und Schandbildern des späten Mittelalters und der frühen Neuzeit (ca. 1350 bis 1600); Mit einem illustrierten Katalog der Überlieferung* (Hanover, 2004), 207, no. 60.
[36] See n. 16 above.

to law and uses other subterfuges.'[37] Feuds, on the other hand, by the very real costs and dangers they implicated, demonstrated one's good faith and signalled a moral seriousness and uncompromising commitment that could make the desired impact on other actors – reassuring creditors, warning debtors, impressing third parties.[38]

A similar set of pressures and motives was at work in conflicts relating to lordship rights, another widespread cause of feuding in Franconia and elsewhere. What is often striking in these disputes is the apparent asymmetry between the negligible pecuniary value of the rights in question and the intransigence and intense moral indignation that the feuders displayed. As one noble put it during an intrafamilial dispute over a fishpond: 'I want to show myself in this such that it shall be seen that it means much to me and I wish either to be ruined or die for it or to maintain my ancestral and paternal property and my wife's property.' A few years earlier, his rival had stated his position in no less trenchant terms: 'It is proper for me to defend myself when my property is unjustly taken away . . . I have always heard that one should fight and die for one's paternal inheritance before one allows it to be taken away.'[39] This way of thinking about hereditary rights as sacred enough to justify self-sacrifice was common to all aristocrats, from emperor at the top

---

[37] *Shiedsspruch Kurfürst Philipp des Aufrichtigen von der Pfalz in der Irrung zwischen Erasmus Graf von Wertheim und Ritter Georg von Rosenberg* (Bayerische Staatsbibliothek Munich, Ded. 350 c), fol. 7 (1501). For a summary of the correspondence between the parties see Georg Veesenmeyer, 'Nachricht von zwei Rosenbergischen Fehden: (1) Jörgen, Adolphs und Friedrichs von Rosenberg mit dem Bistume Würzburg, 1486; (2) Jörgen von Rosenberg mit Asmus, Grafen von Wertheim, 1501–1502', *Verhandlungen des Vereins für Kunst und Alterthum in Ulm und Oberschwaben* 12 (1860), 41–56, at 45–55.

[38] Cf. Fehn-Claus, 'Erste Ansätze einer Typologie der Fehdegründe', 115 n. 103; Chapter 2 n. 41.

[39] StAN, Fstm.Ansb., Ansbacher Historica, no. 210, doc. of Palmtag zu Abend [29 March] 1488: 'so wil ich mich darinen bewysen das man sol sehen das es mir leit ist und wil dar ob verderben oder sterben oder wil mein anherlich vetterlich und weyplich gut behaltten und zu mein handen prengen'; ibid., doc. of Montag Antonii [17 June] 1485: 'zimpt mir so mir einer das meyn an recht nymt zu weren . . . wan ich albeg gehort habe, einer soll umb sein vetterich [sic] erbe streyten und sterben ee und er im das nemen laße'.

Illustration 6. Defamatory letter: a cow befouls the coat-of-arms of Heinz von Guttenberg, *c.* 1487. Germanisches Nationalmuseum, Nuremberg, Kk. HB. 2527 / Kaps. 1382

to untitled nobles at the bottom.[40] Hence they willingly accepted the often glaring discrepancy between the economic value of these rights and the costs of protecting and retaining them. Margrave Albrecht Achilles of Brandenburg reported to his brother that a conflict over tolls with the bishop of Würzburg was forcing him to keep 200 or

[40] Cf. William Maltby, *The Reign of Charles V* (Basingstoke, 2002), 12–13.

300 horsemen at the ready, which cost him in a week the equivalent of his income from the toll in a whole month – 'but with the help of God we would not let 4,000 Gulden be taken away from the lordship even if it should cost us three times the worth of the toll'.[41]

The biologist Robert Trivers noted in a now famous article that 'much of human aggression has moral overtones. Injustice, unfairness, and lack of reciprocity often motivate human aggression and indignation. A common feature of this aggression is that it often seems out of all proportion to the offenses committed.' He explained this feature thus: 'Since small inequities repeated many times over a lifetime may exact a heavy toll in relative fitness, selection may favour a strong show of aggression when the cheating tendency is discovered.'[42] This logic applies very well to disputes over lordship rights in Franconia. The foundation of noble status, lordship in late medieval and early modern Franconia was not a solid, monolithic, cohesive entity. Rather, it was a composite structure, the sum total of diverse rights, a *summa iurium*. This meant that any one of its constituent elements could be alienated from one lord by another. Failing to respond forcefully to the threat of alienation of one element, however paltry in itself, was likely to be seen by other lords as a sign of impotence, of a flagging will, of demoralisation. Quiescence or placatory measures were unlikely to bring tranquility. On the contrary, in the competitive world of armigerous lords such behaviour was likely to breed contempt, whet appetites and feed aggression. And this in turn could lead to the disintegration and

---

[41] GStAB, BPH, Rep. 44, no. 1, fol. 40: 'doch lassen wir viertausent gulden gelts der herschafft nicht encziehen mit der hilff gots und solt es uns dreymal als vil kosten als der zol wert wer'. Cf. Johannes Merz, *Fürst und Herrschaft: Der Herzog von Franken und seine Nachbarn 1470–1519* (Munich, 2000), 54 n. 8.

[42] Robert Trivers, 'The Evolution of Reciprocal Altruism', *Quarterly Review of Biology* 46 (1971), 35–57, at 49. Cf. Robert Wright, *The Moral Animal: Evolutionary Psychology and Everyday Life* (New York, 1994), 205–9.

eventual collapse of lordship.[43] Hence any dispute over lordship rights was potentially critical, and it was quite sensible for nobles to respond to challenges vigorously, sometimes in a seemingly disproportionate manner. No feud was in this sense more spectacular than the one which Christoph Fuchs von Bimbach started in 1462 against the prince-bishop of Bamberg over grazing rights.[44] The chronicler of this feud, which ultimately led to a war between princes, noted that the annual income from the disputed right was a mere 3 Gulden. He could not help concluding that 'this was the beautiful Helen over which the two princes . . . went to a veritable Trojan War'.[45] Nobles such as Fuchs not only had to react to current threats, but had to anticipate future ones as well. They feared a situation encapsulated in a maxim of which one feuder reminded fellow nobles in 1470: 'He who sustains the damage must often suffer the scorn as well.'[46] Hence they felt constrained to maintain formidable reputation – that invisible and intangible palisade against prospective encroachers.

However, such edgy behaviour entailed immediate costs, whereas the benefits were to be reaped, if at all, only in the future. Feuding nobles must have faced the problem of summoning enough resolve to make the necessary sacrifices in the present, to put up a credible

---

[43] Hans von Egloffstein complained that, because of a protracted conflict with Nuremberg, he had to evacuate his home 14 times in a space of 18 years, and was eventually forced to put it up for sale: StAB, Hofrat Ansbach-Bayreuth, no. 579, doc. of Freitag nach Egidii [4 September] 1545.

[44] The cartel of defiance in StAW, Standbücher, no. 717, fols. 257r–v.

[45] Lorenz Fries, *Chronik der Bischöfe von Würzburg 742–1495*, vol. IV, *Von Sigmund von Sachsen bis Rudolf II. von Scherenberg (1440–1495)*, ed. Ulrike Grosch, Christoph Bauer, Harald Tausch and Thomas Heiler (Würzburg, 2002), 205–23 (quotation at 223).

[46] StAN, AA-Akten, no. 738, doc. 6. For this proverb see also Joachim Schneider, 'Legitime Selbstbehauptung oder Verbrechen: Soziale und politische Konflikte in der spätmittelalterlichen Chronistik am Beispiel der Nürnberger Strafjustiz und des Süddeutschen Fürstenkriegs von 1458–1463', in *Schriftlichkeit und Lebenspraxis im Mittelalter: Erfassen, Bewahren, Verändern*, ed. Hagen Keller, Christel Meier and Thomas Scharff (Munich, 1999), 219–41, at 228.

show of aggression despite the immediate risks entailed by feud and violence, and thus to bridge the gap between the current costs of such conduct and its future reputational benefits.[47] It must be borne in mind that feuds were not usually declared on the spur of the moment, nor carried out in hot blood. For all the emotions that no doubt played a part, feuds involved careful deliberation, reasoning and calculation. As the negotiations that often preceded and accompanied them suggest, feuds were strategic enterprises. It is here that honour came to play a pivotal role.

Honour is a highly complex, protean concept that can acquire different meanings in different contexts.[48] Accordingly, its invocation in feuds could serve several overlapping purposes, some more self-consciously so than others. The most basic aim, clearly recognisable in virtually all texts produced by feuding parties for third parties, was to isolate the rival, to make it difficult for other noblemen openly to help him. Honour lent itself to such attempts because it is a quintessentially 'mediated acquisition':[49] it turns on the recognition and approbation of one's fellow men. In the case of nobles, honour was accorded by the community of fellow nobles. Given that honour is intersubjective in nature, each nobleman was in a position to grant or withhold it. As anthropologists and sociologists have shown, this

[47] For general theoretical considerations on this pattern of human behaviour see Robert H. Frank, *Passions within Reason* (New York, 1988), 83, 84, 88–9, 169, 211. Cf. Matt Ridley, *The Origins of Virtue* (Harmondsworth, 1996), 127–47. Cf. also Ernst Fehr, Urs Fischbacher and Simon Gächter, 'Strong Reciprocity, Human Cooperation, and the Enforcement of Social Norms', *Human Nature* 13, no. 1 (2002), 1–25, at 18.

[48] Psychologists Jonathan Haidt and Craig Joseph, 'Intuitive Ethics: How Innately Prepared Intuitions Generate Culturally Variable Virtues', *Daedalus* (Fall 2004), 55–66, have argued that honour, like other particular traits and virtues, aqcuires different meanings according to the four fundamental patterns (suffering, hierarchy, reciprocity, purity) of human interaction which between them underlie moral systems. Thus 'the virtue of honour can be incarnated as integrity (in reciprocity), as chivalry or masculine honour more generally (in hierarchy), or as chastity or feminine honour (in purity)'.

[49] The term 'mediated acquisition' is borrowed from Dan Eldar, 'Glory and the Boundaries of Public Morality in Machiavelli's Thought', *History of Political Thought* 7 (1986), 419–38, at 422.

process of recognition by the relevant community classifies people and works also as a mechanism for distinguishing between members and non-members.[50] Nobles understandably were deeply concerned about the opinion of their fellows. As Schwarzenberg himself said during the above-mentioned feud, Ludwig von Hutten was primarily preoccupied with public opinion (*gemain pawern geschray*). True, one cannot measure the effects of pamphlets and letters in moulding noble public opinion. But the very fact that noblemen consistently resorted to this method of dissemination testifies to the importance which they attributed to them. Nobles unquestionably believed in the power of words to validate or to question a noble's conformity to norms, his reliability, and hence his very nobility. Thus what Schwarzenberg was driving at was that Hutten failed to conform to the model of honourable man; albeit of noble stock, he did not deserve to be a member of the community of nobles. For Hutten, according to Schwarzenberg, had (1) broken his word; (2) not kept his father's word; and (3) attacked Schwarzenberg without sending a cartel of defiance. It is noteworthy that these alleged deeds echo the transgressions which the tournament regulations of the fifteenth century stipulated as meriting punishment.[51] How could any nobleman eat and drink in Hutten's company and still call himself a noble, he wondered. The lesson was clear: anyone who helped such a false noble as Hutten would place himself outside the community. The same point was made in numerous other texts composed by rival noblemen. A discredited nobleman deprived of the moral support of fellow nobles was an easy target.

---

[50] Georg Simmel, *Soziologie: Untersuchungen über die Formen der Vergesellschaftung* (Leipzig, 1908), 533–4; J. G. Peristiany (ed.), *Honour and Shame: The Values of Mediterranean Society* (London, 1965); R. A. Nye, 'Honor Codes in Modern France: A Historical Anthropology', *Ethnologia Europae* 21 (1991), 5–17, here 11; Kristen B. Neuschel, *Word of Honor: Interpreting Noble Culture in Sixteenth-Century France* (Ithaca, 1989), 76–7.

[51] See n. 69 below.

But the invocation of honour could, as has been indicated, also serve as a solution to the problem of the gap between the immediate costs of feuding and the expected future reputational gains. This use of honour is in the nature of things not as directly observable as the aim of morally isolating the opponent. But the evidence for the political and social instrumentalisation of honour by nobles suggests that they possessed enough practical consciousness to put honour to this use as well.[52] In the first place, the language of honour could be employed to convert a conflict originally over a material prize into a conflict over a moral or symbolic good. In thus transposing a conflict onto a moral plane, nobles would communicate a serious threat of violence. When a conflict is transferred from the domain of law into the realm of morality, and when the good at stake is as unique and non-negotiable as honour, it is necessarily less inhibited by rules. Conflicts over points of honour could theoretically develop unrestricted virulence. By signalling such a danger, nobles effectively invited the intervention and mediation of princes or fellow nobles in the feud. Not for nothing did Schwarzenberg send a copy of his pamphlet, in which he offered to risk his life in a duel with Hutten, to Duke Albrecht of Prussia.[53] Princely archives are full with copies of letters in which nobles impugned each other's honour. By the same token of brinkmanship, the appeal to one's honour was a

---

[52] See the examples given in Hillay Zmora, 'Adelige Ehre und ritterliche Fehde: Franken im Spätmittelalter', in *Verletzte Ehre: Ehrkonflikte in Gesellschaften des Mittelalters und der Frühen Neuzeit*, ed. Klaus Schreiner and Gerd Schwerhoff (Cologne, 1995), 92–109, at 107. When Schwarzenberg sought to avoid the politically thankless membership in an Estates committee, he was advised to use Hutten's membership in the same body as an excuse for his refusal to sit on it: Uwe Müller, *Die ständische Vertretung in den fränkischen Markgraftümern in der ersten Hälfte des 16. Jahrhunderts* (Neustadt a.d. Aisch, 1984), 203–4. For a penetrating remark on practical consciousness as an intermediate form between naturalised, unconscious knowledge and exteriorised, codified knowledge, see Norman Bryson, *Vision and Painting: The Logic of the Gaze* (Basingstoke, 1983), 69–70.

[53] See n. 16 above.

'commitment device'.[54] By bringing honour into play, a noble bound himself to a certain – ostensibly irrational – course of action that discounted its costs. In fact, the threat involved in invoking honour would not have been credible if honour had not by cultural definition entailed a commitment to behave in such a way. It was as it were a contract which one made with oneself and which one had an interest in advertising; once advertised, it came into force: one could not now renege on one's word of honour without sorely compromising one's reputation.[55]

Reputation was essential for success in life because nobles depended on each other for securing their most vital interests. Reputation – and honour as at once a sentiment closely associated with it and a strategy for defending it – inhered in a web of reciprocal relations of trust within a community. In this understanding, reputation was not so much achieved by agonistic behaviour as preserved by living up to and acting out certain values and norms, and continuously proving oneself an honest and trustworthy person. One was presumed to possess honour so long as one did not lose it by breaching the balance of reciprocities. Reputation and honour were in this sense a set of normative expectations imposed and monitored by a consensus of public opinion.[56] This meant that they demanded social conformism. In the sixteenth century, as Arlette Jouanna pointed out, honour was, among other things, a model of comportment which befitted one's social position and the quality of those who effectively conformed to

---

[54] For commitment devices see Frank, *Passions within Reason*, 4–7, 54, 86–8.

[55] A succinct and for the present purposes relevant game-theoretical definition is that 'a player's reputation [is] the probability that she has a certain privately observed type or will take a certain action': Colin F. Camerer, *Behavioral Game Theory: Experiments in Strategic Interaction* (Princeton, 2003), 445.

[56] Cf. M. Herzfeld, 'Honour and Shame: Problems in the Comparative Analysis of Moral Systems', *Man*, n.s., 15 (1980), 339–51.

this model.[57] To fail to conform to expectations and therefore earn mistrust would in such a world have had the disastrous consequence of being excluded from areas of social life that were indispensable for social survival as a noblemen. As representatives of the nobility in 1501 assured Count Erasmus of Wertheim with regard to his conflict with Georg von Rosenberg: 'Were it to be established that he [i.e. Rosenberg] had acted towards you dishonourably and not as an honest man, we would avoid him and not have his company and act against him, as one who has violated honour and should not live among or enjoy the company of honest people.'[58]

The need to maintain a good reputation is of course a characteristic of every society, but it is particularly strong in relatively small groups where people know each other, have relatively good information about each other, and depend on their relationships with each other more than on formal institutions or central government. For nobles in pre-modern European society there were some additional constraints that increased the pressure to maintain reputation even further. In the first place, standing at the very top of society, the nobles were supposed to be the paragons of honour. As Ludwig von Hutten put it in 1531, 'Human beings have nothing higher or greater in the world than their honour, and it befits everyone, and especially those born to nobility, to protect, defend and safeguard it.'[59] Secondly, nobles set great store by the name of their family, encapsulated in the formula 'maintaining and elevating the name and bloodline' (*Nam*

---

[57] Arlette Jouanna, 'Recherches sur la notion d'honneur au xvιème siècle', *Revue d'histoire moderne et contemporaine* 15 (1968), 597–623, at 603.

[58] *Shiedsspruch Kurfürst Philipp des Aufrichtigen von der Pfalz*, fol. 8: 'wurde sich erfinden das er unerlich und nit als ein biderman gein euch gehandelt hett So wollen wir unns sein nit annemen uns auch sein ewßern und entschlagen und kein gemainschafft mere mit ime haben und uns also gegen ime halten, als dem der wider Ere gethann und nit bei fromen lewten wonen oder gemainschafft haben solle'.

[59] British Library, C.38.k.16. Cf. Alain Guerreau, 'L'honneur blessé (note critique)', *Annales E.S.C* 48, no. 1 (1993), 227–33, at 230–1.

und Stamm).[60] The reputation of a family was an important asset to all its members. To borrow the words of Judge Fabio Salamone on the Mafia, the name of the lineage 'is a "capital" which represents the result of a process of "collective accumulation" and which can provide a "rent" to the individual member even if he did not take part in the process'.[61] One was therefore under pressure, both self-induced and from other members of the family, not to act in ways that might taint that name.[62] In his dialogue *The Robbers* (1521), the Franconian noble and humanist Ulrich von Hutten made Franz von Sickingen say that 'If there was in our family one who, albeit descending from this lineage, still displayed in his life only sordid baseness – such a one I would not recognise as a relation or a kinsman, nor as a noble, and never have anything in common with him.'[63]

A third possible reason why the compulsion to maintain reputation was especially strong among nobles was their living conditions. Although the local nobility constituted a small group,[64] and although they were closely related and tightly interdependent, the nobles mostly lived in their castles apart from each other, or apart from other families. As a foreign observer noted in 1436, 'The nobles live in their castles... and if they had not been able to gather for

[60] Karl-Heinz Spieß, *Familie und Verwandtschaft im deutschen Hochadel des Spätmittelalters: 13. bis Anfang des 16. Jahrhunderts* (Stuttgart, 1993), 10, 425, 454, 498, 532.

[61] Quoted in Diego Gambetta, *The Sicilian Mafia: The Business of Private Protection* (Cambridge, Mass., 1993), 145. See also ibid., 43, on reputation obviating the need to shoulder the burden of proof in every new transaction.

[62] When Margrave Albrecht of Brandeburg called nobles to arms against Duke Charles of Burgundy in 1474, he wrote to them that the honour of taking part in a campaign for the Holy Roman Empire and the German nation would redound 'not only to you but also to your bloodline and lineage' ('das wollen wir zusambt den eren die du nicht allein dir selbst sunder auch deiner stamm und geslecht damit zu aignen wirdest genediglich gein dir erckennen'): StAN, Generalrepertorium Bamberger Abg. 1996, no. 237 I, doc. 7.

[63] Ulrich von Hutten, *Die Räuber*, in *Gespräche von Ulrich von Hutten*, ed. and trans. David Friedrich Strauß (Leipzig, 1860), 315–89, at 318–19.

[64] The Franconian nobility counted just over 400 families in the first half of the sixteenth century: Cord Ulrichs, *Vom Lehnhof zur Reichsritterschaft: Strukturen des fränkischen Nieder-adels am Übergang vom späten Mittelalter zur frühen Neuzeit* (Stuttgart, 1997), 201–6.

[tournaments], they would have not become familiar either with each other or with the rules of knighthood.'[65] The nobles did not lead a communal life and had relatively infrequent occasions for sustained cooperation. Compared with city or village life, nobles suffered from a relative shortage of opportunities either to gauge each other or to demonstrate their characteristics to each other. It is arguable that this tension between close relationships, tight interdependence and a certain familiarity on the one hand, and relative dearth of opportunities to provide and collect information on the other hand, was a factor in making reputation a particularly sensitive issue: in such social circumstances, the presumption was natural that the absence of information as to the existence of a certain quality in an individual reflected the actual absence of that quality. Nobles must therefore have been particularly concerned both with providing information about themselves and with preventing the spread of misinformed opinions about their persons in the community.[66]

The centrality of this concern is reflected in regulations for tournaments. One of the articles of the Heilbronn tournament code of 1485 ordained that 'whoever hits somebody and then says he misrecognised him, should come to the person whom he had hit and

---

[65] K. Stehlin (ed.), 'Ein spanischer Bericht über ein Turnier in Schaffhausen im Jahr 1436', *Basler Zeitschrift für Geschichte und Altertumskunde* 14 (1915), 145–75, at 167. The dispersion of the nobles was one of the factors taken into account by Emperor Maximilian I in his reaction to the Franconian and Swabian knights' refusal to pay the Common Penny tax: Helmut Neumaier, *'Das wir kein anderes Haupt oder von Gott eingesetzte zeitliche Obrigkeit haben': Ort Odenwald der fränkischen Reichsritterschaft von den Anfängen bis zum Dreißigjährigen Krieg* (Stuttgart, 2005), 17.

[66] This concern is evident in statutes of noble confraternities enjoining members to defend each other's honour and to inform each other of defamations that come to their notice: Herbert Obenaus, *Recht und Verfassung der Gesellschaft mit St Jörgenschild in Schwaben: Untersuchungen über Adel, Einung, Schiedsgericht und Fehde im fünfzehnten Jahrhundert* (Göttingen, 1961), 82; Andreas Ranft, *Adelsgesellschaften: Gruppenbildung und Genossenschaft im spätmittelalterlichen Reich* (Sigmaringen, 1994), 107–8; Cyriacus Spangenberg, *Hennebergische Chronica: Der uralten löblichen Grafen und Fürsten zu Henneberg, Genealogia, Stamm-Baum und Historia, ihrer Ankunfft, Lob und denckwürdigen Tathen, Geschichten und Sachen wahre und gründliche Beschreibung* (Meiningen, 1755), 435.

state under oath that he misrecognised him and ask for forgiveness. The pursuivant should announce this in the dance hall, to the effect that the person who was hit today was hit for no other reason than that he was misrecognised.'[67] No less revealing is the catalogue of violations which would result in the infliction of punishments by fellow nobles during tournaments.[68] Heading the list of punishable deeds are perjury, failure to keep one's word and being false to one's sealed pledges.[69] The nobles expressly emphasised trustworthiness as a central element of noble identity. A nobleman was defined by his conduct and relationship with other noblemen no less than by his descent. Good reputation was deemed essential for being a noble.

When a dispute broke out, therefore, nobles' preoccupation with their reputation could not but provide a powerful motivation to feud. Feuds were not merely direct actions taken to counter or enforce legal claims. They were also – and sometimes primarily – about projecting a certain image of oneself. As has already been indicated, nobles sometimes chose to feud even when peaceful ways to settle the dispute were available.[70] Litigation or arbitration, for instance, apparently did not, in certain circumstances, convey the right message to the aristocratic public who observed and appraised the performance of the disputing parties. Even a legal reformer such as Baron Johann von Schwarzenberg, author of the Bamberg penal code (1507) which served as the basis for the *Constitutio criminalis Carolina* (1532), the unified criminal code of the Holy Roman Empire, believed at least

[67] Heide Stamm (ed.), *Das Turnierbuch des Ludwig von Eyb (cgm 961). Edition und Unter-suchung mit einem Anhang: Die Turnierchronik des Jörg Rugen (Textabdruck)* (Stuttgart, 1986), 205–6.

[68] See Chapter 4 nn. 74–5.

[69] Stamm (ed.), *Das Turnierbuch des Ludwig von Eyb*, 169, 219.

[70] See nn. 36–7 above. Cf. Fehn-Claus, 'Erste Ansätze einer Typologie der Fehdegründe', 99, 117; Julius R. Ruff, *Violence in Early Modern Europe, 1500–1800* (Cambridge, 2001), 76–7; Stuart Carroll, 'The Peace in the Feud in Sixteenth-Century France', *Past and Present* 178 (2003), 74–115, at 85.

on one occasion that legal action was inferior to feuding.[71] In 1519 he himself had a feud with Hans-Georg von Absberg. Schwarzenberg at first agreed to appear before the margrave of Brandenburg for adjudication, but later retracted. In a letter to Margrave Kasimir he explained that, since Absberg had in the meantime perpetrated additional hostilities against his tenants, it would now be a disgrace if he, Schwarzenberg, came before the prince notwithstanding this fact.[72] It may well have been prudent for nobles to be conciliatory, but it may equally well have been reckless to appear to be so. In brief, one had to know when and how to carry out a feud. Nobles who failed in these tests of will and skill risked incurring disesteem that could have adverse effects in many other areas of aristocratic existence. Failure could indicate that one was a pushover, and therefore useless as an ally, unattractive as a marriage partner, or unreliable as a client or servitor – in short, more of a liability than an asset. Failure to risk a feud, when the situation called for it, could foreclose essential opportunities for social exchange in other spheres of life.

Feuds, in other words, were about attracting as well as about deterring. Precisely because they reflected certain values and norms, because they required making sacrifices, because they appeared to be driven by passions no less than by rational calculations, feuds were extraordinarily effective vehicles for signalling that the feuder was a man of principle, a man of honour, a moral person who could be trusted by others to do the right thing even at a personal cost. A virtuous man like that would surely cooperate and keep faith even in situations where he could gain more by defecting. Feuds,

---

[71] For Schwarzenberg see Friedrich Merzbacher, 'Johann Freiherr zu Schwarzenberg', *Fränkische Lebensbilder* 4 (1971), 173–85; Karl Fürst zu Schwarzenberg, *Geschichte des reichsständischen Hauses Schwarzenberg* (Neustadt a.d. Aisch, 1963), 58–68.

[72] StAN, Fstm.Ansb., Fehdeakten, no. 209, doc. 10.

whatever their proximate reasons and immediate ends, could help nobles position themselves favourably in the aristocratic network of relations on which their status and fortunes so heavily depended. It was not only that one could not withstand or win feuds without supporters and allies; it was perhaps equally true that one could not win allies and supporters unless one was prepared to pursue feuds and, crucially, was believed to be so. Hence failure to respond to challenges, or a humiliating defeat, could result in grave damage to one's reputation and standing with other nobles, and could diminish one's chances of success in other areas of aristocratic life. Thus the very interdependence of the Franconian nobles provided powerful incentives to resort to feuding. In sum, feuds were closely bound up with a sense of what it meant in practice to belong to a community of nobles.

The community of nobles, or the relevant sections thereof, was the most crucial element of feuding. Feuds were in no small measure signals destined for this community, and difficult or even impossible to carry out effectively without mobilising it. An instructive example is provided, again, by Wilwolt von Schaumberg. His biography relates how he came to his maternal uncle's assistance in a conflict with the brothers Georg and Konrad Schott.[73] Although a feud was not declared, the dispute became uncharacteristically vicious, to such an extent that the Schotts borrowed and used some pieces of artillery. The rivals slugged it out indecisively for a couple of years. Then in 1487 Konrad Schott, in a move that foreshadowed his future notoriety as a ruthless feuder,[74] changed the course of the

[73] The discussion of the feud is based on Keller (ed.), *Geschichten und Taten*, 70–4; Rabeler, *Niederadlige Lebensformen*, 145–6, 171–5.

[74] Joseph Baader (ed.), *Verhandlungen über Thomas von Absberg und seine Fehden gegen den Schwäbischen Bund 1519 bis 1530* (Tübingen, 1873), 71 n. 1; Rochus Freiherr von Liliencron (ed.), *Die historischen Volkslieder der Deutschen vom 13. bis 16. Jahrhundert*, 4 vols. (Leipzig, 1865–69), II, 351–3, no. 193.

feud. As Wilwolt made his way to join the army of Duke Albrecht of Saxony in Austria, Schott took him by surprise and overpowered him. The incident incensed Duke Albrecht of Saxony. He summoned Schott to a hearing. Wilwolt accused Schott of attacking him without declaring a feud; and the duke charged him with acting against his duties and claimed that he, the duke, as the lord of both nobles, had the authority to penalise him. According to Wilwolt's biographer, Schott tried hard to solicit support among the nobility. Yet when the audience took place no one wanted to take up the cudgels for him. So there he stood alone, having nobody to speak for him. He broke down in tears 'like a child' and begged the prince for mercy. Schott proposed to release Wilwolt from the oath he extracted from him in the wake of the ambush and to waive his claim for ransom against an oath by Wilwolt to keep the peace (*Urfehde*). Wilwolt rejected this condition as humiliating. The hearing achieved nothing, as did the duke's subsequent efforts to bring Schott to book.

The matter was now taken up by the rival parties' fellow nobles. According to the biography, Konrad Schott was made to feel unsafe in Franconia, especially by Wilwolt's relatives. When the latter assembled 'in large number' in Coburg, Schott came to meet them. He asked them to write to Duke Albrecht and to Wilwolt to ask them to 'drop their disfavour and displeasure towards him, and for the duke again to be his gracious lord'. Schott offered to release Wilwolt from the oath without an *Urfehde*. He then mounted a bench and formally declared that he released Wilwolt from all obligations. Although both the duke and Wilwolt made it clear that they did not view the conflict as settled, there is no evidence that they pursued it further.

What emerges clearly from this running conflict between Schaumberg and Schott, as from many other feuds, is that naked violence was not enough to win such disputes.[75] That Schott managed to field some artillery pieces in the early phase of the quarrel gave him no decisive edge over Wilwolt. By contrast, his climb-down was surely due to Wilwolt's superior network of relatives – indeed, the Schaumbergs were a distinguished and extraordinarily large lineage.[76] That Schott failed to garner the moral support of fellow nobles to balance out Wilwolt's social network was in the end his decisive weakness. His violent and opportunistic behaviour may have contributed to his isolation. In any case, force without morality, or the semblance of morality, was nearly as ineffective as morality without the capacity and will to use force. Morality was an inseparable feature, and an indispensable instrument, of feuding. Feuding nobles knew this full well, hence all those angst-ridden, angry self-justifying accounts that make modern historians happy. It is not for nothing that these accounts were couched predominantly in a moral idiom, and that the feuding nobles defended themselves and accused their opponents in terms of ethical values and shared beliefs rather than in terms of the law. The accounts they wrote and circulated were of a piece with their belligerent actions.

But, as has been argued, and as Wilwolt's conflicts suggest, physical violence also had deep roots in the moral sensibilities and perceptions of the noble community. And precisely because they derived from and expressed values and morals, feuds could and did serve much larger ends than simply winning disputes and enforcing claims. Nobles who mastered the subtle arts of amalgamating the symbolic and the material could utilise feuds as a vehicle for reinforcing or acquiring prestige, preserving or making a name, and thus for

---

[75] Cf. Alexander Jendorff and Steffen Krieb, 'Adel im Konflikt: Beobachtungen zu den Austragungsformen der Fehde im Spätmittelalter', *ZHF* 30 (2003), 179–206, at 197–8, 204–5.

[76] See Chapter 4 nn. 53–4.

maintaining their social position or indeed improving it. As Wilwolt's biographer put it:

As such clashes seldom cease in the land of Franconia, some barons and nobles who were at loggerheads captured fortified places, burned down villages, and seized cattle . . . Wilwolt determinedly served his good companions who asked for [his help] in these affairs . . . and he made a big name (*groß geschrai*) for himself and earned recognition from the princes and the nobles.[77]

Feuds launched Wilwolt on the brilliant military career that made him an edifying example for young nobles, and a most proper subject of a contemporary biography.

[77] Keller (ed.), *Geschichten und Taten*, 60.

CHAPTER FOUR

The wages of success

Reproduction and the proliferation of conflicts

The concept of 'inimical intimacy' centres on the relationship and communication among nobles and between nobles and princes. As indicated in the preceding chapter, its analytical content is drawn from the social, institutional and economic constraints that shaped noblemen's lives, and from the preferences and norms that influenced their behaviour. Together, it has been suggested, these dimensions form as realistic a context as possible for understanding the individual motivations for feuding. It might be objected, however, that like other general interpretations of the phenomenon of the feud, this approach provides only a conceptual framework but cannot authentically account for each and every feud. This is undeniable: as the following pages will make clear, there is a variety of empirical observations regarding feuds that are insufficiently explained by any of the available general interpretations. It is also inevitable: like any theoretical strategy designed to explain complex human behaviour, the 'inimical intimacy' thesis covers specific, particular historical variations of human behaviour only in a general, abstract manner.[1] It is not a historical 'Theory of Everything' that purports to capture and clarify all manners and aspects of feuding behaviour.

---

[1] Cf. Stephen K. Sanderson, *The Evolution of Human Sociality: A Darwinian Conflict Perspective* (Lanham, Md, 2001), 144.

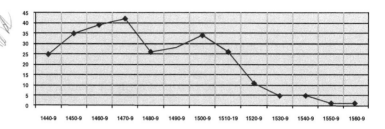

Figure 4.1. Incidence of nobles' feuds in Franconia, 1440–1570

talk about
incline of
feud

In order to make better sense of the feud, one has also to formulate specific questions and offer specific propositions. And indeed, once the empirical data on feuds are analysed, the need for such a twofold method becomes readily apparent.

Between 1440 and 1570 Franconian nobles conducted 278 feuds.[2] Plotting the incidence of feuding in Franconia over these years shows that violence was rising steeply from 1440 onwards until it peaked in the years 1460–79 (Figure 4.1). The level of violence declined in the next two decades (1480–99), but then rose again to a second though lower peak in 1500–9.[3] After this date feuding began to dwindle until it died out after 1570.

It is not difficult to explain the explosion of feuds in the 1460s: this decade witnessed a bitter and prolonged war between German princes in Franconia and beyond.[4] Many of the feuds that broke out in this decade were either integral components of this war or its offshoots. As Figure 4.2 suggests, the political and territorial struggles between the princes were responsible for a substantial proportion of the feuds. It was in the 1460s that noblemen's feuds

---

[2] See Appendix.

[3] A rise in feuding in the early years of the sixteenth century was also noted by Helgard Ulmschneider, *Götz von Berlichingen: Ein adeliges Leben der deutschen Renaissance* (Sigmaringen, 1974), 49.

[4] See Chapter 5.

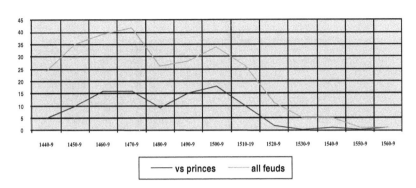

Figure 4.2. Nobles' feuds against princes in relation to the total, 1440–1570

against princes peaked for the first time (16 = 41 per cent of all feuds).[5]
They continued on the same level in 1470–9 (16 feuds = 38 per cent),
and only the decade 1500–9 saw a higher number of noblemen's feuds
against princes (18 = 53 per cent). It is also worthy of note that, in
the 1460s, the number of feuds by nobles against princes was higher
than the number of feuds among nobles (15), some of which were
themselves the consequence of the struggle between the princes.
Clearly then, the efforts of the princes to consolidate their states
and the concomitant conflicts offer the most apposite explanation of
feuding in the 1460s.[6]

However, princely state formation cannot explain the proliferation
of feuds in the 1470s. On the one hand, this decade, with 42 feuds,
witnessed the absolute peak of feuding in general throughout the
entire period 1440–1570; and whereas the number of feuds against
princes in this decade remained the same as in the previous decade,
the number of feuds between nobles, as Figure 4.3 shows, rose to 21 –
the highest in the whole period 1440–1570. On the other hand, the
1470s were otherwise a period of political stability in Franconia in

[5] There were eight feuds against cities/commoners in 1460–9.
[6] For the state-formation interpretation of the feud see the introduction to this book.

The Feud in Early Modern Germany

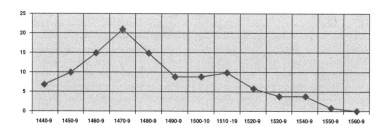

Figure 4.3. Incidence of feuds between nobles, 1440–1570

the aftermath of the wars of the previous decade. As Johannes Merz has pointed out, 'one notices around 1470 a clear localisation and substantially less belligerence as far as the intra-Franconian conflicts are concerned . . . The dispute in 1468 [between Bishop Rudolf of Würzburg und Margrave Albrecht of Brandenburg] over the Gulden Toll ushered in a new phase, in which sustainable separate solutions were fundamentally preferred to power-political confrontations.' All in all, 'the period roughly between 1470 and 1519 was a relatively mild phase in the consolidation of the principalities'.[7] If this view is correct, then the process of state formation does not provide a cogent account of the exceptionally high level of feud violence in the 1470s. A different explanation is needed in order to make sense of the empirical findings.

In many different societies at different historical periods, the number of unmarried young men has proved to be a good predictor of violence.[8] This is apparently true of both random individual fights and organised collective conflicts. One comparative study has found that states in which the age group 15–29 constitutes a large proportion

---

[7] Johannes Merz, *Fürst und Herrschaft: Der Herzog von Franken und seine Nachbarn 1470–1519* (Munich, 2000), 48, 49, 50.

[8] Cf. Robert Wright, *The Moral Animal: Evolutionary Psychology and Everyday Life* (New York, 1994), 100.

of the male population are more likely to go to war.[9] A salient trait of suicide attackers is that, apart from being more educated than other members of their communities, they are mostly young unmarried males.[10] Case studies of medieval groups or societies also demonstrate a close link between youth and violence. David Herlihy has traced the violent disturbances characteristic of Tuscan cities in the late Middle Ages to the large number of young males who delayed marriage until well into their thirties but did not have a legitimate outlet for their sexual desire.[11] Georges Duby argued that aristocratic youths formed the spearhead of feudal aggression in the twelfth and thirteenth centuries. The spread of primogeniture in northern France diminished prospects for younger sons of inheriting family estates and setting up an independent household. Left to their own devices, they took to a life of itinerancy and tried their luck in the tournament arenas and theatres of war.[12]

As far as the German aristocratic feud is concerned, however, the young played merely a subsidiary role in the production of violence. A case in point is Wilwolt von Schaumberg, the well-documented protagonist of the previous chapter. His biography extolled his exploits in feuds in the 1470s and 1480s. But in fact he was involved in those conflicts only as a helper, not as a principal. And he continued to provide violent assistance to others well into

---

[9] Based on a sample of eighty-eight nation-states: Christian G. Mesquida and Neil I. Wiener, 'Human Collective Aggression: A Behavioral Ecology Perspective', *Ethology and Sociobiology* 17 (1996), 247–62, quoted in Sanderson, *The Evolution of Human Sociality*, 328.

[10] Diego Gambetta, 'Can We Make Sense of Suicide Missions?' in *Making Sense of Suicide Missions*, ed. Diego Gambetta (Oxford, 2006), 259–99, at 270.

[11] David Herlihy, 'Some Psychological and Social Roots of Violence in the Tuscan Cities', in *Violence and Civil Disorder in Italian Cities 1200–1500*, ed. Lauro Martines (Berkeley, 1972), 129–54, esp. 141–50, 152.

[12] Georges Duby, 'Youth in Aristocratic Society: Northwestern France in the Twelfth Century', in *The Chivalrous Society*, trans. Cynthia Postan (Berkeley, 1977), 112–22.

his thirties.[13] The main reason for this secondary role was that he was not established as a lord with his own household until later in life. He had at that time no land and property worth feuding over. Nearly 30 years old, he still 'struggled with poverty'.[14] This was not the usual social profile of the rivals in feuds. Rather, the principals were mostly middle-aged, married men.[15] This finding squares well with the prevalence of the custom of partible inheritance among the untitled nobility in Germany. The custom of multigeniture not only increased the likelihood of struggles over the resources needed for success (not least, reproductive success);[16] it also entailed that such struggles would primarily involve not the landless young but rather the nobles who, having inherited all or part of the property of their father, were already set up as lords. Feuding clearly had a close link to the inheritance system. This in turn suggests that the demographic fortunes of noble families must be taken into consideration. It is obvious that the practice of dividing the landed resources of the family among its lay sons facilitated demographic growth and hence the survival of the family; it is equally obvious that, at the same time, it reduced the size and economic viability of each unit of property, could sow discord in the family, and in the long run even endanger the survival of the family.[17] Now demographic growth did indeed take place among the Franconian nobility in the second half

---

[13] Sven Rabeler, *Niederadlige Lebensformen im späten Mittelalter: Wilwolt von Schaumberg (um 1450–1510) und Ludwig von Eyb d.J. (1450–1521)* (Würzburg, 2006), 132–46, 151.

[14] Adalbert von Keller (ed.), *Die Geschichten und Taten Wilwolts von Schaumburg* (Stuttgart, 1859), 44. For the meaning of 'poverty' in this context see Rabeler, *Niederadlige Lebensformen*, 153.

[15] It has been possible to establish the date of marriage of 12 of the 45 Franconian nobles who feuded against other nobles in the 1470s. Ten of them had been married before the feud broke out. The average age of those feuders of the 1470s for whom enough biographical data exist to permit reliable assessment was 37.

[16] Cf. Andreas Ranft, 'Einer von Adel: Zu adligem Selbstverständnis und Krisenbewußtsein im 15. Jahrhundert', *HZ* 263 (1996), 317–43, at 332.

[17] Karl-Heinz Spieß, *Familie und Verwandtschaft im deutschen Hochadel des Spätmittelalters: 13. bis Anfang des 16. Jahrhunderts* (Stuttgart, 1993), 201–2, 278, 427.

of the fifteenth century. This growth, though, followed a particular pattern that reflected fundamental social and political changes in the Franconian nobility.

In a groundbreaking study of the body of vassals (*Lehenhof*) of the bishops of Würzburg between 1303 and 1519, Hans-Peter Baum established that demographic growth was limited to those noble families that held particular types of property in feudal tenure. Baum reached this conclusion by constructing a model of social stratification of the noble vassals of Würzburg according mainly to the quality of their fiefs.[18] The model divides the vassal families into five strata: (1) families rated as belonging to the Top Stratum (*Spitzen-schicht*) are defined by the possession of property which involved the exercise of lordship (*Herrschaft*). The prime example of such lordship-conferring fiefs are castles.[19] Not for nothing were castles the quintessential status symbol of nobility: throughout the whole period under discussion, only one castle was granted in fee to a non-noble family. Below the top stratum is (2) the Elevated Stratum (*Gehobene Schicht*), which is also determined by the holding of a castle and some other, less extensive lordship-conferring property in fee (the Top and Elevated Strata form together the Upper Stratum). The next two categories are the (3) Upper Middle Stratum (*Obere Mittelschicht*) and the (4) Lower Middle Stratum (*Untere Mittelschicht*). And finally, beneath them all is (5) the Lower Stratum (*Unterschicht*).

An analysis of the development of these groupings over the period 1303–1519 reveals one particularly startling change: the Top Stratum expanded from 12 families and 37 individuals at the beginning of the

---

[18] Hans-Peter Baum, 'Der Lehenhof des Hochstifts Würzburg im Spätmittelalter (1303–1519): Eine rechts- und sozialgeschichtliche Studie', 3 vols. (*Habilitationsschrift*, University of Würzburg, 1990), I, 163–9.

[19] Ibid., 163. See also ibid., 169; Matthias Bachmann, *Lehenhöfe von Grafen und Herren im ausgehenden Mittelalter: Das Beispiel Rieneck, Wertheim und Castell* (Cologne, 2000), 45.

period to 51 families and 513 individuals by its end. By 1519 this group constituted an imposing 28 per cent of the total of untitled noble lineages but a staggering 53 per cent of all individual vassals.[20] Their proportion within the *Lehenhof* had thus risen by nearly 1,000 per cent since 1303. The Würzburg *Lehenhof* was absorbed, as it were, by some 50 large families endowed with superior fiefs. What explains this development is, on the one hand, the decline of the total of vassal families from 421 in 1303 to 182 in 1519, and, on the other hand, the rise of the average number of vassals per family from 1.73 to 5.28. This rise was mainly due to expansion of the Top Stratum: the average number of vassals per family in this echelon went up from 3.1 in 1303 to 10.1 in 1519.[21] The crucial point to emerge from this analysis is that the number of vassals representing a lineage in the Würzburg *Lehenhof* was likely to increase with the amount of superior fiefs this lineage held.

Baum's findings, though striking, are not historically anomalous. That reproductive success in pre-industrial societies goes hand in hand with social status is a central hypothesis of evolutionary biology. The more power men have, and the more resources they control, the greater is the number of their offspring. Anthropological and ethological case studies support this hypothesis.[22] Historical studies of various European societies or groups in the late Middle Ages and early modern period have come to similar conclusions.[23]

---

[20] Baum, 'Der Lehenhof des Hochstifts Würzburg', 1, 171, 176.   [21] Ibid., 171, 176.

[22] J. Hill, 'Prestige and Reproductive Success in Man', *Ethology and Sociobiology* 5 (1984), 77–95; Paul W. Turke and L. L. Betzig, 'Those Who Can Do: Wealth, Status, and Reproductive Success on Ifaluk', *Ethology and Sociobiology* 6 (1985), 79–87; Hillard Kaplan and Kim Hill, 'Hunting Ability and Reproductive Success among Male Ache Foragers: Preliminary Results', *Current Anthropology* 26, no. 1 (1985), 131–3; Sanderson, *The Evolution of Human Sociality*, 145–6, 161–4; Wright, *The Moral Animal*, 246–7; Laura Betzig, 'Medieval Monogamy', *Journal of Family History* 20, no. 2 (1995), 181–216.

[23] Roger Sablonier, *Adel im Wandel: Eine Untersuchung zur sozialen Situation des ostschweizerischen Adels um 1300* (Göttingen, 1979), 194; James L. Boone, 'Paternal Investment and Elite Family Structure in Preindustrial States: A Case Study of Late Medieval – Early

The correlation between status and reproductive success has been confirmed for other regional or local nobilities in Germany of the same period. As Joachim Schneider has shown, the proportion of the elite families in Electoral Saxony rose from 16 per cent in 1445 to 27 per cent in 1527, whereas the proportion of individual nobles from these families rose from 23 per cent to 36 per cent.[24] Furthermore, examining the top six families, Schneider has found that the average number of persons in such families rose from 5.33 in 1454 to 9.83 in 1527/30 – a figure nearly four times higher than that of the other families in the elite of Electoral Saxony. Still, even this impressive figure was just about one half of the average of 17.5 persons in the six top families of the Würzburg *Lehenhof* in 1495–1506.[25]

Baum has considered possible objections to his findings regarding the Top Stratum. He has argued that its astounding expansion was not merely apparent, the result, say, of an improved documentation on the part of the Würzburg chancellery.[26] The recorded rise in the number of lordship-conferring fiefs that the prince could distribute among his noble vassals was too large to be accounted for by assuming a patchy registration of the fiefs in the earlier periods. Moreover, since the number of such high-quality fiefs could not be multiplied at will, it cannot be claimed that the more males a noble family produced, the larger the number of fiefs it received from the prince-bishop of Würzburg. Thus, the growth of the Top Stratum

---

Modern Portuguese Genealogies', *American Anthropologist* 88 (1986), 859–78; Anthony Molho, *Marriage Alliance in Late Medieval Florence* (Cambridge, Mass., 1994), 211–12.

[24] Joachim Schneider, *Spätmittelalterlicher deutscher Niederadel: Ein landschaftlicher Vergleich* (Stuttgart, 2003), 441. Heinz Noflatscher, *Räte und Herrscher: Politische Eliten an den Habsburgerhöfen der österrreichischen Länder, 1480–1530* (Mainz, 1999), 202–3, found that noble top councillors in the service of the Habsburgs had an average of 5.8 children, twice as high as that of non-noble top councillors.

[25] Schneider, *Spätmittelalterlicher deutscher Niederadel*, 445 (based on Baum's research). The six top families in the Würzburg *Lehenhof* were Fuchs (31 individual vassals), Seckendorff (20), Stein (16), Berlichingen (14), Hutten (13), Rüdt (11), Stetten (11), Giech (11).

[26] Baum, 'Der Lehenhof des Hochstifts Würzburg', I, 172–3.

was a socially and economically meaningful reality. Indeed, although the number of castles granted in fee quintupled between 1303 and 1519, it was still unable to keep up with the number of Top-Stratum vassals. And the increase in the number of other kinds of valuable fiefs was slower still. All this could not but imply that individual nobles from the leading families were on average provided with fewer high-quality fiefs than their forefathers.[27] On the other hand, over the fifteenth century allodial property was losing ground to feudal property as the dominant form of landholding among the untitled nobility.[28] It seems safe to assume that the mounting demographic pressure on feudal property was accompanied by stiffer competition between the noble families.

The question now is whether and how many of the families of the nobles who feuded in the 1470s belonged to the elite of the nobility that was particularly exposed to the demographic pressure on feudal property. A valid answer to these questions depends on two further considerations which concern the use of Baum's stratification model. One is essentially practical: Baum's model is based on a study of the Würzburg *Lehenhof*, yet some of the families of the nobles who feuded in the 1470s had their landed estates concentrated in other parts of Franconia and consequently had only weak links, if any, to the principality of Würzburg. They held the bulk of their feudal property from other Franconian princes, in particular the bishop of Bamberg and the margrave of Brandenburg.[29] The second and related consideration is essentially methodological: assessing the degree to which Baum's model genuinely reflects the hierarchical structure of the Franconian nobility in general, and the social and

[27] Ibid., 172, 176–7. [28] Ibid., 270–1. See nn. 41–4 below.
[29] Systematic studies of the *Lehenhöfe* of the margraves of Brandenburg and the bishop of Bamberg are not available.

economic situation of the leading noble families in particular. These two problems, albeit of a different order, share a solution.

Baum's model is based on just one variable: feudal property. Even though feudal property was in all probability the predominant form of landholding among the Franconian nobility by the late fifteenth century, this still does not mean that there were no other important determinants of status and stratification. Once these determinants are identified, they can be employed as criteria for establishing the social status of those families that were not orientated towards the Würzburg *Lehenhof*. This procedure in itself reveals nothing about the size of the families in question, nor therefore about the possible demographic pressure on them. However, if these determinants of status could be shown to correlate closely with the possession of high-quality fiefs, then this would not only corroborate Baum's stratification model, but also render his findings applicable beyond the Würzburg *Lehenhof*. In other words, it could be assumed that pre-eminent families, whether qualified as such by feudal property or by some other measure, were equally likely to have been large and hence under demographic pressure.

One criterion of high status that recommends itself is office-holding in the princely territorial administrations or in the princely courts. It is generally acknowledged that office-holding was an indicator of wealth and political power, and a factor in social differentiation.[30] It has the methodologically important advantage that it was a universal feature: all of the Franconian principalities had territorial administrations and courts, and the functions of the office-holders and the mechanisms of their recruitment were akin. Secondly, the sheer number of office-holders makes statistical

---

[30] Cord Ulrichs, *Vom Lehnhof zur Reichsritterschaft: Strukturen des fränkischen Niederadels am Übergang vom späten Mittelalter zur frühen Neuzeit* (Stuttgart, 1997), 118–19, 130–1; Schneider, *Spätmittelalterlicher deutscher Niederadel*, 439.

Table 4.1. *Relationship between office-holding and possession of feudal property in the principality of Würzburg*

	No. of governors, 1500–50	No. of vassals in the Top Stratum, 1495–1519
Thüngen	23	17
Truchseß von Wetzhausen	21	14
Fuchs	11	41
Rosenberg	9	41
Stein	8	17
Schaumberg	7	32
Geyer	5	0
Grumbach	5	12
Münster	5	0

Source: Ulrichs, *Vom Lehnhof zur Reichsritterschaft*, 127–8; Baum, 'Der Lehenhof des Hochstifts Würzburg', II, 90–1.

analysis more meaningful.[31] It is true that the odd office-holder, whether in the territorial administration or in the princely court, may not carry sufficient probative weight concerning the station of his family of origin. But several office-holders from a single family in the period under discussion can indeed serve as a trustworthy indication of its position.

A comparison of the noble families which led the pack in the number of Würzburg district governors in the first half of the sixteenth century, with the families strongest on property held in fee from Würzburg, reveals a very tight correlation indeed. As Table 4.1 shows, of the nine families which contributed five or more district governors, seven rank in the Top Stratum of Baum's stratification model. Lordship-conferring fiefs and the holding of high office in

---

[31] Other important criteria, such as membership in the Franconian cathedral chapters of Bamberg, Eichstätt and Würzburg, lack these characteristics and are therefore of more limited value in this context.

the service of the feudal overlord seem nearly interchangeable as indicators of high status.[32]

With this preliminary result, the analysis can be extended to the office-holders of the two Brandenburg principalities, the Upper Margraviate (Kulmbach) and the Lower Margraviate (Ansbach).[33] For several reasons, it is the latter that lends itself most readily to an examination of the correspondence between office-holding and fief-holding. In the first place, as in the Kulmbach margraviate, the majority of office-holders in Ansbach were recruited from the local families.[34] But unlike Kulmbach, the principality of Ansbach was contiguous with the see of Würzburg. This territorial proximity, coupled with the pervasiveness of multiple vassalage in Franconia, means that office-holders of Ansbach were likely to have been vassals of the bishop of Würzburg as well as of the margrave.[35] Hence, even though the two princes in question were traditionally rivals, the elite of office-holders in Ansbach can be compared with the elite of the Würzburg vassals.

In the reign of Margrave Albrecht (1440–86), four families provided the prince with three or more top office-holders, which indicates a consistent high standing rather than the random recruitment

---

[32] Close correlation existed also between the extent of feudal property in the possession of a family and the number of canons the same family managed to introduce into the socially exclusive cathedral chapter of Würzburg: Ulrichs, *Vom Lehnhof zur Reichsritterschaft*, 99, 105.

[33] This analysis is based on an extensive roster of district governors and court officials in 1440–1550. This roster has been put together mainly from StAN (Ansbacher Bestallungen [Rep. 117 I]; Ansbacher Beamtenkartei; the relevant Herrschaftliche Bücher and Gemeinbücher) and StAB (A 205; C 3, no. 1563), but also from many other diverse kinds of documents which for reasons of space cannot be referred to here.

[34] Ulrichs, *Vom Lehnhof zur Reichsritterschaft*, 124.

[35] As Baum, 'Der Lehenhof des Hochstifts Würzburg', I, 190–1, noted, the more property held by a family in fee from one prince in Franconia, the more likely was this family to hold property in fee from one or more other local princes. See also Ulrichs, *Vom Lehnhof zur Reichsritterschaft*, 49–50.

Table 4.2. *Leading margravial office-holders' families,*
Ansbach, 1440–1486

Family	Margravial office-holders	Status and number in Würzburg *Lehenhof,* 1455–66	
Seckendorff	13	Top Stratum	25
Absberg	5		
Wollmershausen	3	Elevated Stratum	5
Lüchau	3	Lower Middle Stratum	1

Source for *Lehenhof:* Baum, 'Der Lehenhof des Hochstifts Würzburg',
II, 86–9.

of one or two individuals.[36] As Table 4.2 shows, two of the four families also belonged to the Upper (i.e. Top and Elevated combined)
Stratum of the Würzburg vassals in the episcopate of Bishop Johann
von Grumbach (1455–66).

Making the same comparison for the reign of Margrave Friedrich
of Brandenburg (1486–1515) and the term in office of Bishop Lorenz
von Bibra of Würzburg (1495–1519) yields proportionally similar
results (Table 4.3).

Five of ten families with three or more top office-holders in Ansbach also belonged to the Upper Stratum of the Würzburg vassals.
A further two families belonged to the Middle Stratum. Bearing in
mind that some of these families had weak ties to Würzburg, or not
at all,[37] this sample appears to confirm Baum's stratification model:
high-status families in terms of holding property in feudal tenure

---

[36] For the sake of rigour, only the four top offices were considered: district governor, master
of the household, marshal and major-domo (*Hausvogt*). For the importance of these offices
see Ulrichs, *Vom Lehnhof zur Reichsritterschaft,* 118–20; Klaus Rupprecht, *Ritterschaftliche
Herrschaftswahrung in Franken: Die Geschichte der von Guttenberg im Spätmittelalter und zu
Beginn der Frühen Neuzeit* (Neustadt a.d. Aisch, 1994), 296.

[37] The Lentersheim, Knöringen and Absberg had a long and strong tradition of margravial
service. None of their members was a vassal of Würzburg in 1495–1519. See Baum, 'Der
Lehenhof des Hochstifts Würzburg', III, List A.

Table 4.3. *Leading margravial office-holders' families,*
Ansbach, 1486–1515

Family	Margravial office-holders	Status and number in Würzburg *Lehenhof*, 1495–1519	
Seckendorff	13	Top Stratum	34
Knöringen	4		
Lentersheim	4		
Wollmershausen	4	Elevated Stratum	2
Heßberg	3	Top Stratum	7
Lüchau	3	Lower Middle Stratum	5
Rosenberg	3	Top Stratum	14
Absberg	3		
Lichtenstein	3	Top Stratum	30
Vellberg	3	Upper Middle Stratum	10

Source for *Lehenhof*: Baum, 'Der Lehenhof des Hochstifts Würzburg', II, 90–4.

tended also to enjoy high status in terms of office-holding, be it in the service of the same prince or in that of another, even a rival Franconian prince.

In the last leg of this examination, this result can be applied to the margravial officialdom in the Upper Margraviate of Kulmbach in 1440–86. Five families stand out as having three or more office-holders in that period (Table 4.4). As one might expect, none of the five families belonged to the Upper Stratum of the Würzburg *Lehenhof*. However, they were undoubtedly part of the elite of the nobility in Upper Franconia, as indeed other indicators show.[38]

It is now finally possible to draw some conclusions as to the families of those who feuded in the 1470s. Of the 37 Franconian families from which the feuders originated, 22 (59.5 per cent) were of high status, whether defined by princely service or by the possession of

---

[38] Rupprecht, *Ritterschaftliche Herrschaftswahrung in Franken*, 37 n. 131, 41 n. 138, 63–6. Cf. Schneider, *Spätmittelalterlicher deutscher Niederadel*, 427–8.

Table 4.4. *Leading margravial office-holders' families,*
Kulmbach, 1440–1486

Family	Margravial office-holders	Status and number in Würzburg *Lehenhof*, 1455–66	
Wallenrod	4		
Schirnding	4		
Aufseß	3		
Lüchau	3	Lower Middle Stratum	1
Wirsberg	3		

Source for *Lehenhof*: Baum, 'Der Lehenhof des Hochstifts
Würzburg', II, 86–9.

high-quality feudal property, or both.[39] Given the close correlation
between status and reproductive success, it can be assumed with a
high degree of confidence that most of these 22 families had enjoyed –
or rather suffered from – the demographic growth that was such a
notable characteristic of this group in the second half of the fifteenth
century. But this is not to say that the foregoing analysis covers
just under two-thirds of the feuds in the 1470s. For it must be taken
into consideration that only in 3 of the 21 feuds (14 per cent) that
broke out between nobles in the 1470s did both sides come from
families which did not belong to the top of the nobility. Nobles from
leading families were also the majority of those who feuded against
princes in that decade (11 out of 16).[40] In other words, the feuding

---

[39] Five feuders' families are identified as high-status according to the criterion of office-
holding in margravial service (Aufseß, Lüchau, Seckendorff, Wallenrod, Wirsberg);
fourteen families according to the criterion of holding lordship-conferring fiefs from
Würzburg (Berlichingen, Bibra, Heßberg, Hutten, Lichtenstein, Rosenberg, Schaumberg, Seinsheim, Steinau genannt Steinrück, Stetten, Thüngen, Vestenberg, Wolfskeel,
Zollner); a further three families (counts of Henneberg and Hohenlohe, and barons of
Schwarzenberg) must be included among the high-status families by dint of belonging to
the titled nobility.

[40] Konrad von Aufseß, Darius von Heßberg, Georg von Rosenberg, Hans von Schaumberg, Ulrich von Schaumberg, Karl von Schaumberg, Hans von Seckendorff, Veit von
Vestenberg, Veit von Wallenrod, Wolf von Wolfskeel, Reinhard Zollner.

scene in the 1470s was dominated by the large, wealthy, pre-eminent families.

These families were victims of their own success, reproductive and otherwise. Their predicament was compounded by the fact that lordship-conferring fiefs, at the same time as they were becoming scarce relative to the number of progeny, were increasingly becoming the principal form of landholding. For between 1300 and 1500, and especially in the fifteenth century, Franconia underwent a process of feudalisation: fiefs proliferated because noblemen tended more and more to transform allodial property into fiefs to be then received from the princes.[41] One probable motive behind the trend was to enhance the legal protection of the patrimony,[42] which may perhaps be seen as a sign of the intensifying demographic pressure under which it was coming. The princes for their part turned substantial portions of their cameral domains into fiefs to be distributed among noblemen.[43] The cumulative effect was that by the year 1500 the allodial landscape of Franconia had been eroded in favour of a feudal one.[44] As a result, the economic and social importance of fiefs, and in particular of lordship-conferring fiefs, cannot but have grown. Indeed, it has been demonstrated that feudal property was a factor of selection in the struggle of noble families for survival: families which had endured into the sixteenth century are conspicuously overrepresented in the Top Stratum of the Würzburg *Lehenhof*; in

---

[41] Baum, 'Der Lehenhof des Hochstifts Würzburg', I, 72–4, 270–1.

[42] Ulrichs, *Vom Lehnhof zur Reichsritterschaft*, 48–9. For the titled nobility see Spieß, *Familie und Verwandtschaft*, 203. Joseph Morsel, *La noblesse contre le prince: L'espace sociale des Thüngen à la fin du Moyen Âge (Franconie, vers 1250–1525)* (Sigmaringen, 2000), 173–83, has argued that the transformation of allods into fiefs served, among other things, the purpose of excluding daughters from the inheritance.

[43] Baum, 'Der Lehenhof des Hochstifts Würzburg', I, 173.

[44] Rolf Sprandel, 'Die territorialen Ämter des Fürstentums Würzburg im Spätmittelalter', *JffL* 37 (1977), 45–64, at 51; Baum, 'Der Lehenhof des Hochstifts Würzburg', I, 270–2. See also Erich von Guttenberg, *Das Bistum Bamberg*, part I (Berlin, 1937), 265–6, 269, 274, 278, 283–4; Rupprecht, *Ritterschaftliche Herrschaftswahrung in Franken*, 145, 151, 221, 302–5.

fact, these families made up no less than 92 per cent of the Top Stratum in 1455–66 and 98 per cent in 1495–1519.[45] The conclusion seems inevitable that the increase in the weight of fiefs in the property portfolio of elite families, coupled with the increase in the average number of males in such families, must have put a substantial strain on their resources. It seems hardly surprising that these families became entangled in numerous conflicts and that the spate of feuds in the 1470s was largely their doing.

It is perhaps appropriate to conclude this analysis by returning to Wilwolt von Schaumberg and his family. His biographer reports that when Wilwolt came back to Franconia in 1476, after a spell in the service of a foreign prince, he found a nearly empty house, 'for his late father had left behind many children, some of whom had to be assisted into the Church, others in the world. Hence the saying: "[division into] many parts makes for little property"'.[46] Wilwolt was one of seven sons. Two of his brothers died before the property was parcelled out, and three were placed in cathedral chapters – a clear indication of the standing of the Schaumbergs. But the costs of securing their canonries were high, and what remained was inadequate as a basis for setting up an independent household.[47] Fortunately for Wilwolt, the times were such that he did not have to wait for long for opportunities to prove his mettle. The political difficulties of the Hohenzollerns in the east gave him the chance to see action in the service of Margrave Albrecht of Brandenburg

---

[45] Baum, 'Der Lehenhof des Hochstifts Würzburg', I, 178–80, 185. See also Hans-Peter Baum, 'Soziale Schichtung im mainfränkischen Niederadel um 1400', *ZHF* 13 (1986), 129–48, at 147–8: the chances of a noble family, which survived from 1400 to the sixteenth century, to have belonged to the Upper Stratum in terms of property were 1 to 8. On the other hand, the probability ratio of a family which did not last that long to have belonged to this stratum was 1 to 80. For families with ambivalent noble status or with strong ties to towns, such chances were virtually nonexistent.

[46] Keller (ed.), *Geschichten und Taten*, 33. Cf. Rabeler, *Niederadlige Lebensformen*, 120.

[47] Rabeler, *Niederadlige Lebensformen*, 121–3.

in 1478. In 1479 began the series of the nine spectacular supra-regional tournaments of the Four Lands,[48] in which Wilwolt spared no extravagant effort to shine and draw attention to himself, not least by taking up the cudgels for a relative too young to throw down the gauntlet himself.[49] Other kin called on his help, and Wilwolt usually obliged.[50] Wilwolt was there for Karl von Schaumberg when he took on Duke Otto II of Mosbach-Neumarkt because of a dispute over a castle.[51] Karl was not the only Schaumberg embroiled in a feud. A further three members of the family pursued a feud of their own in the 1470s.[52] The Schaumbergs were by no means more bellicose than other noble families; they were, quite simply, more numerous: few Franconian noble families were more prolific. They contributed 16 men to the pool of vassals of Würzburg in 1455–66, belonging to the Top Stratum according to Baum's stratification model. By the turn of the century they were represented by 32 vassals in the Würzburg *Lehenhof*.[53] These figures, while reflecting the demographic trend, are incomplete: the Schaumbergs' actual strength at the end of the fifteenth century was in the region of 60 males.[54] It is not surprising, perhaps, that they were so heavily represented in the sample of feuders, and that two of their four feuds were over castles, that is over the ultimate lordship-conferring fiefs.

---

[48] See below.   [49] Keller (ed.), *Geschichten und Taten*, 47–50, 64–5. See Chapter 3.

[50] Keller (ed.), *Geschichten und Taten*, 60; Rabeler, *Niederadlige Lebensformen*, 143–6.

[51] Rabeler, *Niederadlige Lebensformen*, 138–43.

[52] Felix Priebatsch (ed.), *Politische Correspondenz des Kurfürsten Albrecht Achilles*, 3 vols. (Leipzig, 1894–8), II, 332, no. 334; 351, no. 356; 545–6, no. 586; 559, no. 606; Joseph Würdinger, *Kriegsgeschichte von Bayern, Franken, Pfalz und Schwaben von 1347 bis 1506*, 2 vols. (Munich, 1868), II, 107. The Schaumbergs were second only to the counts of Henneberg, who fought six feuds in the 1470s.

[53] Baum, 'Der Lehenhof des Hochstifts Würzburg', II, 90.

[54] Oskar von Schaumberg, *Neuaufstellungen der Stammtafeln des uradelig fränkischen Geschlechts von Schaumberg* (Bamberg, 1953). The Schaumbergs were one of the top ten Franconian noble families in terms of multiple vassalage: Ulrichs, *Vom Lehnhof zur Reichsritterschaft*, 51.

The examples of Wilwolt and the von Schaumberg clan evince an atmosphere of vulnerability. These circumstances, shared by other large and influential noble families, must have created numerous flashpoints. But there was, perhaps, more to the resultant feuds than that. It may not be implausible to conjecture that the build-up of demographic pressure in elite families exacerbated competition not just over property but also over access to women. In one sense this is a tautology. These two types of competition are not as far apart as one might be tempted to believe.[55] Aristotle Onassis is credited with the dictum that 'if women didn't exist, all the money in the world would have no meaning'. While few men have been in a better position to pronounce judgment on this existential question, it reflects a truth that goes deeper than the private wisdom of a shipping tycoon. A study of thirty-seven cultures around the globe has found that, in choosing a mate, women put a premium on economic resources – and express this preference about 100 per cent more than men do. Women fancy good providers.[56] This cannot but affect the behaviour of men. Hence the competition between men over resources is often, at bottom, intimately intertwined with female mate choice, or, historically, with the choice of the female's family.

While this is a general human tendency, different social structures, traditions and norms shape the criteria for choosing spouses in a whole a variety of ways. Thus endogamous marriages were a salient characteristic of aristocracies in late medieval and early modern

---

[55] For the distinction between a narrow (sexual) and broad (resources and conditions for attracting women and rearing offspring) senses of reproduction, see Azar Gat, *War in Human Civilization* (Oxford, 2006), 58–61, 416.

[56] David M. Buss, *The Evolution of Desire: Strategies of Human Mating* (New York, 1994), 19–48 (esp. 22–5). Geoffrey Miller, *The Mating Mind: How Sexual Choice Shaped the Evolution of Human Nature* (New York, 2000), 209–11, has argued that the traits which women prefer are not necessarily those that indicate male ability to provide but rather heritable fitness. Some traits can of course indicate both.

Europe. Few noble fathers were prepared to marry their children off to a non-noble, no matter how rich he or she was. In Germany, nearly 90 per cent of the counts and barons married their equals in the period between the thirteenth and sixteenth centuries; only 6 per cent married below their rank.[57] Yet among the nobility, the material resources of the groom were a crucial consideration. This was to a large extent dictated by the customs governing the dotal system. As a rule, the noble bride's dowry was reciprocated by the groom with a matching sum (*Widerlegung*). In addition the groom gave the bride a 'morning-gift' (*Morgengabe*) whose value was at his discretion. The conjugal fund thus created was commuted into rents and secured on the groom's property as the bride's dower. Feudal property was usually pledged as security for at least part of the conjugal fund, an operation for which the permission of the princes was requested and normally granted.[58] Under this dotal system, nobles without an adequate material foundation had bleak prospects of finding a spouse and ensuring genealogical continuity. The men from leading families were affected, too: they could hardly hope to take a wife from an equally eminent family unless they possessed a certain minimum of property against which to secure the generous marital prestations conventionally expected of such alliances.[59] This predicament must have felt all the more frustrating because of the pride of place which nobles gave to the perpetuation of the lineage – an ultimate value

---

[57] Spieß, *Familie und Verwandtschaft*, 398–400.   [58] Cf. ibid., 146.

[59] One of the complaints which the nobles raised against the bishops of Bamberg and Würzburg in 1503 and 1507, respectively, was that princely permissions to secure dowers against a fief were limited to one half or even one third of its value: StAW, Stb, no. 892, fol. 99r; StAB, B 28, no. 1, fol. 4r. Cf. Rupprecht, *Ritterschaftliche Herrschaftswahrung in Franken*, 305, 507. A random sampling of dowries among the Franconian nobility in the late fifteenth century suggests that 1,000 Gulden was the average in matrimonial alliances between leading families. One thousand Gulden was the average dowry also among the nobility of south-west of Germany: Markus Bittmann, *Kreditwirtschaft und Finanzierungsmethoden: Studien zu den Verhältnissen des Adels im westlichen Bodenseeraum* (Stuttgart, 1991), 238.

encapsulated in the formula 'maintaining and elevating the name and bloodline' (*Nam und Stamm*).[60]

This is where feuds could come in. As a previous chapter has suggested,[61] in a social environment shaped by relationships of inimical intimacy, feuds functioned, among other things, as cues designed not only to deter rivals but also to attract potential allies, including prospective marriage partners. As signals, feuds had the important advantage of being hard to fake: because they were costly – in the short run often conspicuously wasteful – undertakings, they provided clues as to the feuder's economic situation; because they could not be carried out without the support of family, friends and followers, they advertised the extent and quality of the feuders' social network; and because they involved real risks and at times demanded sheer physical courage, they conveyed information on the character of the man. In short, they exhibited traits that indicated wealth, personality and fitness all at once. Now it may be assumed that such signals grew all the more valuable as this social environment became crowded and as the precise landed resources that were critical for preserving 'name and bloodline' became ever scarcer. In these circumstances of heightened competition, feuds could be used to provide evidence of one's ability to set up and maintain a household, or to provide one's offspring with the means to do so.

Contests over women as a major cause of violence between men is a universal human theme. It is a matter of nature, not of nurture.[62] No society has managed to do without it, and for a good reason. The reward of success is huge: reproductive success. One of the most violent societies studied by anthropologists provides a remarkable

---

[60] Spieß, *Familie und Verwandtschaft*, 10, 425, 454, 498, 532.   [61] Chapter 3.

[62] Cf. Matt Ridley, *The Red Queen: Sex and the Evolution of Human Nature* (Harmondsworth, 1993), 195–8.

example: Yanomamö men who killed other men have more wives than their peaceful brethren.[63] While such valorisation of aggression may be extreme, and indeed translates into an exceptionally high rate of fatalities, the basic attitude which underlies it is by no means confined to the Amazon rainforest. Sexual rivalries between men are also a major motive for homicide in monogamous Western societies.[64] How far a link of this kind between violence and mating is true of feuding nobles in late medieval society is difficult to ascertain.[65] A helpful intimation, however, is offered, yet again, by Wilwolt von Schaumberg. His biography touches on this issue in a crucial passage whose subject matter, tellingly, is feuds in Franconia:

Since this war came to an end and Wilwolt von Schaumberg had nothing to do either for himself or for his relations, the time was one of minor raids. As such clashes seldom cease in the land of Franconia, some barons and nobles who were at loggerheads captured fortified places, burned down villages, and seized cattle... Wilwolt determinedly served his good companions who asked for [his help] in these affairs... and he made a big name (*groß geschrai*) for himself and earned recognition from the princes and the nobles. Now it is very true, and is often demonstrated, that, as Ovid writes, every honourable woman shows love and inclination to manly, fearless, lively, serious men, thinking that they will take bolder risks because of women than stay-at-home or effeminate men.[66]

The association here between violence and sex is explicit: feuding is not just about legal claims, nor just about earning the esteem of princes and fellow noblemen. It is also about impressing women, or

---

[63] Ibid, 196; Sanderson, *The Evolution of Human Sociality*, 323.

[64] Margo Wilson and Martin Daly, 'Competitiveness, Risk Taking, and Violence: The Young Male Syndrome', *Ethology and Sociobiology* 6 (1985), 59–73, at 63.

[65] Virtually no research has been done on this topic. One reason may well be a certain scholarly attitude which was described by Napoleon Chagnon, a leading authority on the Yanomamö, thus: 'You are allowed to admit the stomach as a source of war, but not the gonads': quoted by Ridley, *The Red Queen*, 196.

[66] Keller (ed.), *Geschichten und Taten*, 60.

rather impressing women's fathers. In fact, Wilwolt's biographer, the otherwise eminently sober Ludwig von Eyb, went further: the story of Wilwolt's adventurous military life culminates in his wedding ceremony, described at the very end of the book.[67] The hero has arrived. He has gained enough prestige and wealth to attract the daughter of one of the richest and most respected nobles in Franconia. The event is modelled on princely weddings, lavish and glamorous, with allegedly one thousand guests, some very prominent, and the indispensable paraphernalia of tourneying and dancing, where one could see 'eighty-six elegant women and maidens'.[68]

Some supportive evidence for a possible link between feuding and mating indeed comes from tournaments, especially those of the Four Lands – Franconia, Bavaria, Swabia and the Rhineland.[69] Initiated and organised by the nobles themselves, the tournaments of the Four Lands began in 1479, that is precisely at the end of that decade in which feuds between nobles reached an unprecedented level. There are indeed some hints that these tournaments originated as a response to the rampant violence.[70] Chivalric culture was drawn upon and a tradition of military sport revivified in an effort to cultivate a spirit of communion and discipline among the

---

[67] It is noteworthy in this respect that Emperor Maximilian I commissioned an epic verse, *Theuerdank*, published in 1517, which allegorically represented his venturesome journey to woo Maria of Burgundy, his future wife.

[68] Keller (ed.), *Geschichten und Taten*, 199. For more on the wedding and for Hans Fuchs, the bride's father, see Rabeler, *Niederadlige Lebensformen*, 332–8. Other successful nobles also put on tournaments at their weddings. The two-day joust staged by margravial district governor Sixt von Seckendorff to celebrate his wedding in 1485 was honoured by the participation of Margrave Friedrich of Brandenburg and a count of Württemberg: StAN, Geheimregistratur, Bamberger Zugang, no. 39, docs. 101–2.

[69] Andreas Ranft, 'Turniere der vier Lande: Genossenschaftlicher Hof und Selbstbehauptung des niederen Adels', *Zeitschrift für die Geschichte des Oberrheins* 142 (1994), 83–102; Werner Paravicini, *Die ritterlich-höfische Kultur des Mittelalters* (Munich, 1994), 94–101. See also the discussion of tournaments in Chapter 5.

[70] Ulrichs, *Vom Lehnhof zur Reichsritterschaft*, 135–6.

nobles.[71] The tournaments were also supposed to serve as a forum for addressing disputes between nobles, and were indeed treated as a substitute for feuds, or a means of regulating them.[72] In the tournament in Heidelberg in 1481, for example, Melchior Süzel levelled an accusation at Erasmus von Rosenberg before the Knightage (*Ritterschaft*). Rosenberg responded with a recrimination of his own. Four years later, in the tournament in Ansbach, a jury of nobles heard the case and pronounced that 'after complaint, defence, verdict and appeal, we judge that Sir Erasmus has sufficiently answered for his honour, and that Melchior Süzel's honour is not diminished either, and the two parties should consequently . . . be reconciled'.[73] Not only was the exercise of unauthorised violence proscribed during the tournaments themselves, both in and outside the games, on pain of permanent expulsion; certain activities, such as highway robbery and unfair feuds, were branded in the tournament regulations as misdemeanours that merited punishments.[74] These were meted out in the form of beating with truncheons administered by other nobles, or of pulling the culprit from his horse and placing him on the barrier

[71] Joseph Morsel, 'Le tournoi, mode d'éducation politique en Allemagne à la fin du Moyen Âge', in *Education, apprentissages, initiation au Moyen Âge: Actes du premier colloque international de Montpellier*, vol. II (Montpellier, 1993), 309–31, esp. 311, 316.

[72] Andreas Ranft, *Adelsgesellschaften: Gruppenbildung und Genossenschaft im spätmittelalterlichen Reich* (Sigmaringen, 1994), 111, 174–5; Ulrichs, *Vom Lehnhof zur Reichsritterschaft*, 135–6, 140–1.

[73] 'Als melchior sutzel hern aßmusen vonn rosenberg ritter vor der Ritterschaft zu jungsten thurner zu haydelberg beschuldigt hat, das sie von bedenteiln in rechtfertigung geineinander kommen sein, sprechen wir nach clag antwurt gesprochen urtailn und ergangen appelation das her aßmus sein ere gnugsamlich verantwurt hab, und das auch melchior sutzeln sollgs an seinen eren unschedlich sei und sollen dorauff von beden teiln sie und alle die darundter verwandt und verdacht sind, der sachen und was sich bisher zwischen ir begeben hat gericht und gesont sein': StAN, Geheimregistratur, Bamberger Zugang, no. 39, doc. 115.

[74] Heide Stamm (ed.), *Das Turnierbuch des Ludwig von Eyb (cgm 961). Edition und Untersuchung mit einem Anhang: Die Turnierchronik des Jörg Rugen (Textabdruck)* (Stuttgart, 1986), 207, 223; Ranft, *Adelsgesellschaften*, 176; Ulrichs, *Vom Lehnhof zur Reichsritterschaft*, 144.

surrounding the lists.[75] No one was allowed to give him assistance in the face of this rough justice.[76]

It was in this context of ordering the behaviour of men and the relationships between them on the basis of chivalrous ideals, that women were accorded an important role. This is how an invitation to one tournament, which otherwise contained instructions of highly technical nature, began:

Hear, hear, hear!

We counts, barons, knights and squires, all those who want to joust tomorrow for the favour of beautiful women and fair maidens, should come to our gracious lord's armoury . . . And whichever knight excels will be awarded a prize (*Dank*) . . . by the most beautiful woman . . . ; whichever worthy squire excels will be awarded a prize . . . by the fairest maiden.[77]

The language evokes a venerable literary topos,[78] and harks back to earlier times, but the imitation of art does not make life any less real for that. Playing, literally, to the gallery (of women) was clearly a strong motive for men to take part in tournaments. Given the physical prowess required for a successful performance, and the expensive horses and equipment, tournaments presented noblemen with a precious opportunity to parade their health and wealth simultaneously. Nobles who wrote about their experience in the tournaments echoed the language of the invitation in the attention they paid to the presence of women. Sigmund von Gebsattel recorded that each member

---

[75] Stamm (ed.), *Turnierbuch des Ludwig von Eyb*, 207; Matthias Thumser (ed.), *Ludwig von Eyb der Ältere (1417–1502): Schriften. Denkwürdigkeiten, Gültbuch, Briefe an Kurfürst Albrecht Achilles 1473/74, Mein Buch* (Neustadt a.d. Aisch, 2002), 402–6. See William H. Jackson, 'Tournaments and the German Chivalric *renovatio*: Tournament Discipline and the Myth of Origins', in *Chivalry in the Renaissance*, ed. Sydney Anglo (Woodbridge, 1990), 77–91, at 81–3.

[76] Ranft, *Adelsgesellschaften*, 192–3. For the wider social and political implications of this ruling see Chapter 6.

[77] StAN, Geheimregistratur, Bamberger Zugang, no. 39, doc. 70 (see illustration 8).

[78] Cf. Maurice Keen, *Chivalry* (New Haven, 1984), 91.

Illustration 7. Chastisement for moral failings: a tournament participant is placed on the barrier surrounding the lists. *Das Wappenbuch Conrads von Grünenberg, Ritters und Bürgers ʒu Constanʒ* (*c.* 1480), Bayerische Staatsbibliothek, Munich, Cgm. 145, p. 237

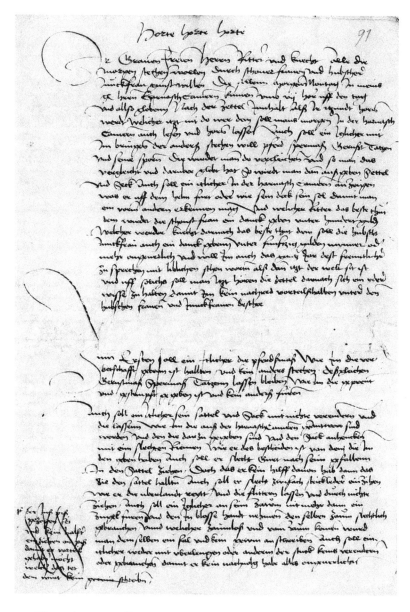

Illustration 8. A call to a tournament, *c.* 1485. StAN, Geheimregistratur, Fstm.Ansb., Bamberger Zugang, no. 39, doc. 70

of the Society of the Unicorn had to bring along a woman or maiden to the tournament in Bamberg. 'The Franconians', he added, 'had many beautiful women and maidens there.'[79] Fellows of the select Society of the Ass were required to bring their womenfolk with them or pay a 10-Gulden fine. Counts and barons were expected, in keeping with their rank, to attend with between four and six women in their company.[80]

The women were no mere passive spectators. They were assigned a part pregnant with meaning: they took part in the inspection of the helms (*Helmschau*), an occasion which preceded the jousting and served to control admittance. The ladies pointed at the helms of prospective participants who allegedly breached the norms of aristocratic conduct articulated in the tournament codes, or were considered ineligible on grounds of pedigree. These nobles could then be debarred from the tournament.[81] Exclusion could take the form of ritual dishonouring: in the tournament in Bamberg in 1486, on the day before the jousting began, Wolf von Seinsheim's wife hacked at the helm of Michael von Seinsheim in the presence of various nobles and then flung it to the ground.[82]

[79] *Eigenhändiger Aufzeichnung des Siegmund von Gebsattel über die Turniere von 1484–1487*, in *Anzeiger für Kunde der deutschen Vorzeit*, n.s. 1, no. 4 (1853), coll. 67–9, at 68. See also Sven Rabeler (ed.), *Das Familienbuch Michels von Ehenheim (um 1462/63–1518): Ein niederadliges Selbstzeugnis des späten Mittelalters. Edition, Kommentar, Untersuchung* (Frankfurt am Main, 2007), 67; Keller (ed.), *Geschichten und Taten*, 33, 37, 40, 47, 53, 55, 61, 64–6, 157, 158–9.

[80] Ranft, *Adelsgesellschaften*, 170. See also Paravicini, *Die ritterlich-höfische Kultur*, 98.

[81] For a contemporary description of the inspection of the helms in tournaments see *Le Livre des Tournois du Roi René de la Bibliothèque nationale (ms. Français 2695)*, ed. F. Avril (Paris, 1986), n.p. See also K. Stehlin (ed.), 'Ein spanischer Bericht über ein Turnier in Schaffhausen im Jahr 1436', *Basler Zeitschrift für Geschichte und Altertumskunde* 14 (1915), 145–75, at 158, 162.

[82] Cf. Ludwig Adalbert von Gumppenberg (ed.), 'Nachrichten über die Turniere zu Würzburg und Bamberg in den Jahren 1479 und 1486', *AU* 19, no. 2 (1867), 164–210, at 209 and Stamm (ed.), *Turnierbuch des Ludwig von Eyb*, 193, 195.

Illustration 9. Inspection of the helms. *Das Wappenbuch Conrads
von Grünenberg, Ritters und Bürgers zu Constanz* (*c.* 1480).
Bayerische Staatsbibliothek, Munich, Cgm. 145, p. 233

The role of women in tournaments can be variously interpreted.
One historian of the Franconian nobility has seen women's func-
tion as the integration of the nobility into a cohesive social group.[83]
Yet the description of women's tasks and activities at tournaments

[83] Morsel, *La noblesse contre le prince*, 340.

seems to warrant a complementary proposition: it is arguable that, in accordance with the avowedly moralising and disciplining concerns of the tournaments, women came in chiefly as objects of a sublimated competition between men.[84] The women's participation in the selection process that heralded the jousting may have symbolised that it was in their power to decide which noblemen were (and were not) to be given the opportunity to attract females.[85] This is underscored by an incident at a tournament in Schaffhausen in 1436: at the inspection of the helms the ladies identified one which belonged to a commoner whose riches had enabled him to marry a countess. Then and there he found out that money did not buy him acceptance into the community of the nobles: at the behest of the women his helm was hurled out of the hall where it was displayed and then dragged through the dirt. The reason given by the women was that there were many nubile maidens available who came from good but relatively poor families; if noblemen chose to marry burghers' daughters for their wealth, poorer maidens of nobler stock would never be wedded.[86] Indeed, in explaining the rationale of tournaments, the Spanish author of the report on Schaffhausen pointed out that, among other things, they served the purpose of negotiating and concluding matrimonial alliances. With a discerning eye for telling sociological detail, he stressed that 'you must know that not all who came to the feast brought their wives along . . . for [those who came] were mostly [either] unmarried young men or widowers'.[87] That

---

[84] On the erotic undercurrents of tournaments see Keen, *Chivalry*, 91–2.

[85] The fact that married men also took part in tournaments does not invalidate this interpretation. A happy marriage may restrain or dampen but not altogether eradicate the desire of men to impress and attract other women. Moreover, given the life expectancy at the time, noblemen could expect to have to return to the marriage market. Of the 318 marriages of counts and barons studied by Spieß, 63 (19.8 per cent) were second or third marriages: Spieß, *Familie und Verwandtschaft*, 422.

[86] Stehlin (ed.), 'Ein spanischer Bericht', 163.

[87] Ibid., 164, 167. Cf. also Spieß, *Familie und Verwandtschaft*, 38.

the ladies represented an object of playful competition seems also to be suggested by the function which some of them performed in the awards ceremony that concluded the tournament: if the men came to the tournament, as they proclaimed, for the 'favour of beautiful women and fair maidens', then the prizes that the women handed to the winners could well be seen as standing for the real trophies – the women themselves.[88]

All in all, the tournaments of the Four Lands give the impression that one of the aims of the nobles was to bring the (indirect) contest for mates under control by redirecting it towards less violent outlets, and by celebrating the unity of the nobility. It was surely no coincidence that the large families which dominated the feuding scene dominated the tournament scene as well.[89] It is of course true that the prominence in the tournaments of the larger, richer lineages reflected their advantages of sheer size and wealth: they simply had more members who could afford the hefty costs involved in taking part in tournaments. But numbers and wealth do not explain their motivation to organise the tournaments in the first place. For these families clearly did not need the tournaments to confirm their status: the twenty-six families of the Society of the Clasp, which initiated the tournaments of the Four Lands, were top-ranking by virtually any standard of social stratification.[90] Their aim was not to distinguish themselves from other nobles. On the contrary, they strove

---

[88] The report on the Schaffhausen tournament relates that a woman elected to award the first prize was led between the tournament officials and other nobles; she was followed by twenty women. They crossed the hall towards the winner. The leading lady spoke to him, then put the ring on his finger and danced with him: Stehlin (ed.), 'Ein spanischer Bericht', 172.

[89] For the social profile of the tournament nobility see Schneider, *Spätmittelalterlicher deutscher Niederadel*, 431–3, 438–9.

[90] On the Society of the Clasp see Ranft, *Adelsgesellschaften*, 35–116. The Society of the Clasp became nearly synonymous with the tournaments. A contemporary drawing (see illustration 10) carries the following caption: 'Item zu wissen das die löblich geselschafft zu franngcken gehaissen in Spenniche den Turnyr Erdacht und Erfunden und den Erstn gethann habenn'.

to open the tournaments to as wide a circle of nobles as possible by enforcing egalitarian sumptuary restrictions.[91] It is hard to avoid the conclusion that these 'elevated lineages', as one prince dubbed them,[92] used the tournaments for dealing with the pressures and tensions which beset them as a result of their very success, reproductive and otherwise.

The tournaments were but one aspect of the communal movement of the nobility. It is remarkable that other landmarks in the evolution of this movement such as the presentation of common grievances by the Würzburg and Bamberg nobilities to the prince-bishops, or the formation of the Rothenberg co-heirship (*Ganerbschaft*), also date from the end of the 1470s.[93] These collective enterprises, like the various aristocratic leagues and unions of the period, were all expressions of the nobles' attempt to define and secure their place in the conflict-ridden political setting of southern Germany. They were driven primarily by difficulties in the relationship between the nobles and the princes, but the relationship among the nobles themselves was also an important aspect of them. As a later chapter will show,[94] one recurrent concern of these collective efforts of the nobles, regardless of their initial aims, was to hinder feuding. That is precisely what happened after 1480: feuding between nobles began to taper off, at first slowly, then faster.[95] This change is

---

[91] Stamm (ed.), *Turnierbuch des Ludwig von Eyb*, 215–17; Ranft, *Adelsgesellschaften*, 104.

[92] '[die] hohen geschlechten, die den thurnier suchen': Margrave Albrecht to Bishop Johann of Würzburg, StAW, Misc. 1029, fol. 118r. The letter is reproduced in Lorenz Fries, *Chronik der Bischöfe von Würzburg 742–1495*, vol. IV, *Von Sigmund von Sachsen bis Rudolf II. Von Scherenberg (1440–1495)*, ed. Ulrike Grosch, Christoph Bauer, Harald Tausch and Thomas Heiler (Würzburg, 2002), 149–51.

[93] For the grievances of 1478 see Klaus Rupprecht, 'Vom Landfriedensbündnis zur Adelseinung: Genossenschaftliche Organisationsformen im spätmittelalterlichen Franken', in *Franken im Mittelalter: Francia orientalis, Franconia, Land zu Franken: Raum und Geschichte*, ed. Johannes Merz and Robert Schuh (Munich, 2004), 101–19, at 113. For the Rothenberg see Chapters 5 and 6.

[94] Chapter 6.   [95] See Figure 4.3 above.

Illustration 10. The banners of the twelve tournament societies of
the Four Lands: Swabia, Franconia, Rhineland and Bavaria. *Das
Wappenbuch Conrads von Grünenberg, Ritters und Bürgers zu
Constanz* (c. 1480). Bayerische Staatsbibliothek, Munich, Cgm.
145, p. 235

all the more remarkable given that the demographic growth of most elite families continued unabated. It is hard to identify any possible factor that could at that time have worked to reduce the level of violence among the nobility other than the progressive consolidation of the group in the wake of the communal movement of the nobles. This movement, in its different guises, dangled the carrot of protective solidarity, brandishing beside it the stick that nobles perhaps feared the most: social marginalisation or even exclusion from the aristocratic community. As the above-mentioned Sigmund von Gebsattel admitted at the end of his memoirs, he was moved to write them by the troubles he had experienced in proving his eligibility at the great tournaments of the Four Lands; by recording his participation in them he hoped to provide his descendents with the proof that would spare them similar travails.[96] Non-compliance with the rules which were then being hammered out for the various domains of aristocratic social and political life put one at risk of losing vital ties of intimacy and cooperation, and of being left to face enmity and conflict alone. This was one of the lessons which the tournaments imparted through the exemplary punishments inflicted on those who contravened the rules. While the political and educational work of the communal movement of the nobles by no means removed the material causes of strife, it did begin to shift the ways in which nobles perceived these issues and dealt with them. This was a complex process that would take decades to complete, not least because some of the biggest obstacles to it were created by the biggest men in Germany: the princes.

---

[96] *Eigenhändiger Aufzeichnung des Siegmund von Gebsattel*, col. 69.

CHAPTER FIVE

Enemies of the state? Feuding nobles, ruling princes and the struggle for mastery in early modern Germany

Early in 1459, a summit of princes took place in Bamberg. Its purpose was to reduce the tension between two coalitions of princes, which had reached a fever pitch in the preceding year. It took remarkably short time for irritation to swell up and break through the surface of goodwill. Margrave Albrecht of Brandenburg accused Duke (and Elector) Friedrich of the Rhine Palatinate of aiding, abetting and protecting Horneck von Hornberg, 'who is a notorious rogue, as are all those who shelter him'. Duke Friedrich replied that the margrave 'was lying like a butcher', whereas he himself was an honest and respectable prince. He then drew his sword; Margrave Albrecht unsheathed his. Only the intervention of their men prevented the confrontation from turning lethal.[1] Thus began the countdown to the Princes' War that engulfed and ravaged the south of Germany for several years (1459/60–3).

From the margrave's perspective, Horneck von Hornberg and the feuds that he and his accomplices carried out from their castle Widdern were a major cause of the great war between the princes. In

[1] *Speierische Chronik*, in *Quellensammlung der badischen Landesgeschichte*, ed. Franz Joseph Mone, vol. 1 (Karlsruhe, 1848), 367–520, at 424. The research on which the first part of this chapter is based was supported by the Israel Science Foundation (grant no. 560/08: Margrave Albrecht Achilles: War, Finance and Princely State-Formation in Germany, 1440–1486).

1463, in a letter to his ally Count Ulrich of Württemberg, he pointed out that he had become involved in this war three times on his, Ulrich's, behalf, and that castle Widdern was very much the source of it all.[2] And Ludwig von Eyb the Elder, the senior margravial statesman, claimed many years later in his memoirs that the war between Margrave Albrecht and the duke of Bavaria originated in castle Widdern and the activities of Horneck von Hornberg.[3] This view is too narrow to be taken at face value. The causes of the war were more complex and closely connected with truly fundamental political developments in Germany. Indeed, Horneck von Hornberg had been an apparently inexhaustible source of nuisance and mayhem ever since the late 1430s, but the remarkably large number of feuds and conflicts he had his hand in never threatened to ignite a war.[4] Yet the margravial view of Widdern as a major cause of the war should not be rejected out of hand. There was more to it than propaganda and convenient self-justification. It did reflect the significant role that feuds played in shaping political relationships among the German princes, and the crucial role that the German princes played in the production of feud violence.

The years after the war between the cities and the princes (1449–53) saw far-reaching changes in the pattern of rivalries in the Holy Roman Empire, and led to a series of political adaptations and realignments. The main division was no longer between princes and cities,

---

[2] Constantin Höfler (ed.), *Das kaiserliche Buch des Markgrafen Albrecht Achilles: Vorkurfürstliche Periode 1440–1470* (Bayreuth, 1850), 95, no. 33. Missing parts of this letter are given in Carl August Hugo Burkhardt, *Correcturen und Zusätze zu Quellenschriften für hohenzollerische Geschichte, 1, Das kaiserliche Buch des Markgrafen Albrecht Achilles herausgegeben von Constantin Höfler* (Jena, 1861), 13–14.

[3] Matthias Thumser (ed.), *Ludwig von Eyb der Ältere (1417–1502): Schriften. Denkwürdigkeiten, Gültbuch, Briefe an Kurfürst Albrecht Achilles 1473/74, Mein Buch* (Neustadt a.d. Aisch, 2002), 89–90.

[4] Hermann Ehmer, 'Horneck von Hornberg: Raubritter oder Opfer fürstlicher Politik', in *'Raubritter' oder 'Rechtsschaffene vom Adel'? Aspekte von Politik, Friede und Recht im späten Mittelalter*, ed. Kurt Andermann (Sigmaringen, 1997), 65–88.

but among the princes themselves.[5] As the princes expanded their rule and sought to consolidate their power, flashpoints multiplied. The rising tensions had two political centres. One was the rivalry between Margrave Albrecht Achilles of Brandenburg-Ansbach on the one side, and Duke Ludwig of Bavaria and the bishops of Würzburg and Bamberg on the other. Based on a poorly formulated imperial privilege, Margrave Albrecht claimed that the jurisdiction of his Territorial Court (*Landgericht*) extended to cover the entire Holy Roman Empire. He went energetically on to translate these claims to jurisdictional superiority into a politically expansionist practice that gravely antagonised neighbouring princes.[6]

The second centre of political volatility was the intensifying contest between Duke Friedrich of the Palatinate and his neighbours, in particular Mainz, Veldenz and Württemberg. A prime tactic employed by Duke Friedrich in extending and consolidating his hegemonial position in the area was to cultivate noblemen and use them as his long – and often hidden – arm in conflicts with other princes.[7] Under his wide wings, smaller powers which had fallen under the control of another prince could regain some

---

[5]   Thomas Fritz, *Ulrich der Vielgeliebte (1441–1480): Ein Württemberger im Herbst des Mittelalters. Zur Geschichte der württembergischen Politik im Spannungsfeld zwischen Hausmacht, Region und Reich* (Leinfelden-Echterdingen, 1999), 176.

[6]   Reinhard Seyboth, *Die Markgraftümer Ansbach und Kulmbach unter der Regierung Markgraf Friedrichs des Älteren (1486–1515)* (Göttingen, 1985), 108–11; Joachim Schneider, 'Legitime Selbstbehauptung oder Verbrechen: Soziale und politische Konflikte in der spätmittelalterlichen Chronistik am Beispiel der Nürnberger Strafjustiz und des Süddeutschen Fürstenkriegs von 1458–1463', in *Schriftlichkeit und Lebenspraxis im Mittelalter: Erfassen, Bewahren, Verändern*, ed. Hagen Keller, Christel Meier and Thomas Scharff (Munich, 1999), 219–41, at 224; Dieter Weiss, 'Franken am Ausgang des späten Mittelalters', in *Handbuch der Bayerischen Geschichte*, vol. III, part 1, *Geschichte Frankens bis zum Ausgang des 18. Jahrhundert*, ed. Andreas Kraus (Munich, 1997), 427–50, at 436–7.

[7]   An illuminating case study is Kurt Andermann, 'Der Überfall im württembergischen Geleit bei Markgröningen im Jahre 1459 – ein klassischer Fall von Straßenraub?' in *Aus südwestdeutscher Geschichte. Festschrift für Hans-Martin Maurer. Dem Archivar und Historiker zum 65. Geburtstag*, ed. Wolfgang Schmierer, Günter Cordes, Rudolf Kieß and Gerhard Taddey (Stuttgart, 1994), 273–86.

room for manoeuvre and make a bid for greater independence. His support of Count Ulrich of Helfenstein against Count Ulrich of Württemberg offers a revealing instance of this policy at work. A conflict between the two Ulrichs led Helfenstein to sell to Eberhard von Neipperg some militarily significant rights in castle Beilstein. Beilstein belonged, however, to Württemberg and was held by Helfenstein only in his capacity as the district governor. Helfenstein's action was not merely a breach of contract with economic implications; it was a political provocation of the first order: castle Beilstein was of eminent strategic importance, and the buyer, Neipperg, was a straw man for Duke Friedrich of the Palatinate. Present at the signing of the agreement were the Palatinate Master of the Household and Horneck von Hornberg; and Helfenstein received a position in Palatinate service immediately thereafter.[8]

Given this policy on the part of the Rhine Palatinate, it is not surprising that Count Ulrich of Württemberg found that the number of local lords bold enough to challenge him was growing by the day, and that their feuds against him were assuming a more aggressive character than before.[9] The hub of these hostile activities was castle Widdern in the Jagst valley. Held in fee from both the bishop of Würzburg and the counts of Hohenlohe, Widdern was a co-heirship (*Ganerbschaft*) in which numerous nobles had a part. This gave the enemies of Württemberg better opportunities to cooperate and coordinate their feud operations. Philipp von Hohenried, who was in dispute with Count Ulrich, invited another enemy of Württemberg to use Widdern as a base for his raids on the count's territory. These two were joined by Helfenstein, who fled to Widdern after forces sent by Count Ulrich evicted him from castle Beilstein.[10]

---

[8] Fritz, *Ulrich der Vielgeliebte*, 157. [9] Ibid., 166.

[10] Ibid., 167–8; Christoph Friedrich von Stälin, *Wirtembergische Geschichte*, part 3: *Schwaben und Südfranken. Schluß des Mittelalters, 1296–1496* (Stuttgart, 1856), 507.

Another old foe of Württemberg, Horneck von Hornberg, was also ensconced in the castle, from which he also attacked lands and people of Margrave Albrecht Achilles. In May 1457 Count Ulrich proclaimed a feud against the co-heirs of Widdern. However, some of them were servitors of Duke Friedrich of the Rhine Palatinate. The duke demanded that Count Ulrich call off the feud and that the case be heard by his own councillors. Ulrich, who at that time had no reliable allies to call on, had no alternative but to give in and abort his feud.[11]

The sense of isolation and impotence in the wake of his humiliating climb-down over Widdern must have greatly concentrated Count Ulrich's mind. He could no longer avoid the conclusion that his once dominant position in Swabia had gravely deteriorated over the preceding few years; that this was due to the influence and policies of the Rhine Palatinate; and — perhaps worst of all — that his weakness was now so visible as to invite further attempts to whittle down his power in the region.[12] His only hope of remedying this situation was Margrave Albrecht of Brandenburg-Ansbach. Ulrich could not have failed to realise that whereas the Wittelsbachs were the ever-flowing fountainhead of his troubles, the Hohenzollern margrave was a constant source of political succour. Ulrich's recent neglect of this relationship had cost him dearly.[13] But this error of political judgment was not irreversible, for Margrave Albrecht's chief policy objective at that time was to keep in check, and if possible undermine, the power of the Wittelsbach party in the Holy Roman Empire. Margrave Albrecht and Count Ulrich of Württemberg shared, then, vital strategic interests. Ulrich had to wait only a short time to have his assessment vindicated.

In the summer of 1457, the simmering conflict between Württemberg and the Rhine Palatinate escalated to the point where

[11] Fritz, *Ulrich der Vielgeliebte*, 167–8.   [12] Ibid., 168–9.   [13] Ibid., 158–9, 161–2.

both sides began to mobilise their forces for war. Some Palatinate
nobles, among them Horneck von Hornberg, already sent the customary cartels of defiance to Count Ulrich. Only the last-minute
diplomatic intervention of Margrave Albrecht averted a war and,
most probably, saved Württemberg from defeat.[14] The two rival
coalitions in the Holy Roman Empire were thus gradually taking
shape. In early 1458 they were given a formal political structure: In
February Duke Ludwig of Bavaria and his fellow Wittelsbach Duke
Friedrich of the Rhine Palatinate signed two treaties, the second
of which was explicitly directed against Margrave Albrecht and the
encroachments of his Territorial Court. Two months later, in Mergentheim, Margrave Albrecht and Count Ulrich of Württemberg
signed an alliance for their lifetimes.[15] It was in this context that
castle Widdern assumed a political importance out of all proportion
to its objective military and strategic value.

Margrave Albrecht and Count Ulrich of Württemberg sought to
demonstrate the strength and value of their alliance.[16] They needed
to signal to other powers that it was wiser to join them rather
than the political constellation dominated by Duke Friedrich of the
Rhine Palatinate. The opportunity presented itself – if it was not
manufactured – when Count Albrecht of Hohenlohe and some of
the von Stetten family instituted proceedings against Philipp von
Hohenried and Horneck von Hornberg at the Territorial Court
of Margrave Albrecht.[17] The plaintiffs were servitors and vassals
of Margrave Albrecht and Count Ulrich.[18] The Territorial Court
discounted the protests of Hohenried and Horneck that as Palatinate
vassals they were not subject to its jurisdiction, and proceeded to

---

[14] Ibid., 140–8.   [15] Ibid., 178–9.   [16] Ibid., 180.
[17] Cf. Joachim Schneider, *Spätmittelalterlicher deutscher Niederadel: Ein landschaftlicher Vergleich* (Stuttgart, 2003), 479.
[18] StAN, Fstm.Ansb., Fehdeakten, no. 84, doc. of Sonntag vor Viti [11 June] 1458; Stälin,
Wirtembergische Geschichte, part 3, 507. Count Albrecht of Hohenlohe was councillor and
courtier of Margrave Albrecht.

proclaim a ban (*Acht*) on castle Widdern.[19] If Margrave Albrecht and Count Ulrich were spoiling for a fight and in search of a pretext to justify it, then this was given to them rather unexpectedly as they made their way to Mergentheim to seal their treaty:[20] Philipp von Hohenried lay in wait for them, planning to disembarrass himself of his two persecutors in one fell swoop. He failed, and his abortive ambush managed to turn a likely expedition against Widdern into a foregone conclusion.[21]

This much was now clear to anyone. Duke Friedrich of the Rhine Palatinate put himself immediately to frustrating the expected onslaught on Widdern. He warned Count Ulrich of Württemberg against attacking Widdern, since the majority of the joint owners of the castle were his own vassals and servitors. He vouched for their peaceful behaviour in the future, and added that they proposed that the dispute be brought to a hearing.[22] But if he hoped for a rerun of his successful intimidation of Count Ulrich of Württemberg in 1457, then he failed to appreciate the extent to which circumstances had changed in the meantime. A similar letter aimed at putting Margrave Albrecht off a military venture was met with a strong-minded retort: the attempt on him and the count of Württemberg, 'an unjust and in these lands unprecedented incident', was only the last in a series of misdeeds perpetrated against him and his men by the Widdern

---

[19] Lorenz Fries, *Chronik der Bischöfe von Würzburg 742–1495*, vol. IV, *Von Sigmund von Sachsen bis Rudolf II. Von Scherenberg (1440–1495)*, ed. Ulrike Grosch, Christoph Bauer, Harald Tausch and Thomas Heiler (Würzburg, 2002), 145.

[20] See n. 15 above.

[21] Fritz, *Ulrich der Vielgeliebte*, 181; StAN, Fstm.Ansb., Fehdeakten, no. 84, doc. of Freitag vor Johannis baptiste [23 June] 1458 (declaration of feud by Margrave Albrecht against Philipp von Hohenried).

[22] Johann Ulrich Steinhofer, *Neue Wirtembergische Chronik*, vol. II (Stuttgart, 1746), 1002–3. Cf. Duke Friedrich of the Rhine Palatinate to Count Ulrich of Württemberg, 8 June 1458: Karl Menzel (ed.), *Regesten zur Geschichte Friedrich's I. des Siegreichen, Kurfürsten von der Pfalz*, in *Quellen und Erörtungen zur bayerischen Geschichte*, vol. II (Munich, 1862), 209–499, at 295; Fritz, *Ulrich der Vielgeliebte*, 182.

co-heirs, for which 'our Imperial Territorial Court placed them under a ban'. Since the plaintiffs, namely his 'councillor and courtier the count of Hohenlohe and our servitors the von Stetten have called on us, as their lord, to help bring the wrongdoers to justice', he and Count Ulrich of Württemberg 'agreed to punish with the help of God the above-mentioned evil deed. You write that you regret that we are forced to defend ourselves against those who cause us damage; it would have been more appropriate if you had regretted that such damage was caused in the first place.'[23]

Duke Friedrich was correct to conclude that Margrave Albrecht and Count Ulrich of Württemberg were bent on marching on Widdern, and that force alone could deter them. He sounded out other princes about their intentions in case of a military conflict, and swallowed their assurances of neutrality. He believed that with the support of Duke Ludwig of Bavaria he could face down Count Ulrich of Württemberg and Margrave Albrecht of Brandenburg and destroy their 'pride and reputation' (*bracht und geschray*).[24] His next letter to Margrave Albrecht was accordingly intransigent. While it reflects the rapidly deteriorating political situation, it also reveals the attitude of a prince – and an elector of the Holy Roman Empire at that – towards feuding: 'you do not name in your letter who did that [i.e. the attacks on him and the count of Württemberg, the count of Hohenlohe and the von Stetten]. Therefore no answer is required, for we have heard it said that some had become enemies of Württemberg and had to do that because they were denied recourse to the law.' The duke also made a point of clarifying that, in his

---

[23] StAN, Fstm.Ansb., Fehdeakten, no. 84, doc. of Samstag vor Viti [11 June] 1458. The letter of Duke Friedrich to Margrave Albrecht in ibid., doc. of octavo Corporis Christi [8 June] 1458.

[24] Duke Friedrich of the Rhine Palatinate to Duke Ludwig of Bavaria, 14 June 1458: Menzel (ed.), *Regesten zur Geschichte Friedrich's I. des Siegreichen*, 296; Fritz, *Ulrich der Vielgeliebte*, 182.

previous letter, he did not mean to say that he regretted that the margrave had to defend himself against those who had caused him damage; he actually meant that he was unwilling to allow the margrave to assail those who were under Palatinate jurisdiction.[25]

Another effort to dissuade the margrave from an attack on Widdern was made by the bishop of Würzburg, a feudal lord of three-quarters of castle Widdern. Neighbours and old rivals, the bishop and the margrave were constantly in conflict, with only the immediate causes changing every now and then. Bishop Johann fielded several arguments why Margrave Albrecht should call off his planned offensive. In the first place, the co-heirs of Widdern were subject to his jurisdiction. Secondly, such an action by the margrave would be against the treaty of alliance between them,[26] which provided for legal settlement of eventual disputes. Indeed, the treaty would obligate the margrave to give assistance to the bishop if Count Ulrich of Württemberg undertook to attack Widdern, as the rumour had it.[27] The response of the margrave was in the best tradition of the long-standing conflict between him and Würzburg: an angry exercise in one-upmanship:

you announce that the administration of justice is your responsibility, and that we have nothing to do with it, but you fail to mention those who have harmed our men and robbed on our roads . . . and you want to protect them from us through the sham offer of a legal process, and you do not see that we do not want to do violence to them, as you write; rather, a legal action has been brought against them and their property in our law-court, and they have been placed under the ban, and our undertaking is in accordance with the law, and is not violence.

---

[25] StAN, Fstm.Ansb., Fehdeakten, no. 84, secunda feria post beat. viti [19 June] 1458.

[26] Allusion to an alliance between the margraves of Brandenburg, the bishop of Würzburg and the bishop of Bamberg, dating from 2 February 1457: StAN, Fstm.Ansb., Herrschaftliche Bücher, no. 5, fols. 196r–197r; Fries, *Chronik der Bischöfe von Würzburg*, 140.

[27] StAN, Fstm.Ansb., Fehdeakten, no. 84, doc. of Samstag nach Viti [17 June] 1458; StAW, Stb, no. 717, fols. 605v–607v. The letter is reproduced in Fries, *Chronik der Bischöfe von Würzburg*, 146–8.

Margrave Albrecht's interpretation of the treaty was the polar opposite of the bishop's: it stipulated that none of the princes was to permit his men to act against any of the other allied princes. Now if the offenders were men of the bishop, then he should have helped the margrave to obtain satisfaction; if they were not, then not only was his protection of them unjust, but he ought actually to assist the margrave in punishing them. In the end the margrave came back to the issue of jurisdiction: he did not deny that Widdern belonged to the bishop, but he stressed that his Territorial Court nevertheless had the competence to judge cases from lands other than those he called his own: 'if we had possessed all the lands over which we are authorised to judge, we would no doubt have been a mighty prince'.[28]

Margrave Albrecht's letter to Bishop Johann was sent from Mergentheim. The margrave was there for the purpose of formalising an alliance directed explicitly against Duke Friedrich of the Rhine Palatinate. Signed on 20 June 1458, the alliance included the count of Württemberg and the archbishop of Mainz, the Primate of Germany, who just a few days earlier had assured Duke Friedrich of his neutrality in the event of war.[29] Three days later Margrave Albrecht sent declarations of feud to Horneck von Hornberg and Philipp von Hohenried. The declaration briefly recapitulated the offences of the nobles: the ambush, the actions against Count Albrecht of Hohenlohe, the damages to the von Stettens – all of them perpetrated from castle Widdern, in which 'you have also maintained horsemen who rob people on our roads. We take all this to heart and undertake to punish this as befits and behoves an

---

[28] StAW, Misc. 1029, fol. 118r; StAW, Stb, no. 717, fols. 610v-612r; StAN, Fstm.Ansb., Fehdeakten, no. 84, doc. of Montag nach Viti [19 June] 1458. The letter is reproduced in Fries, *Chronik der Bischöfe von Würzburg*, 149–51. On the issue of jurisdiction see also Schneider, 'Legitime Selbstbehauptung oder Verbrechen', 227.

[29] StAN, Fstm.Ansb., Herrschaftliche Bücher, no. 5, fols. 191r–v; Fritz, *Ulrich der Vielgeliebte*, 182.

upright prince to do, since the activities took place in our land and on our roads.'[30] Just before the end of June a large joint army of Württemberg and Brandenburg captured what Margrave Albrecht took to calling the 'robber castle' of Widdern without encountering any resistance, and razed it to the ground.[31]

The fate of Widdern was a triumph to the Mergentheim alliance, and a blow to Duke Friedrich. The omission of his duty to protect his vassals and servitors, for which he offered an unconvincing military justification, was compounded by his failure to engage the army of Württemberg on its way back, although a good opportunity for doing so had presented itself. The explanation put out from Heidelberg this time was that Duke Friedrich had been advised by his councillors of the illegality of such an attack, since he had not yet sent a formal cartel of defiance to the count of Württemberg.[32] With his reputation dented,[33] Duke Friedrich evidently could not let matters rest there. He reportedly vowed to turn Margrave Albrecht into a subject peasant of his.[34] He gave Horneck another castle, from which he 'made war on the [count] of Württemberg as before'.[35] This was the reason for Margrave Albrecht's outburst against Duke Friedrich of the Rhine Palatinate, which according to the single source that mentions it derailed the princely peace talks in Bamberg in early 1459.[36]

---

[30] StAN, Fstm.Ansb., Fehdeakten, no. 84, docs. of Freitag vor Johannis baptiste [23 June] 1458.

[31] The precise date is in dispute, but 29 June seems the most probable. See Fritz, *Ulrich der Vielgeliebte*, 184. On 2 July Margrave Albrecht sent a letter from Widdern to an anonymous addressee, informing him that the castle had been taken without resistance: StAN, Fstm.Ansb., Fehdeakten, no. 84, doc. Sonntag unsers Frauentag Visitationis 1458. 'Raubschloß' was used repeatedly in Margrave Albrecht's correspondence.

[32] Fritz, *Ulrich der Vielgeliebte*, 185–6; Joseph Würdinger, *Kriegsgeschichte von Bayern, Franken, Pfalz und Schwaben von 1347 bis 1506*, 2 vols. (Munich, 1868), II, 4.

[33] Schneider, 'Legitime Selbstbehauptung oder Verbrechen', 228.

[34] Thumser (ed.), *Ludwig von Eyb der Ältere (1417–1502): Schriften*, 90.

[35] *Speierische Chronik*, 421.   [36] Ibid., 424.

Illustration 11. Margrave Albrecht Achilles of
Brandenburg. Predella of the altar of the Order of the
Swan, 1484, St Gumpert, Ansbach; from Günther
Schuhmann, *Die Markgrafen von Brandenburg-Ansbach*
(Ansbach: Selbstverlag des Historischen Vereins für
Mittelfranken, 1980), p. 48

It cannot be ruled out that Margrave Albrecht's was a stage-managed fit of anger, an exercise in diversionary diplomacy of emotions, for some serious charges regarding the responsibility for the political crisis were laid at his door in Bamberg. The Wittelsbach princes fastened upon the intrusions of his Territorial Court into their jurisdictions as a central point at issue.[37] Widdern was not high, if at all, on the agenda. For as has already been indicated, Widdern and the feuds of its nobles were not the cause of the looming Princes' War. They were rather the consequence of the two problems which divided the princes into contending camps: the hegemonial pretensions of the Palatinate and the jurisdictional claims of Margrave Albrecht. Both played a major role already in the events surrounding castle Widdern. The various arguments made and actions taken by the rival princely parties were by way of a smokescreen for the real interests and intentions in play. Horneck von Hornberg could pursue so many feuds for so long only because they were part of a larger political contest and he therefore enjoyed the protection of a powerful prince.[38] When that prince became unhappy about the trail of troubles Horneck usually left in the wake of his activities, he had him taken into custody.[39] The same goes for the other side: Horneck's noble rivals, the Hohenlohes and von Stettens, found the administration of justice so unusually swift and effective in enforcing their legal claims against him only because they chose to bring their suits at the Territorial Court of Margrave Albrecht of Brandenburg.

---

[37] The nature of the charges against the margrave emerges from his responses to them: StAN, Fstm.Ansb., Fehdeakten, no. 84, n.d.

[38] Duke Friedrich disapproved of attempts by the Widdern nobles to reach a compromise with Margrave Albrecht, urged them to hold out, and promised to supply them weapons and amunition: StAW, Misc. 1029, fol. 115.

[39] *Speierische Chronik*, 424; Schneider, 'Legitime Selbstbehauptung oder Verbrechen', 231 n. 61.

Indeed, the judicial expedition of the margrave against Widdern was in nearly every respect such an unprecedented overkill as to leave little doubt that the disinterested enforcement of the law was not its primary objective. All of these actions by princes and nobles were calculated moves in a political game played by the strongest men in Germany for exceedingly high stakes. Castle Widdern and the feuds of its joint owners became politically so volatile a business because at least some of the princes judged that war was inevitable anyway, and perhaps also desirable.[40] The conflict over Widdern was in essence a trial run of the two opposing coalitions of princes.

The Widdern affair affords a number of insights into the causes and nature of feuding in the late 1450s and 1460s. A prominent aspect of the dispute was the politicisation of the law. It is not only that the conflict turned to a considerable extent on the question of jurisdictional competence as a constituent of the princes' authority; between them the rival princes ran the gamut of harnessing law courts and legal arguments to political ends. Much of this activation of the law revolved around the feud, which was at once treated as a cause, used as a pretext, and wielded as an instrument. Duke Friedrich of the Rhine Palatinate supported and even fomented noblemen's feuds in order to put pressure on other rulers. He also appealed to the formalities of feuding to absolve himself from a mortifying failure to take decisive military action. But he found his match in Margrave Albrecht, who exploited the feuds backed, or fuelled, by Duke Friedrich as a *casus belli* against Widdern. And whilst his justification was the illegality of the feuds of Horneck von Hornberg and his associates, he proceeded to enforce the sentence pronounced by his own court by means of a formally declared feud against

---

[40] Fritz, *Ulrich der Vielgeliebte*, 186–7.

the culprits. His pragmatic, not to say propagandistic, approach to
noblemen's feuds was brought out even more clearly by statements he
made to some nobles who found themselves in a typically Franconian
quandary: they were both allied with the margrave and vassals of
the bishop of Würzburg, by whom they were now called upon
to render military service in view of the impending advance on
Widdern.[41] Having made several arguments to the effect that the
bishop's position on Widdern was legally indefensible, Margrave
Albrecht concluded on a slightly different note:

> [concerning the question] whether it is fair to protect and safeguard [the
> Palatinate men in Widdern] from the princes and other nobles in the land
> of Franconia, anyone should [ask himself] whether he would judge it as a
> proper or improper thing to do if he himself was a victim [of such attacks] –
> let alone the unfair undertaking to subjugate the nobility so that they would
> be unable to serve their lords and relatives in the land, which is harmed . . . by
> foreigners, offer resistance to them, defend the land and its inhabitants from
> harm and maintain its valorous reputation.[42]

Not only did Margrave Albrecht not consider feuding as an inher-
ently illegal means of conflict resolution, he also made out a moral
case for the right of nobles to wage feuds in certain circumstances.[43]
He and other princes did not see an incongruity between the law and
their duty to enforce it on the one hand, and the feud on the other.
In fact, feuds were one of their tools of the trade. The princes may
have claimed a higher authority to wage feuds, but not an exclusive
right to do so. Given this outlook, and the practical political value of
noblemen's feuds, it is hardly surprising that the princes so readily

---

[41] Schneider, *Spätmittelalterlicher deutscher Niederadel*, 481–2.
[42] GStAB, BPH, Rep 27 E. I. 6, doc. 2.
[43] A similar case was made by Duke Friedrich of the Rhine Palatinate for the Widdern
nobles: StAN, Fstm.Ansb., Fehdeakten, no. 84, doc. of secunda feria post beat. viti [19
June] 1458.

exploited and manipulated them in their own dynastic and territorial struggles.

The nobles were by no means mere playthings of the princes. The intense rivalry between the princes allowed the nobles ample interstitial room for manoeuvre. Playing on the conflicts between the princes, they could gain or retain a degree of independence. Their feuds often enough served this purpose, among other things.[44] But as the fate of Widdern suggests, it was a dangerous game, precisely because it was to a large extent controlled by the princes. It was well-nigh impossible to feud against a prince without the support of another prince. Every such feud could therefore compromise the independence of the nobles involved in it. Noblemen's feuds, especially but not only those against princes, were closely tied to and substantially shaped by princely interests and intentions. The princes had a major influence on the rate of feud violence in Germany.

This contention is borne out by a comparison between the incidence of feuds in general and the incidence of feuds by nobles against princes in particular. The three most violent decades in Franconia, the 1460s, 1470s and the first decade of the sixteenth century, also saw the three peaks in the number of feuds against princes.[45] As the previous chapter has indicated, it is easy to account for the spate of feuds in the 1460s, the most violent decade in the entire period under examination: a large proportion of the feuds were either integral parts or offshoots of the Princes' War. Essentially this was a continuation with some intensification of the pattern of events leading up to the crisis over Widdern. Much of the war was fought by proxy, made up more

---

[44] See Chapter 1 nn. 49–50.

[45] See Chapter 4, Figure 4.2. The 1490s, though in general less violent than the other three decades, were also characterised by a relatively high number of feuds against princes: 15, which constituted 53.6 per cent of the 28 feuds recorded for those years.

by a chain of feuds of nobles from the rival camps than by set battles between armies.[46]

By contrast, the first decade of the sixteenth century, which witnessed the highest number of feuds between nobles and princes, presents something of a puzzle.[47] After a decline between 1480 and 1490, feud violence between princes and nobles bounced back to a previous level in the 1490s (15 feuds), and then peaked in the following decade (18 feuds). However, the Franconian princes were not at war in these years, and although tensions and disputes between them persisted, they were not as general and severe as those which filled the late 1450s and early 1460s.[48] Moreover, it is striking that this upsurge in feuds against princes occurred precisely at a time when feuds were being banned completely by the Imperial Diet in Worms in 1495, thus curtailing the nobles' right to feud as part of imperial reforms that generally seemed to enhance the clout and authority of the princes.[49] Given these conditions, it is intriguing that noble feuds against princes, rather than subsiding, climaxed at the turn of the century (Figure 5.1).

One explanation put forward by historians is that it was precisely the prohibition and criminalisation of the feud that was a cause of the increase in feuding because it took away from the nobles a right which they deemed to be a defining element of their status. In reaction, the nobles feuded with a vengeance so as to demonstrate their nobility.[50] There is some circumstantial evidence for this argument.

---

[46] See Chapter 3 n. 8.   [47] For an explanation of the feuds in the 1470s see Chapter 4.

[48] Johannes Merz, *Fürst und Herrschaft: Der Herzog von Franken und seine Nachbarn 1470–1519* (Munich, 2000), 48–50.

[49] Mattias G. Fischer, *Reichsreform und 'Ewiger Landfrieden': Über die Entwicklung des Fehderechts im 15. Jahrhundert bis zum absoluten Fehdeverbot von 1495* (Aalen, 2007), 204–41.

[50] Reinhard Seyboth, '"Raubritter" und Landesherren: Zum Problem territorialer Friedenswahrung im späten Mittelalter am Beispiel der Markgrafen von Ansbach-Kulmbach', in *'Raubritter' oder 'Rechtschaffene vom Adel'?*, 115–31, at 121. See also

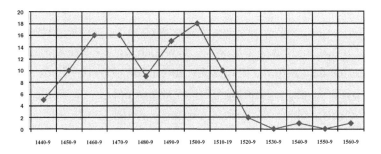

Figure 5.1. Incidence of nobles' feuds against princes, 1440–1570

Nobles protested vehemently at the reforms of 1495, especially at the intended imposition on them of the Common Penny tax, and formed the association of the Franconian Knightage in order to protect their rights and liberties. They also made collective preparations for the possibility of an armed struggle.[51] Some works written by nobles in the early sixteenth century suggest that nobles continued to regard feuding as a birthright and to celebrate feuds as an expression of the noble ethos, ignoring the imperial legislation against it.[52] A comment by the biographer of Wilwolt von Schaumberg brings out the nobles' attitude to the decrees of the Imperial Diet of 1495:

Christine Reinle, 'Fehden im Spannungsfeld von Landesherrschaft, Adel und bäuerlicher Bevölkerung', in *Tradition und Erinnerung in Adelsherrschaft und bäuerlicher Gesellschaft*, ed. Werner Rösener (Göttingen, 2003), 173–94, at 178, 194; Christine Reinle, 'Umkämpfter Friede: Politischer Gestaltungswille und geistlicher Normenhorizont bei der Fehdebekämpfung im deutschen Spätmittelalter', in *Rechtsveränderung im politischen und sozialen Kontext mittelalterlicher Rechtsvielfalt*, ed. Stefan Esders and Christine Reinle (Münster, 2005), 147–74, at 172.

[51] Klaus Rupprecht, *Ritterschaftliche Herrschaftswahrung in Franken: Die Geschichte der von Guttenberg im Spätmittelalter und zu Beginn der Frühen Neuzeit* (Neustadt a.d. Aisch, 1994), 390–1; Cord Ulrichs, *Vom Lehnhof zur Reichsritterschaft: Strukturen des fränkischen Niederadels am Übergang vom späten Mittelalter zur frühen Neuzeit* (Stuttgart, 1997), 181. For the opposition of the untitled nobility to the Common Penny tax see Peter Schmid, *Der Gemeine Pfennig von 1495: Vorgeschichte und Entstehung, verfassungsgeschichtliche, politische und finanzielle Bedeutung* (Göttingen, 1989), 399–407.

[52] That the feud was a defining privilege of nobility was argued in 1521 by Ulrich von Hutten, *Die Räuber*, in *Gespräche von Ulrich von Hutten*, ed. David Friedrich Strauß (Leipzig, 1860), 315–89, at 319–20.

'it was weighed and resolved', he wrote, 'especially by the Franconians, that they would not let themselves be put on a level with the French [nobility], who once were also free'.[53] Not inconsistent with this defiance, the biography all but idealises the feuds carried out by Wilwolt, presenting them as an example of the noble values and virtues which the protagonist personified in all his deeds and dictums. This edifying work gives no sign whatever of unease about feuding.[54] All the same, in the final analysis this evidence is far from conclusive. To argue that nobles feuded partly in order to make a point and broadcast their defiance against emperor and princes, is to offer an underdetermined interpretation. A more exhaustive and systematic analysis of the evidence suggests that the rise in feuding against Franconian princes around 1500, while by no means divorced from the issue of Imperial reforms, had much deeper origins. It was not the direct outcome of a reactionary, in-your-face behaviour of the nobles. Rather, it was of a piece with a complex social and political development within the nobility which began long before 1495.

The preceding discussion has established that the earlier peak in feuding against princes, in the 1460s, was closely related, first, to the rivalries between the princes and, secondly, to the feuding nobles' ties of vassalage and office-holding to one prince or another. This pattern reflects the enormous importance of princes in the life of nobles. Nobles largely depended on princely service for their economic wellbeing and social status.[55] Not for nothing did some of them

---

[53] Adalbert von Keller (ed.), *Die Geschichten und Taten Wilwolts von Schaumburg* (Stuttgart, 1859), 156.

[54] See Chapter 3.

[55] See Hillay Zmora, 'The Princely State and the Noble Family: Conflict and Co-operation in the Margraviates Ansbach-Kulmbach in the Fifteenth and Sixteenth Century', *The Historical Journal* 49, no. 1 (2006) 1–21, at 3–4.

instruct their sons to 'serve princes and counts'.[56] In many cases the career of nobles in princely service was preceded by a spell of education at the princely court, which could give this relationship a lasting emotional tinge: nobles and princes would mention this in order to remind each other of the moral debts they owed.[57] It is not surprising that nobles, especially those who went on to hold important offices in princely service, derived from it a strong sense of identity. Indeed, some noble office-holders had the position they had held inscribed on their tombstones.[58] The commemorative plaque for Ludwig von Eyb the Younger, one of the most successful nobles of his time, read like a proud résumé of his career:

In the year of the Lord 1521 ... died the gracious noble and knight Ludwig von Eyb zu Herrenstein, who was the master of the household of Bishop Wilhelm of Eichstätt for 8 years, then master of the household of Count Palatine Otto, Duke of Bavaria, for 13 years, then of Count Palatine Philipp, Duke of Bavaria, Elector, for 12 years, then lieutenant of the Upper Margraviate for Margrave Friedrich of Brandenburg, for 2 years, then once again master of the household of Count Palatine Friedrich, for 3 years.[59]

Death was a timely occasion to point out that success in life required maintaining a close relationship with one or more princes. This necessarily bore on feuding. Nobles, even if they wanted, could not

---

[56] Sven-Uwe Bürger, 'Burg Amlishagen – Anmerkungen zur Besitzgeschichte', *Württembergisch Franken* 76 (1992), 39–60, at 48.

[57] When one noble asked Margrave Albrecht of Brandenburg for help in a dispute he had with another noble, he called the prince 'my rightful hereditary lord who has brought me up' (StAN, Fstm.Ansb., Ansbacher Historica, no. 1, doc. 75 [1471]); Margrave Albrecht complained that a noble waged a feud against him although 'we have brought him up and showed his father great favour' (StAN, Fstm.Ansb., Fehdeakten, no. 143, doc. 3 [1471].

[58] Isolde Maierhofer (ed.), *Die Inschriften des Landkreises Hassberge* (Munich, 1979), passim; Karl Borchardt (ed.), *Die Würzburger Inschriften bis 1525* (Wiesbaden, 1988), passim; Rudolf M. Kloos (ed.), *Die Inschriften des Landkreises Bamberg bis 1650* (Munich, 1980), passim. See also Sven Rabeler, *Niederadlige Lebensformen im späten Mittelalter: Wilwolt von Schaumberg (um 1450–1510) und Ludwig von Eyb d.J. (1450–1521)* (Würzburg, 2006), 267.

[59] Rabeler, *Niederadlige Lebensformen*, 392–3.

easily avoid becoming caught up as feuders in the greater conflicts of
their princes. As the Franconian humanist noble Ulrich von Hutten
complained in his famous 'letter' to Willibald Pirckheimer (1518):
a nobleman who does not enter service with a prince and does not
enjoy his protection is regarded by anyone as easy prey; a nobleman
who is employed in the service of a prince is regarded by that prince's
enemies as a legitimate target. 'So I encounter enmity because I have
hoped for protection.'[60]

This nexus between the relationship of princes and nobles on
the one hand, and feuding on the other, underwent a remarkable
transformation in the last quarter of the fifteenth century. The late
1470s stand out as a particularly creative period in the formation of
the nobility as a group capable of collective action. Whether as cause
or effect, this went hand in hand with a change in self-conception.
A defining moment in this evolution was the organisation by the
nobles of the series of tournaments of the Four Lands, which began
in 1479.

What is particularly striking about these tournaments, which
brought together nobles from Franconia, Swabia, Rhineland and
Bavaria, is that they were initiated and organised not by princes, but
by noble confraternities.[61] This was a bid for independence. Paradoxically however, the attendance of the princes was essential for its
success. For the tournaments were meant to convey, among other
things, the idea of common aristocratic values and a shared heritage
that transcended the hierarchal chasms between princes, titled nobles
and untitled nobles. The princes had to participate, without taking
over. Hence, for example, Margrave Albrecht of Brandenburg was

---

[60] Winfried Trillitzsch, 'Der Brief Ulrich von Huttens an Willibald Pirckheimer', in *Ulrich
von Hutten: Ritter, Humanist, Publizist. Katalog zur Ausstellung des Landes Hessen anläßlich
des 500. Geburtstag*, ed. Peter Laub (Kassel, 1988), 211–29, at 218.

[61] See Chapter 4 n. 90.

invited 'only as a Franconian',[62] that is not primarily as a prince. Taking care to defer to the exalted status of the princes, the nobles in effect contrived to place themselves, in some respects, on an equal footing with them. [63] In other words, they were not to be treated as subjects of the princes.[64]

This attempt to keep the princes at arm's length was not entirely new: as individuals nobles always sought distance from some princes, while at the same time seeking proximity to other princes. As a group, too, nobles had a history of taking collective action to protect or enhance their interests in the face of princely policies.[65] What was particularly new was that this chivalrous quest for independence went together with an effort to define and formalise noble status. The nobles laid down exacting social criteria for admission into the tournaments, without paying heed to the princes.[66] Unlike the 'new monarchies' of France, Castile or England, where various marks of noble status, such as exemption from taxation, hunting rights,

---

[62] Heide Stamm (ed.), *Das Turnierbuch des Ludwig von Eyb (cgm 961). Edition und Unter-suchung mit einem Anhang: Die Turnierchronik des Jörg Rugen (Textabdruck)* (Stuttgart, 1986), 212; Heinrich Gradl, 'Die Bamberger Turnierordnung von 1478', *Bericht des Historischen Vereins Bamberg* 45 (1883), 87–97, at 89. See also Rupprecht, *Ritterschaftliche Herrschaftswahrung*, 372.

[63] Ulrichs, *Vom Lehnhof zur Reichsritterschaft*,140; Joseph Morsel, 'Le tournoi, mode d'éducation politique en Allemagne à la fin du Moyen Âge', in *Education, apprentissages, initiation au Moyen Âge: Actes du premier colloque international de Montpellier*, vol. II (Montpellier, 1993), 309–31, at 317.

[64] Cf. Morsel, 'Le tournoi', 320. See also Klaus Rupprecht, 'Vom Landfriedensbündnis zur Adelseinung: Genossenschaftliche Organisationsformen im spätmittelalterlichen Franken', in *Franken im Mittelalter: Francia orientalis, Franconia, Land zu Franken: Raum und Geschichte*, ed. Johannes Merz and Robert Schuh (Munich, 2004), 101–19, at 114.

[65] Ulrichs, *Vom Lehnhof zur Reichsritterschaft*, 153–73.

[66] Stamm (ed.), *Turnierbuch*; Ludwig Adalbert von Gumppenberg (ed.), 'Nachrichten über die Turniere zu Würzburg und Bamberg in den Jahren 1479 und 1486', *AU* 19, no. 2 (1867), 164–210. Rupprecht, *Ritterschaftliche Herrschaftswahrung*, 371–3. Cf. Horst Carl, *Der Schwäbische Bund, 1488–1534: Landfrieden und Genossenschaft im Übergang vom Spätmittelalter zur Reformation* (Leinfelden-Echterdingen, 2000), 106. For criteria of nobility from a prince's perspective see Karl-Heinz Spieß, 'Aufstieg in den Adel und Kriterien der Adelszugehörigkeit im Spätmittelalter', in *Zwischen Nicht-Adel und Adel*, ed. Kurt Andermann and Peter Johanek (Stuttgart, 2001), 1–26, at 10.

titles and certain privileges, were predicated on royal legislation, the distinguishing criteria which the German nobles elaborated as conditions for entrance into the circle of the jousting companions were fundamentally self-contained: noble ancestry, noble marriage, and indeed a record of participation in past tournaments. The tournaments, then, were a potent symbolical realisation of the confraternal spirit of the nobility, and a lively demonstration that the princes were not the arbiters of noble status.

With these social and political ambitions, coupled with a supraregional scope and an unprecedented level of cooperation, the tournaments of the Four Lands ushered in an altogether new stage in the self-understanding of the nobles. All this was not lost on the princes. Margrave Albrecht considered aspects of the tournament activity as dangerous to his position and tried to bring it under control.[67] And it was possibly no mere coincidence that several months after the first of these great tournaments had taken place in Würzburg, Bishop Rudolf suggested to the margrave that the Franconian princes should make an alliance and thus become the 'lord(s) of the lords' (*der hern herr*).[68] As the wording suggests, the princes now saw themselves confronted by a group of nobles who understood themselves as lords in their own right, and who were busy forging a social and political identity that did not have its ultimate source in the princes.[69]

Another contemporaneous milestone in the consolidation of the Franconian nobility as a social group, and in the emergence of a more autonomous self-conception, was the establishment of the co-heirship (*Ganerbschaft*) of Rothenberg. The Rothenberg castle, with

---

[67] Rupprecht, *Ritterschaftliche Herrschaftswahrung in Franken*, 374–6; Schneider, *Spätmittelalterlicher deutscher Niederadel*, 501–2.
[68] StAN, Fstm.Ansb., AA-Akten, no. 768, Fasz. II., doc. 41. Cf. Felix Priebatsch (ed.), *Politische Correspondenz des Kurfürsten Albrecht Achilles*, 3 vols. (Leipzig, 1894–8), II, 532, no. 571.
[69] Further to the construction of a lordly identity see below.

its lordship over extensive lands, was purchased in 1478 by forty-four noblemen from the Wittelsbach Duke Otto II of Mosbach-Neumarkt (who retained feudal overlordship). The nobles covenanted to hold it in joint ownership.[70] Direct evidence for the motives behind the transaction is wanting, but it appears plausible to assume that one particular aim of the noble buyers was to counteract the endeavours of Margrave Albrecht of Brandenburg to dominate them. The castle lay just outside his territory and under the protection of a prince from a rival dynasty. Secondly, nobles from Upper Franconia, an area where the margrave's position was robust, were prominent among the joint owners.[71] More generally, the castle seems to have been intended to serve as a safe haven and military base in the event of feuds against territorial powers.[72] Thus, like other jointly owned castles in Germany,[73] the Rothenberg was a manifestation of the tendency among the nobility to preserve autonomy, or enlarge their room for manoeuvre, by means of associations – in this case one with prominent military and lordly qualities. Indeed, the nobles of the Rothenberg were now lords of a swathe of territory which the princes had to reckon with. And in fact, as if to confirm a widespread fear among its neighbours,[74] the Rothenberg soon became a hub of

[70] The names of the buyers are given in Martin Schütz, 'Die Ganerbschaft Rothenberg in ihrer politischen, juristischen und wirtschaftlichen Bedeutung' (PhD thesis, University of Erlangen, 1924), 121. For an overview of the history of the Rothenberg see Robert Giersch, Andreas Schlunk and Berthold von Haller, *Burgen und Herrensitze in der Nürnberger Landschaft* (Lauf, 2006), 367–74.

[71] Rupprecht, *Ritterschaftliche Herrschaftswahrung*, 378–81.

[72] Schütz, 'Die Ganerbschaft Rothenberg', 7, 126–7.

[73] Cf. Joachim Schneider, 'Die Wetterauer Ganerbenverbände im Zusammenhang landschaftlicher Adelseinungen und Hoforden: Zu einer vergleichenden Landesgeschichte des Reiches im späten Mittelalter', *ZHF* 31 (2004), 529–49.

[74] For the concerns of Nuremberg see Rabeler, *Niederadlige Lebensformen*, 92. Emperor Friedrich III tried, at the behest of Nuremberg, to foil the plan of the nobles and warned that the castle would be a hotbed of robbery: Elfie-Marita Eibl (ed.), *Die Urkunden und Briefe aus den Archiven und Bibliotheken des Freistaates Sachsen*, Regesten Kaiser Friedrichs III. (1440–93) nach Archiven und Bibliotheken geordnet, ed. Heinrich Koller und Paul-Joachim Heinig, part 11 (Vienna, 1998), 261–2, no. 495.

Illustration 12. Castle Rothenberg, *c.* 1550. Germanisches Nationalmuseum, Nuremberg, Inv.-Nr. SP 9703

feuding. While some of the worst violence by nobles against the city of Nuremberg was carried out from the castle, most of the feuds waged by its members were against princes.

These observations are of vital pertinence to the upswing in feuds by nobles against princes in the years from 1490 to 1510, for of the 33 feuds against princes in these two decades, 18 (54.5 per cent) were carried out by members of the Rothenberg.[75] It is this remarkably

---

[75] Eukarius von Aufseß (2 feuds); Konrad von Bibra; Eberhard von Brandenstein; Konrad von Gebsattel; Christoph von Giech; Wolf Gottsmann (2 feuds); Philipp and Moritz von Guttenberg (1 feud); Jobst von Lüchau; Silvester von Schaumberg; Christoph vom Stein; Albrecht Stiebar; Ewold Stiebar; Sebastian Stiebar; Melchior Süzel; Albrecht von Wirsberg and Balthasar von Redwitz (1 feud); Stefan Zobel. StAA, Ganerbschaft Rothenberg, no. 2538a, passim. The number of the Rothenberg feuds as a proportion of the total number of feuds (18 out of 33, or 54.5 per cent) was much higher than the number of Rothenberg nobles as a proportion of the total number of nobles capable of declaring a feud in this

high proportion that probably induced the joint owners to send two emissaries to Emperor Maximilian I in 1508 to disclaim any responsibility for the rampant brigandage and highway robbery in Franconia.[76] Moreover, the fact has to be taken into account that, as has been indicated above, Franconian nobles were not equally represented in the Rothenberg. If one considers only the feuds against the margrave of Brandenburg and the bishop of Bamberg, the princes from whose Upper Franconian dominions most of the co-heirs came, then the proportion is even higher: two-thirds of the feuds (10 out of 15) were by Rothenberg nobles.

At first sight this might seem to confirm the notion that the recrudescence of feuding around 1500 was a reaction of the nobles against the curtailment of their right to feud by the Diet of Worms in 1495. Given that the Rothenberg co-heirship was a manifestation of the communal movement of the nobility, and of its effort to keep the princes at a healthy distance, it appears reasonable to interpret in this light the feuds of its members against princes. However, as in other parts of Europe, the relationship between nobles and rulers in Germany was not exclusively marked by antithesis. Conflict was only one aspect, and though its intrusions on the normal business of political life are the stuff of high drama, it did not normally overshadow cooperation.[77] The Rothenberg was no exception to this pattern. For all the feuds undertaken by its joint owners, it was

period (*c.* 70 out of *c.* 400, or 17.5 per cent). A statistical significance test of the hypothesis that 54.5 percent of 33 is the same as 17.5 per cent of 400 is strongly refuted: we can be more than 99 per cent confident that the two proportions are indeed different from one another, and hence that the Rothenberg nobles were significantly over-represented among feuders in this period. I am grateful to Professor Sheilagh Ogilvie and Dr Jeremy Edwards for carrying out the statistical significance test. Sheilagh Ogilvie, email to author, 16 May 2008.

[76] Ibid., Montag nach Antonii [24 January] 1508.

[77] Cf. Hillay Zmora, *Monarchy, Aristocracy, and the State in Europe, 1300–1800* (London, 2001).

by no means a bastion of political opposition to the princes. Many of the Rothenberg nobles were holders of high office in princely service. Of the eleven nobles who, in the period under discussion, occupied the top position in the castle, namely that of the burgrave, five held also top positions in princely administrations.[78] The above-mentioned Ludwig von Eyb the Younger, the esteemed servitor of many princes, exercised important functions in the Rothenberg, and acted as an intermediary between his fellow joint owners and his employer, the Duke of the Upper Palatinate, who was the feudal overlord of the castle.[79] The noble joint owners were as much at home in the princely courts as in the Rothenberg.

Collaboration of a violent kind was also in the nature of things. In 1501, following a series of exceedingly brutal feuds between certain co-heirs and Nuremberg, Margrave Friedrich, who had his own differences with the city, supplied the Rothenberg with weaponry and ammunition against the common enemy.[80] Moreover, Margrave Friedrich of Brandenburg was unmistakably behind some of the thirteen feuds which the prince-bishop of Bamberg faced during the period 1490–1510, and he interfered in a number of other affairs in

---

[78] Lamprecht von Seckendorff (Gerhard Rechter, *Die Seckendorff: Quellen und Studien zur Genealogie und Besitzgeschichte*, 3 vols. (Neustadt a.d. Aisch, 1987–1997), I, 127); Heinz von Guttenberg (Johannes Bischoff, *Genealogie der Ministerialen von Blassenberg und Freiherren von (und zu) Guttenberg 1148–1970* (Würzburg, 1971), 78); Konrad Schott (*Neues Württembergisches Dienerbuch*, ed. Walther Pfeilsticker, vol. II (Stuttgart, 1963), § 2616); Sixt von Seckendorff (Rechter, *Die Seckendorff*, I, 158); Sebastian Stiebar (Otto Seefried, *Aus dem Stiebar-Archiv: Forschungen zur Familiengeschichte von Bauer, Bürger und Edelmann in Ober- und Mittelfranken* (Nuremberg, 1953), 48). Another burgrave, Hans von der Tann, was possibly the one who lent 3,500 Gulden to Margrave Friedrich (StAN, Fstm.Ansb., Brandenburger Literalien, no. 643); Konrad Schott was also a lender (StAN, Fstm.Ansb., Herrschaftliche Bücher, no. 35, fol. 1 v). For a list of the burgraves see Schütz, 'Die Ganerbschaft Rothenberg', 100–1.

[79] StAA, Ganerbschaft Rothenberg, no. 2538a, passim. Rabeler, *Niederadlige Lebensformen*, 411.

[80] Seyboth, '"Raubritter" und Landesherren', 124.

the bishopric.[81] A good example is provided by the conflict over
castle Streitberg. In 1486 Eberhard von Streitberg, a member of
the Rothenberg,[82] made the family onomastic castle an open house
for the margrave.[83] Other members of the family strongly objected
to this measure. They were backed by the bishop of Bamberg, in
whose territory the fortress lay and from whom it was held in fee.
In 1497 a domestic feud broke out between the Streitbergs, which
in turn brought the bishop and the margrave to the brink of war.[84]
Meanwhile, Eberhard von Streitberg was appointed a margravial
governor and councillor. In 1507 his son, Georg, also a member
of the Rothenberg, sold the castle he did not own to Ludwig von
Leineck, a margravial office-holder who acted as a straw man in this
transaction: in 1508 Leineck 'sold' the castle to the margrave. Georg
von Streitberg was named a margravial district governor.[85]

As this crisis shows, the situation around 1500 was seemingly not
unlike that which had produced the peak in feuds against princes
in the 1460s. Princes again had a strong interest in using nobles
as their proxies in conflicts with other princes or with nobles. The
underlying cause was the imperial reforms and legislation, in particular the Common Penny scheme, of the late fifteenth century.
The changes these entailed conspired to raise a range of interre-
lated fundamental issues, from the 'sovereignty' of the princes, to

---

[81] The bishop hinted at the margrave's involvement in complaints made to Emperor Maximilian I: StAB, Fehde-Akten, no. 152, doc. 25. For an example of covert cooperation,
mediated by Ludwig von Eyb the Younger, between Margrave Friedrich and the Franconian Knightage to help Count Wilhelm of Henneberg against the bishop of Würzburg,
see Rabeler, *Niederadlige Lebensformen*, 323–5.

[82] StAA, Ganerbschaft Rothenberg, no. 2538a, passim. Streitberg was one of the 44 initial buyers of the Rothenberg: Schütz, 'Die Ganerbschaft Rothenberg', part 2, 121,
appendix 5.

[83] Paul Oesterreicher, *Die Burg Streitberg* (Bamberg, 1819), 15.

[84] Heinz Gollwitzer (ed.), *Deutsche Reichstagsakten, mittlere Reihe*, vol. VI, *Reichstage von
Lindau, Worms und Freiburg 1496–1498* (Göttingen, 1979), passim; Seyboth, *Die Markgraftümer Ansbach und Kulmbach*, 317–20.

[85] Oesterreicher, *Burg Streitberg*, 26–9, 40, 55–7.

the relationship between the neighbouring principalities, to the legal and 'constitutional' status of the nobles in the Holy Roman Empire in general and in the princely territories in particular. Such problems were inevitably all the more acute in the politically fragmented core zones of the Empire: Franconia, Swabia and the Rhineland. Hence the years around 1500 were characterised by growing tensions and intensified conflicts among princes, and between them and nobles.[86] And as in the 1460s, these conflicts not only drew nobles in; they also created opportunities for them. Having experienced this first-hand, the bishop of Bamberg rebuked his nobles in 1503 for having converted allodial property located in the diocese into fiefs to be held from other princes; for having placed their Bamberg fiefs under the protection of other princes; for making their castles 'open houses' for other princes; and for seeking, by means of service contracts with other princes, to evade Bamberg authority and jurisdiction.[87] And, he could as well have added, for using feuds to gain proximity to princes.

However, the feuds against princes at the turn of the century, even if they could and did serve the interests of other princes, were not carried out at their bidding to the same extent as those of the 1460s. As the case of the Rothenberg suggests, they were part of a much more complex pattern. What indeed made for the significant differences was the communal movement of the nobles. By the late fifteenth century it was a great deal more highly developed than in the former period. In 1494, the movement, which had previously been active in the territories of Würzburg and Bamberg, made itself felt for the first time among nobles closely associated with the margraves

---

[86] Rupprecht, *Ritterschaftliche Herrschaftswahrung*, 70–117. For political conflicts in Swabia see Carl, *Der Schwäbische Bund*, 112–14.

[87] StAB, B 28, no. 1, fols. 15v, 16r–v. For Würzburg see Ulrichs, *Vom Lehnhof zur Reichsritterschaft*, 50–1.

of Brandenburg.[88] One of the clauses of their prospective league enjoined that 'on behalf of no prince or lord should any nobleman do damage to life and limb and property of another'.[89] It was this clause in particular that vexed Margrave Friedrich. His objections, the language in which they were couched, and the measures he subsequently took to ensure the allegiance of nobles, leave no doubt as to the tension that now existed between prince and nobility.[90] The organised Knightage had become a force to be reckoned with. Indeed, five years later, when a military conflict with Nuremberg seemed imminent, it was with an assembly of the Knights that the margrave treated in order to secure their military aid.[91] This reflected and reinforced the new self-understanding of the nobles. As one noble put it to the margrave in 1499, 'Your Princely Grace cannot maintain his princely estate without the nobility.'[92] The nobles had by now come to see themselves as pan-Franconian and free lords.[93] As the tournaments had already demonstrated, however much the nobles benefited from princely service, they had been working to

---

[88] While the names of the members of the planned union are unknown, those who appear to have played a leading part were predominantly margravial office-holders. Of the nine envoys sent on 15 March 1495 to alleviate Margrave Friedrich's misgivings, five held top positions in the margravial administration: StAB, Neuverzeichnete Akten, no. 70143, unnumbered doc. Cf. Rupprecht, *Ritterschaftliche Herrschaftswahrung*, 385 n. 1019.

[89] Constantin Höfler, 'Betrachtungen über das deutsche Städtewesen im XV. und XVI. Jahrhunderte', *Archiv für Kunde österreichischer Geschichts-Quellen* 11 (1853), 177–229, at 186.

[90] Ibid., 187–8. Rupprecht, *Ritterschaftliche Herrschaftswahrung*, 384–6; Ulrichs, *Vom Lehnhof zur Reichsritterschaft*, 171–2.

[91] StAB, Neuverzeichnete Akten, no. 70142, docs. 1, 4, 7.

[92] StAN, Fstm.Ansb., Fehdeakten, no. 227. The letter was printed in *Verhandlungen zwischen der Stadt Nürnberg und der fränkischen Ritterschaft wegen Christoph von Giech und Contz Schott* (Nuremberg, 1500): 'Als auch ewr fürstlich gnad auß fürstlichen tugenden zuthun schuldig sind dy on adel fürstlichen stand nit füren sollen.' The charter of the 1517 union of the Franconian nobility similarly declared that the princes could not maintain their rule 'an frumme getrewe Ritter und Knecht': Johann Christian Lünig, *Des Teutschen Reichs-Archiv partis sepecialis continuatio III*, part 2 (Leipzig, 1713), 7, no. 1.

[93] See Rupprecht, 'Vom Landfriedensbündnis zur Adelseinung'. See also Ulrichs, *Vom Lehnhof zur Reichsritterschaft*, 172–3.

forge a social and political identity that did not have its ultimate source in their relationship with the princes. Thus, at the same time as the princes accentuated their claims to jurisdictional supremacy over the nobles, whom they increasingly tended to treat as subjects, the nobles stressed their lordly freedom and strove harder to preserve their liberties.

It is noteworthy in this connection that some of the most telling evidence for the emergence among the nobles of a lordly self-image comes from members of the Rothenberg. When in 1504 Ludwig von Eyb the Younger was called to arms by Duke Ruprecht of the Palatinate in the Landshut War of Succession, he replied to the prince that 'I am not Your Grace's indentured servitor.' A similar rebuff of a presumptuous imposition of formal obligations was issued in 1495 by Wilwolt von Schaumberg: in response to a letter that purported to fix the terms of his military service to the duke of Saxony, he wrote back to the ducal councillors that the messenger's fee was a waste of money – 'should my Gracious Lord want me to do something, he would know to speak to me, since I have been closer to him... than others'.[94] A few years later Wilwolt excelled himself. His sense of self-worth was at that time apparently so overweening that his letter of invitation to the dukes of Saxony to come to his veritably princely wedding addressed them as 'fellows' (*gesell*). Whether this unsolicited familiarity was the reason for their failure to oblige is impossible to say. But if they did regard it as a transgression of the customary hierarchical boundaries that aimed at signalling, as the tournaments had done, a shrinking social disparity between princes and nobles, they were probably right.[95]

---

[94] Quotations from Rabeler, *Niederadlige Lebensformen*, 307, 270, respectively.
[95] Ibid., 334–5.

This assertive self-conception of the nobles as lords, inferior in status to the princes but by no means their subjects, was richly played out in one of the most dramatic and violent feuds that took place between nobles and princes around 1500 in Franconia. The feud, which pitted members of the von Guttenberg family against Margrave Friedrich of Brandenburg, was all about the autonomy of a noble family.[96] The construction of a well-fortified castle by Philipp von Guttenberg, a co-heir of the Rothenberg, in a border area of strategic significance to several princes sent the margravial clerks scouring the archive for old documents. They emerged with written proof that Margrave Friedrich had a legal right to use the fortress in wartime. This legal claim was supposed to allow the prince to bring the noble family and their castle under his thumb. Fearing for their independence, Philipp von Guttenberg and his nephew Moritz, also a co-heir of the Rothenberg, rejected the claim out of hand. They knew full well what the consequences would be. In a parley with the margrave Philipp declared that one would have to strangle them to secure their consent to the prince's demands. The latter erupted in rage and a duel was averted at the last moment. The Guttenbergs offered to have the dispute heard by margravial nobles, but their request was answered with force: Margrave Friedrich proceeded to storm the castle. Philipp, Moritz and the other Guttenbergs who chose to defy him had however long gone underground.[97] They would resurface every now and then only to attack men and property of the prince.

As usual, the small war between the two parties was accompanied by a propaganda campaign. While the Guttenbergs could not match

---

[96] The following description is based on Rupprecht, *Ritterschaftliche Herrschaftswahrung*, 72–117.

[97] Philipp was later captured and died, in suspicious circumstances, in margravial gaol.

the resources of the prince, their actions and arguments were any-thing but those of old-fashioned nobles fighting a quixotic battle for outdated conceptions. Not only did they make use of the printing press to show the margrave in as bad a light as possible, their main point was utterly 'modern': in using force in complete disregard of their offer of legal settlement, the margrave, they argued, was acting in contravention of 'the General Peace and the [legal] order which has recently been set up by prince-electors, princes and the Holy Empire'. Letters to this effect were sent to the Franconian Knightage and to King Maximilian I. Thus, rather than a perceived attack on noble status, the resolutions of the 1495 Imperial Diet of Worms were appealed to as ideally safeguarding it against the superior power of a prince. The margrave, however, had greater influence on the King of the Romans and managed to block royal intervention on behalf of the Guttenbergs. In an apologia published in 1500, Moritz von Guttenberg remonstrated that he had been placed under an imperial ban only because the prince was the infinitely stronger side. His right was up against a superior might. The whole affair, he concluded, was a travesty of justice that left him with no other option but to wage a feud: 'The Law of Nature permits self-defence, and it is said "pugna pro patria", that is "you should struggle and fight for your fatherland and paternal property".'[98] If the imperial law of 1495 did not apply to all equally, then it was better not to include the nobility in the General Peace. As a historian of the Guttenbergs has observed, few other documents testify so well to the lordly self-conception of the nobles.[99]

This new self-conception, buttressed by the communal move-ment, could not fail to generate clashes between princes and nobles which, in the tense atmosphere then prevailing in Franconia, could

---

[98] Rupprecht, *Ritterschaftliche Herrschaftswahrung*, 499.   [99] Ibid., 96.

easily segue into feuds. But while it accounts for some conflicts, it does not on its own explain the peak in feuding against princes that was reached around 1500. As has been indicated above, nobles were intimately associated with the princes, depended on them for their economic wellbeing and social status, and derived a strong sense of identity from service to them. The key to this apparent paradox is provided by the Rothenberg co-heirship, which was its perfect embodiment: most of the noble feuds against princes around 1500 were by its co-heirs, yet co-heirs of the Rothenberg counted among the most successful and most respected princely servitors in Franconia.

The Rothenberg, in fact, witnessed a convergence of two sometimes competing tendencies that characterised the noblemen's relationship with princes throughout the fifteenth century. One tendency was towards conflict between nobility and princes, and it involved efforts by nobles to keep the princes at arm's length and retain a degree of independence. The other tendency was towards increasing cooperation and interdependence between prince and nobles.[100] Both tendencies were set in motion by the process of state formation and both intensified in the late fifteenth and early sixteenth centuries as a result of the changes and reforms designed to bring better order to the relations between the Empire and its constituents.[101] And both produced a good deal of violence. The nobles at that time had more conflicts with the princes than before, and more fundamental conflicts at that; the princes, too, now had more conflicts with

[100] For a more detailed discussion of these two tendencies see Hillay Zmora, 'The Formation of the Imperial Knighthood in Franconia: A Comparative European Perspective', in *The Holy Roman Empire, 1495–1806*, ed. R. J. W. Evans, Michael Schaich and Peter H. Wilson (Oxford, 2011), 283–302.

[101] See n. 86 above.

each other than in the previous thirty years or so. Frictions of all kinds multiplied, and so did the prospects for gaining support in the event of a feud: the princes were more likely to find nobles at loggerheads with rival princes, and therefore had more opportunities to use nobles as weapons in proxy war. The Franconian humanist noble Ulrich von Hutten observed at the time that 'the princes need [feuding nobles] as a shield for their own power; indeed, the power of all princes rests on them. Hence, among [the princes], he who becomes enemy of another calls upon [the noblemen], using them as weapons of war.'[102] The nobles, on the other hand, were more likely to find princes at loggerheads with each other, and therefore had more opportunities to receive covert, and sometimes overt, backing in a feud against one of the princes. The Rothenberg provided most of the feuders against princes not primarily because its military and geostrategic advantages and its semi-autonomous status constituted a 'facilitating environment'; rather, the Rothenberg was at the forefront of feuding activities against princes because its members were precisely those nobles who led the noble movement towards greater independence, yet were at the same time prominent servitors of princes and therefore likely to be deeply involved in their conflicts.

As the case of the Rothenberg co-heirship suggests, then, what explains the rising tide of noble feuds against princes around 1500 was neither the tendency towards closer cooperation of the nobles with the princes, and its concomitant dependence on them, nor the newer tendency towards autonomy, and its concomitant stiffer resistance to princely politics. Rather, the underlying cause was the convergence between these two tendencies. In other words,

---

[102] Ulrich von Hutten, 'Die Anschauenden', in *Ulrich von Hutten: Deutsche Schriften*, ed. Peter Ukena (Munich, 1970), 136–61, at 149–50.

the drive towards individual proximity to princes, which made for collaboration between nobles and princes, came to interact dynamically with the drive towards collective distance from them, which set nobles against princes. Within the context of the fundamental political tensions then at work in the Holy Roman Empire, the tradition of cooperation between princes and nobles exacerbated the conflicts between them over issues of jurisdiction and 'sovereignty'. It was this convergence of opposing interests that produced the explosion of feud violence between 1490 and 1510 in Franconia.

CHAPTER SIX

The politics of civility

The decay of the feud

The early modern period was characterised by significant changes in attitudes to violence and by increasing socio-political control and regulation of behaviour. Historians and sociologists have advanced a number of theories to explain this transformation. Confessionalisation, social disciplining, the 'civilising process', state formation and the expansion of state justice – these are all conceptual frameworks with which historians have sought to account for the growing internal as well as external restraints imposed on violent behaviour in Western Europe over the early modern period.[1] Some of these theories have been operationalised to explain the decline of the feud or the vendetta in different countries. For Scotland, Keith Brown maintained that Calvinism was part of the solution to the problem of endemic bloodfeud: 'The world of the bloodfeud was being turned upside down as the corporate society of kinsmen, friends, dependants, and ancestors was replaced with the awful isolation of the individual sinner standing before the judgment of God. In this new world men inherited nothing from their parents, not even their feuds.'[2] For the Friuli region in Italy, Edward Muir argued along

---

[1] See Julius R. Ruff, *Violence in Early Modern Europe, 1500–1800* (Cambridge, 2001), 3–9.

[2] Keith M. Brown, *Bloodfeud in Scotland: Violence, Justice and Politics in an Early Modern Society* (Edinburgh, 1986), 207.

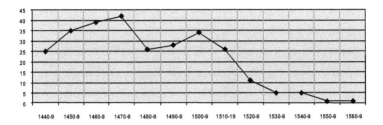

Figure 6.1. Incidence of nobles' feuds in Franconia, 1440–1570

the lines of Norbert Elias's *The Civilising Process* that the adoption
by nobles of new courtly manners put an end to the culture of violent revenge. Friulan nobles, who previously stooped to feeding
their murdered enemies to the dogs, now embraced the precept that
'revenge is a dish best eaten cold'.[3] Hot-blooded enormities gave
way to the elegant cruelties of palace intrigue.

None of these grand theories can be unproblematically applied
to the decay of the noble feud in Germany. Confessionalisation and
its attendant campaign of social disciplining simply do not fit the
chronology: as Figure 6.1 shows, the steady fall in the number of
noble feuds in Franconia had already begun before the Reformation,
let alone before the consolidation of confessional identities. And the
incidence of feuding among the nobles in particular already began
to de-escalate at the end of the fifteenth century.[4] The protocols of
the co-heirship of Rothenberg, for example, reveal that the religious
problem did not begin to claim the attention of its members before
1528.[5] State formation, by contrast, was closely related to feuding.

[3] Edward Muir, *Mad Blood Stirring: Vendetta & Factions in Friuli during the Renaissance* (Baltimore, 1993), 247–72 (quotation at 272).
[4] See Chapter 4, Figure 4.3.
[5] Martin Schieber, '"Auf das sie also die Milch Gottes Worts mit Nutz und Freuden mugen drincken": Die Ganerbschaft Rothenberg als lutherisches Territorium 1529–1629', in *Frömmigkeit, Theologie, Frömmigkeitstheologie: Contribution to European Church History: Festschrift für Berndt Hamm zum 60. Geburtstag*, ed. Gudrun Litz (Leiden and Boston, 2005), 483–96, at 486.

But as the preceding chapter has shown, state formation was at least as much a part of the problem of the feud as its solution. The 'Civilising Process' theory, with its emphasis on courtly society as the trend-setting centre of change in behavioural norms, is at first sight perhaps the most germane to an explanation of the decline of the feud. Indeed, moral improvement was one of the main concerns of the tournaments of the Four Lands in the late fifteenth century;[6] and reforming some of their social habits and manners was high on the agenda of the nobles in the early sixteenth century.[7] However, the 'Civilising Process' theory rests on some questionable assumptions about the relationship between civilisation and violence. As Robert Conquest pointed out, 'the first truly "cultured" man in English politics was the revolting John Tiptoft, Earl of Worcester, translator of Cicero, patron of humanists, the purity of whose Latin brought tears to the eyes of Aeneas Sylvius himself, but who is known to political history, according to different criteria, as "the Butcher Earl", owing to his record as impaler of prisoners and slaughterer of infants, new phenomena in medieval England'.[8] The same objection, *mutatis mutandis*, applies to noble feuds in Franconia. The nobles most likely to be involved in feuds were precisely those who held high offices in princely administrations or courts. As has already been mentioned, even a man of parts such as Baron Johann von Schwarzenberg, who a held a top court position and composed a satirical work on drunkenness as well as a poem on the 'murderous depravity of robbing', preferred feuding to litigation in 1519.[9] A more fundamental objection, perhaps, is that the 'Civilising Process'

---

[6] Chapter 4; Cord Ulrichs, *Vom Lehnhof zur Reichsritterschaft: Strukturen des fränkischen Niederadels am Übergang vom späten Mittelalter zur frühen Neuzeit* (Stuttgart, 1997), 138.

[7] Ulrichs, *Vom Lehnhof zur Reichsritterschaft*, 172, 184.

[8] Robert Conquest, *Reflections on a Ravaged Century* (London, 1999), 209. Cf. Stuart Carroll, *Blood and Violence in Early Modern France* (Oxford, 2006), 310.

[9] See Chapter 3 nn. 71–2. Johann von Schwarzenberg, *Das Büchlein vom Zutrinken*, ed. Willy Scheel (Halle, 1900); *Ain Lied mit vorgehender anzaygung / wider das mordlaster des raubens*

was far too long-drawn-out to account for the relatively quick fall in the incidence of feuding after 1510. In the final analysis, the theory does not provide a cogent conceptual framework for understanding why nobles abandoned feuding over the first half of the sixteenth century.

Variations in the occurrence of noble feuds are best explained by formulating specific propositions that are compatible with the general interpretation of the feud.[10] The preceding chapters have indentified three forces that shaped the motives and provided strong incentives for nobles to resort to this form of violence: first, the relationship of 'inimical intimacy' among the nobles, and the concomitant preoccupation with reputation; second, the nobles' proximity to princes, which involved them in the rivalries between state-making rulers. These two forces overlapped. Both were closely bound up with the structures, practices, necessities and compulsions of the social and economic life of the aristocracy; both sustained as well as reflected a particular outlook on the proper relationships within this world. It is a characteristic of these social models that, on the one hand, they had the capacity to support solidarity and cooperation among nobles and between nobles and princes; and, on the other hand, they were also likely to engender conflict and violence. While nobles' economic situation and social standing heavily depended on service to princes, it was precisely against these feudal overlords and employers that they often felt compelled to feud. As the prince-bishop of Bamberg complained in responding to grievances presented by the nobles in 1503, the nobles who were associated with the bishopric waged feuds

(1513). It is true, however, that some other nobles at the very top of princely service seem not to have been involved in feuding. Nobles like Masters of the Household Hans von Seckendorff-Aberdar, Ludwig von Eyb the Younger and Hans Fuchs are not recorded as feuding against either other nobles or princes.

[10] Cf. Chapter 4.

against it more than anyone else.[11] Moreover, as the 'biography' of Wilwolt von Schaumberg suggested, feuds could be very handy in gaining the kind of reputation that helped launch a noble into lucrative positions in princely service.[12] Thus, either in combination or alone, both the desire to attain proximity to princes and the desire to achieve or maintain reputation were as likely to conduce to conflict as to cooperation.

The third force that shaped the motives and provided the incentives for nobles to feud was the emergence of a self-perception of the nobles as free lords. An integral aspect of the communal movement of the nobles and the consolidation of its confraternal structure, this made itself especially felt in the last quarter of the fifteenth century.[13] The signs were legion: noble unions and leagues, the presentation in 1474 and 1478 of collective remonstrations to the princes, the establishment in 1478 of the Rothenberg co-heirship, and the tournaments of the Four Lands which began in 1479. As has been argued on the basis of the feuds of the Rothenberg co-heirs, not only did the rising lordly identity which the communal movement embodied and bolstered collide with the growing claims of the princes to jurisdictional supremacy and their state-making ambitions; the nobles' bid for autonomy interacted with a venerable tradition of service to the princes to create a wave of feuds against princes between 1490 and 1510.[14]

This was the storm before the calm. For the confraternal movement of the nobility, for all its resistance to princely policies, contained elements that militated against feuding. This was already apparent

---

[11] StAB, B 28, no. 1, fol. 15v (the grievances and the bishop's responses are reproduced in Klaus Rupprecht, *Ritterschaftliche Herrschaftswahrung in Franken: Die Geschichte der von Guttenberg im Spätmittelalter und zu Beginn der Frühen Neuzeit* (Neustadt a.d. Aisch, 1994), appendix 3).
[12] See Chapter 3 n. 77.　　[13] Chapter 5.　　[14] Ibid.

in the tournaments of the Four Lands. A central plank of the tournament codes concerned the prevention and settlement of feuds.[15]
The nobles in effect took the idea of a community of peace and law,
which was a fundamental principle of the noble confraternities,[16] and
extended it to all the participants in the tournaments. A telling example is the prohibition on helping nobles who were to be punished
during tournaments. This ruling, which was designed to obviate
acts of revenge and the spread of violence outside the tournament,
overrode the all-important aristocratic principle of solidarity and
mutual help among family and friends.[17] This and other measures
were necessarily ad hoc and temporary. But as the nobles worked
out the mechanisms for self-regulation and for enhancing their independence from the princes, so did this principle of a community of
law and peace become increasingly institutionalised.

The working out of the principle of confraternal limitation of
feuding was apparent in the co-heirship of Rothenberg. Indeed, no
other issue preoccupied the Rothenberg co-heirs in their meetings
more than whether or not to permit this or that member to use the
castle during his feud. That the Rothenberg was in the joint ownership of several dozen noblemen with common interests meant that
the private interests of nobles embroiled in conflicts with princes
or other territorial powers could not be given free rein. All of the
Rothenberg nobles had ties of one kind or another with princes, and

---

[15] Chapter 4.

[16] Herbert Obenaus, *Recht und Verfassung der Gesellschaft mit St Jörgenschild in Schwaben:
Untersuchungen über Adel, Einung, Schiedsgericht und Fehde im fünfzehnten Jahrhundert*
(Göttingen, 1961), 17; Rupprecht, *Ritterschaftliche Herrschaftswahrung*, 372; Klaus Rup-
precht, 'Vom Landfriedensbündnis zur Adelseinung: Genossenschaftliche Organisations-
formen im spätmittelalterlichen Franken', in *Franken im Mittelalter: Francia orientalis,
Franconia, Land zu Franken: Raum und Geschichte*, ed. Johannes Merz and Robert Schuh
(Munich, 2004), 101–19, at 110–11.

[17] Andreas Ranft, *Adelsgesellschaften: Gruppenbildung und Genossenschaft im
spätmittelalterlichen Reich* (Sigmaringen, 1994), 192–3; Ulrichs, *Vom Lehnhof zur
Reichsritterschaft*, 144.

for every noble who was happy to begin a feud against a prince, there were other nobles who were openly unhappy about the possible consequences of such a decision. A letter from the duke of Braunschweig and the archbishop of Magdeburg prompted the co-heirs to instruct Eberhard von Brandenstein to release, without demanding ransom, the captives he had brought to the Rothenberg from Saxony.[18] That the castle became a hotbed of feuds by Franconian nobles against princes should not therefore blind one to the fact that, paradoxically, it also marked the beginning of the end of feuding.

A pact (*Burgfrieden*) made in 1479 with a view to regulating the relationship among the joint owners laid down that a member would be allowed to use the castle in a feud only if he had first sought a legal settlement of the conflict and this had been refused by the opponent.[19] The *Burgfrieden* of 1493 made the conditions for use of the castle even stricter: even if the rival party refused a legal settlement, the Rothenberg noble still would not be allowed to use the castle before a period of nearly half a year had passed in which the burgrave would seek to mediate a settlement of the dispute.[20] These conditions did not remain a dead letter. They were invoked each time a member sought the consent of the other joint owners to operate from the castle. And members who wished to do so invariably found it difficult to obtain such permission from their fellow co-heirs. When Matern von Vestenberg wanted to use the castle in his feud against the prince-bishop of Würzburg, the other members refused his request, 'because the [bishop] suggested to him, in accordance with our *Burgfrieden*, that the case be heard by three of His Grace's lay noble councillors'. They added that if the proceedings were to

---

[18] StAA, Ganerbschaft Rothenberg, no. 2538a, Mittwoch nach Galli [22 October] 1505.

[19] Martin Schütz, 'Die Ganerbschaft Rothenberg in ihrer politischen, juristischen und wirtschaftlichen Bedeutung' (PhD thesis, University of Erlangen, 1924), 127, appendix 7, articles 5–8.

[20] Rupprecht, *Ritterschaftliche Herrschaftswahrung*, 380 n. 1004.

be dragged out by the bishop, then on receiving Matern's complaint the members of the Rothenberg would again write to the prince and demand that the case be heard within the time limit stipulated in the *Burgfrieden*. Only if this did not work either, would Matern be given his rights as specified in the *Burgfrieden*.[21] Another noble who had a conflict with the bishop of Würzburg claimed that the prince failed to respect a prior agreement between them and that therefore he, the nobleman, should be entitled to use the castle in a feud. He was told that because the bishop made another offer of a legal settlement, and 'one cannot find that His Princely Grace was slow in complying with the agreement, one cannot at this time grant the use of the castle against His Grace'.[22] Some nobles found this stringent policy frustrating. The protracted feud of Ernst von Redwitz against the bishop of Eichstätt mutated into a conflict between him and his fellow members of the Rothenberg: Redwitz accused them of withdrawing the consent they had already accorded him to use the castle against the bishop. He gave vent to his anger by vilifying them 'with words and writings'. The differences were in the end composed by other members of the castle.[23]

As a corporate body, then, the Rothenberg joint owners behaved in ways that were opposed to the accustomed principles governing the relations between nobles. As was foreshadowed by the tournament codes, ties of kinship, friendship and patronage, or even plain class solidarity, carried remarkably little weight when it came to making the decision whether or not to permit fellow joint owners to operate from the Rothenberg against princes or other powers. In 1507, for instance, Wolf Gottsmann applied to Burgrave Albrecht Gottsmann for leave to use the castle in his feud against the bishop of Bamberg.

[21] StAA, Ganerbschaft Rothenberg, no. 2538a, Donnerstag nach Judica [6 April] 1514.
[22] Ibid., Montag–Mittwoch, nach unser lieben Frauen geburt [15–17 September] 1522.
[23] Ibid.

The burgrave, having polled the opinion of the members, turned down his relative's request, because the bishop was prepared to seek a legal settlement. He suggested to Wolf that another attempt be made to reach a peaceful resolution.[24] In 1521 Albrecht Gottsmann, the former burgrave, found himself on the other side of the same predicament. His petition to be allowed to operate from the castle against Nuremberg was declined. The joint owners reasoned that his feud had to do with his duties as a Bamberg district governor. They offered instead to discuss the matter on his behalf with the bishop or the city.[25] Lastly, nobles who were involved in feuds and wanted to join the Rothenberg as members were rejected. As it was put to one candidate, 'it has been resolved that he should not be admitted as a co-heir at present, because he is encumbered with open feuds'.[26]

The deliberations of the Rothenberg joint owners demonstrate that the binding together of nobles in a collective structure was likely to hamper feuding. A particularly revealing case in point is the 'system of collective security' that was the Swabian League.[27] In the first place, the Swabian League was seen by contemporaries as primarily an instrument for keeping the peace in the face of feuding nobles. Indeed, not only did an attack by a nobleman in 1487 on a merchant convoy give an important impetus to its establishment; in the early 1520s the League became the nemesis of Franconian feuding nobles. A punitive expedition in June 1523 reduced twenty-three proud castles to smouldering rubble.[28] The deterrent effect

---

[24] Ibid., Sonntag nach Michaelis [3 October] 1507.
[25] Ibid., Montag–Mittwoch nach Michaelis [30 September–2 October] 1521.
[26] Ibid., Sonntag nach Michaelis [3 October] 1507.
[27] Horst Carl, *Der Schwäbische Bund, 1488–1534: Landfrieden und Genossenschaft im Übergang vom Spätmittelalter zur Reformation* (Leinfelden-Echterdingen, 2000), 402.
[28] Ibid., 474–9; Peter Ritzmann, '"Plackerey in teutschen Landen": Untersuchungen zur Fehdetätigkeit des fränkischen Adels im frühen 16. Jahrhundert und ihrer Bekämpfung durch den Schwäbischen Bund und die Reichsstadt Nürnberg, insbesondere am Beispiel

this had on the nobles in Franconia was considerable.[29] The 'war' on the Franconian nobility points to a second remarkable feature of the Swabian League: made up of princes, nobles and cities, the League had to bring its anti-feuding actions into line with the ostensibly differing social attitudes of its members towards feuding.[30] Yet this social heterogeneity of the League did not result in political paralysis. One reason is that the feuding culture was not the preserve of the nobility. All members of the League, irrespective of their social origin, saw in the feud a proper instrument for pursuing the anti-feuding policy of the League. Even the cities shared this ethos. Patricians of Nuremberg, Ulm and Augsburg signed the cartels of defiance issued by the League and led its troops. Another reason is that even if the cities did have some misgivings about the feud, these were not shared by the nobles and the princes in the League. And theirs was usually the more influential point of view. So much so, in fact, that minor breaches of the peace that harmed only cities were treated with relative leniency. Noble feuders could count on the solidarity of noble members of the League. Only when violations of the peace were serious, or when they affected also nobles and princes, did the League mobilise its might in full. Paradoxically, the League's policy of fighting feuds with feuds helped to keep up the practice of feuding, and in some cases exacerbated the problem. As Horst Carl concluded, the Swabian League provides no proof of a change in the mentality of the nobility.[31] It is precisely this conclusion, however, that throws into relief the effect of unions and leagues in restraining noble feuds. For if the Swabian League was itself a cause of feuds with non-members, it was nevertheless remarkably successful in putting an end to feuding in Swabia. Conflicts between members

des Hans Thomas von Absberg und seiner Auseinandersetzung mit den Grafen von Oettingen (1520–31)' (PhD thesis, University of Munich, 1993), 300–41.
[29] See below.   [30] Carl, *Der Schwäbische Bund*, 464.   [31] Ibid., 480–1.

Illustration 13. Destruction of castle Reussenberg by the Swabian League in 1523.
Staatsbibliothek Bamberg, RB.H.bell.f.1, p. 16

of the League were dealt with by its judicial organs. It was nearly impossible for one member to wage a feud against another.[32]

The effect of the League on feuding suggests that the difference between Swabia and Franconia was not in the culture of noble feuding, which remained much the same in both regions, but in the integration of the nobles into some collective structure. The co-heirship of Rothenberg, which did have a comparable effect on its members in Franconia, comprised only a fraction of the regional nobility. But the Rothenberg was a part of the confraternal movement of the Franconian nobility.[33] And it was the institutionalisation of

---

[32] Ibid., 466–7.

[33] In 1507 it was the burgrave of the Rothenberg and his deputies who convoked an assembly of the entire Franconian nobility: StAA, Ganerbschaft Rothenberg, no. 2538a, Sonntag nach Elftausend jungfrauentag [24 October] 1507. Some of the leaders of the Franconian Knightage were members of the Rothenberg. Cf. ibid., Mittwoch nach Sebastiani [26 January] 1519, Schütz, 'Ganerbschaft Rothenberg', 121, and Robert Fellner, *Die fränkische Ritterschaft von 1495–1524* (Berlin, 1905), 115–16 nn. 24, 25 (Martin Truchseß,

this movement in the Franconian Knightage which, as in the case with the Rothenberg, increasingly constrained the feud, but on a much wider scale. Formed to preserve the liberties of the nobles in the wake of the Imperial Diet of 1495 and the Common Penny scheme, in the sixteenth century the Knightage made an about-face. The fiscal-military needs of Emperor Charles V led him in 1528 to ask the Franconian nobles to summon an assembly to discuss a request for military service.[34] The nobles saw the opportunity, and seized it. In 1532 they agreed to contribute in taxes to the war effort against the Ottomans, taking care to dignify as a *subsidium charitativum*, or voluntary subvention, what was for all intents and purposes a Turkish Tax (*Türkensteuer*). In return they demanded imperial protection from the princes, and recognition of their free status.[35] Ten years later the nobles consented to pay what they so strenuously refused in 1495: the Common Penny, revivified to help finance King Ferdinand I's war in Hungary. Unlike 1495, however, the Knights were now approached directly by the king, not through the princes. Ferdinand also decreed that whoever did not pay his assessment through the Knightage could not belong to it and would be regarded as a princely subject (*Landsass*). The Knightage ceased to be a voluntary body.[36] On 24 August 1542 Ferdinand confirmed the Franconian Knightage in their position as 'those who are subordinate to a Roman Emperor and King without any intermediary', and promised them protection and safeguard.[37] This constitutional arrangement formalised and

---

Eberhard von Streitberg, Kaspar von Waldenfels and Hans Fuchs); Ulrichs, *Vom Lehnhof zur Reichsritterschaft*, 185 (Moritz Marschalk).

[34] Joseph Aschbach (ed.), *Wertheimisches Urkundenbuch*, 2nd part of his *Geschichte der Grafen von Wertheim von den ältesten Zeiten bis zu ihrem Erlöschen in Mannsstamme im Jahre 1556* (Frankfurt am Main, 1843), 335–8.

[35] Ernst Schubert, *Die Landstände des Hochstifts Würzburg* (Würzburg, 1967), 127–8.

[36] Volker Press, *Kaiser Karl V., König Ferdinand und die Entstehung der Reichsritterschaft*, 2nd edn (Wiesbaden, 1980), 40–51.

[37] Johann Christian Lünig, *Des Teutschen Reichs-Archiv partis specialis continuatio III*, part 2 (Leipzig, 1713), 310–11.

stabilised the noble status of the Knights and placed them beyond the jurisdictional reach of the princes.

The element of restraint on feuding shown by the Franconian Knightage was even more pronounced than that shown by the Rothenberg. By the last decade of the fifteenth century nobles who were offered contracts as princes' indentured servitors (*Diener von Haus aus*) had begun to insert a clause exempting them from taking action against members of the Franconian Knightage.[38] The Knightage also affected the relationship among its members. When they intervened in a dispute between Georg von Rosenberg and Count Erasmus of Wertheim in 1502, they wrote to the latter that they were concerned about the trouble and disruption that might result from it 'not only to the two of you, but also to the counts, barons and common nobility of the land of Franconia'. They raised the remarkable claim that not only the princes, but also the Knightage had authority to hear the case.[39] Other statements by representatives of the Knightage suggest that they were now considering the feud as a problem that had to be brought under control, and, more importantly, that they were actively engaging with it in search of solutions. Their delegates told the Franconian princes in 1507 that the nobles knew that they were being suspected by the emperor and the princes of being responsible for robberies and other 'surreptitious and malicious deeds'. This, they asserted, was an unfair generalisation, but it nonetheless prompted them to deliberate in their assembly over ways to prevent disorder and misdemeanour.[40] In the early sixteenth century, union after union of the Franconian

---

[38] StAB, C 3, no. 6, fol. 171r; StAN, Fstm.Ansb., Fehdeakten, no. 233; ibid., AA-Akten, no. 1402, fol. 227r; Eberhard Graf von Fugger, *Die Seinsheim und ihre Zeit: Eine Familien- und Kulturgeschichte von 1155 bis 1890* (Munich, 1893), appendix 212.

[39] *Shiedsspruch Kurfürst Philipp des Aufrichtigen von der Pfalz in der Irrung zwischen Erasmus Graf von Wertheim und Ritter Georg von Rosenberg* (Bayerische Staatsbibliothek Munich, Ded. 350 c), fol. 8.

[40] StAW, Stb, no. 892, fols. 107r–108r.

Knightage proscribed feuds and threatened unruly members with sanctions. A 1511 blueprint for a union, for instance, authorised the principal captain to confiscate the property of offenders. Anyone found guilty of assisting a feuder was to be thrown of out of the union.[41] A letter which the Knights sent in 1512 to Emperor Maximilian I reveals the extent to which the feud had become an issue that touched them all. Complaining of attacks by Nuremberg on some nobles suspected of complicity in feuds against the city, the Knights protested:

If the relatives [of these nobles] will now respond with violence against such wrongful actions, why should the Franconian nobility as a whole, who bear no responsibility for that, be blamed and vilified. If those of Nuremberg denied responsibility for the said misdeeds on the ground that they were reacting to an equally evil action, the answer to this would be that even if some nobles in the land of Franconia did commit it, it cannot be blamed on the many other upright nobles, for whom it is a source of deep sorrow and shame, since they are not related to each other in such a way that they should be held responsible for each other's [actions].[42]

This attempt to deny common responsibility shows that, as far as the feud was concerned, the nobles now had a good deal in common: perhaps not so much 'deep sorrow and shame', which are indeed a mark of a community whose members recognise their mutual obligations, but certainly a desire to distance themselves from feuding.

The nobles did not cease to consider the feud as legitimate in principle. The deliberations of the Rothenberg joint owners in the first quarter of the sixteenth century provide ample evidence that they continued to believe that it was perfectly proper to resort to feuding in certain circumstances. None of the reasoned rejections

---

[41] Ibid., fols. 127v–133v; Fellner, *Die fränkische Ritterschaft*, 164–5.
[42] StAW, Stb, no. 948, fols. 396–7.

of the requests to use the castle betrays discomfort about the feud as such, about the legality or legitimacy of the practice. All they betray is discomfort about the possible consequences of this or that feud. There is no indication that the condemnations of the feud by jurists or churchmen dented the nobles' conviction that it was an appropriate means of defending their interests.[43] Indeed, a well-attended assembly of the Knights in 1523 maintained that feuding was a necessary means of self-defence given the impaired state of the judicial system in Franconia.[44] However, the persistence of old principles did not mean that the nobles could not see the need to adapt their approach to the new political realities. The union which the nobles went on to set up in 1523 laid down that members whose feuds were indefensible were not to enjoy its support. Moreover, anyone suspected of misdeeds had to clear himself before a magistrate or else be ejected from the union.[45] The nobles thus drew a formal distinction between just and unjust feuds and between the innocent and the guilty.[46]

The formation of the nobility as a political body, then, made feuding more difficult. It also made it less necessary. The existence of the Knightage counteracted the force of the ties of 'inimical

---

[43] Christine Reinle argues for a change in the legal climate over the fifteenth century which, with the growing acceptance of Roman Law and concepts of 'just war', undermined the legitimacy of feuding. She maintains that this shift was the cause of a temporary increase in feud violence. Christine Reinle, 'Umkämpfter Friede: Politischer Gestaltungswille und geistlicher Normenhorizont bei der Fehdebekämpfung im deutschen Spätmittelalter', in *Rechtsveränderung im politischen und sozialen Kontext mittelalterlicher Rechtsvielfalt*, ed. Stefan Esders and Christine Reinle (Münster, 2005), 147–74; cf. Christine Reinle, *Bauernfehden: Studien zur Fehdeführung Nichtadliger im spätmittelalterlichen römisch-deutschen Reich, besonders in den bayerischen Herzogtümern* (Stuttgart, 2003), 347–8.

[44] Adolf Wrede (ed.), *Deutsche Reichstagsakten, jüngere Reihe*, vol. III (Gotha, 1901), 727–34, no. 116.

[45] Ibid., 914 n. 1, no. 244; Fellner, *Die fränkische Ritterschaft*, 240–55.

[46] The Knights had already broached this theme in 1512 and 1515: StAW, Stb, no. 892, fols. 159r, 171r–v; ibid., Stb, no. 948, fol. 396. A weaker form of this distinction was included in the treaty of the 1517 union: Lünig, *Des Teutschen Reichs-Archiv partis specialis continuatio III*, part 2, 7, no. 1.

intimacy' between nobles. It attenuated the compulsion nobles felt to feud in order to communicate their worth, martial spirit and moral characteristics – and hence their membership in the nobility. On the contrary, they now demonstrated their membership in the politically evolving nobility through cooperation with the group and respect for its common interests. Membership in the nobility became less a matter of continual dramatisation of a noble ethos, and more a matter of structured political life. Ironically, both the belligerent culture of 'inimical intimacy' and the organisation of the Knightage had the same foundation: the interdependence of nobles. The difference was that in the case of the Knightage this interdependence was no longer primarily social and diffuse; it was political – and it was institutionalised. This reversed the logic of action: interdependence ceased to be a powerful incentive to feuding and became instead a no less powerful curb on feuding. In the first place, unlike previous leagues and confraternities, the Knightage included all of the Franconian nobles. Secondly, it raised the stakes tremendously: the private grievances and interests of individual nobles simply could not be permitted to jeopardise the common project of preserving the ancient liberties. Nobles who failed to comply with the new canons of correct behaviour faced isolation, even exclusion from the Knightage.[47] And to be excluded from the Knightage meant, in Franconia, to lose not only its protective solidarity, but also noble status. By the same token, those who belonged to the politically – and later constitutionally – ordered nobility had less need to prove their noble status.[48] They had a quasi-official certificate, as it were, of their social identity. The

---

[47] Cf. Chapter 3 n. 58.

[48] On the status insecurity and status anxiety of the nobles see Hillay Zmora, 'The Formation of the Imperial Knighthood in Franconia: A Comparative European Perspective', in *The Holy Roman Empire, 1495–1806*, ed. R. J. W. Evans, Michael Schaich and Peter H. Wilson (Oxford, 2011), 283–302.

advance of the Knightage meant that the age of feuding was coming to an end.

The continuation of feuds for some decades after 1495 is evidence that the ban on feuding proclaimed by the Imperial Diet of Worms was not the immediate cause of its dwindling over the first half of the sixteenth century.[49] But while the anti-feuding legislation of 1495 was largely ineffective, the attempted fiscal reforms did affect feuding indirectly by leading to the creation of the Knightage in Franconia, Swabia and the Middle Rhine region. The decline of the feud was at bottom a response of the nobles to political and legal developments in the Holy Roman Empire. Other contributory factors were equally part of these general changes. The deposition in 1515 of Margrave Friedrich of Brandenburg by his sons was much more than an inner-dynastic power struggle of mere local relevance. It was itself partly the result of the margrave's cavalier attitude to feuding and of the sorry state of public security under his watch.[50] His successors did not wish or dare to follow his example in exploiting noblemen's feuds against other princes (or against cities). And though they too could at times indulge even the most brazen of feuders,[51] they did not provide the same kind of material and moral support to feuding nobles. Moreover, by 1523 the margrave of Brandenburg and the prince-bishops of Bamberg and Würzburg had joined the Swabian League. The membership of the three Franconian princes in the

---

[49] Cf. Carl, *Der Schwäbische Bund*, 426.

[50] Reinhard Seyboth, '"Raubritter" und Landesherren: Zum Problem territorialer Friedenswahrung im späten Mittelalter am Beispiel der Markgrafen von Ansbach-Kulmbach', in *'Raubritter' oder 'Rechtschaffene vom Adel'? Aspekte von Politik, Friede und Recht im späten Mittelalter*, ed. Kurt Andermann (Sigmaringen, 1997), 115–31, at 126–7, 129.

[51] Christine Reinle, 'Fehden und Fehdebekämpfung am Ende des Mittelalters: Überlegungen zum Auseinandertreten von "Frieden" und "Recht" in der politischen Praxis zu Beginn des 16. Jahrhunderts am Beispiel der Absberg-Fehde', *ZHF* 30 (2003), 355–88, at 361–2.

League meant that feuding now had much less scope in Franconia:[52] on the one hand, the princes were not as likely to take advantage of noblemen's feuds as before; on the other hand, the nobles could no longer rely on the princes to provide them with the necessary protection against the Swabian League. Indeed, the menace of the Swabian League looms large in the protocols of the Rothenberg, and became a stock argument against allowing nobles to use the castle in their feuds.[53] The nobles were thus left very much to their own devices as far as feuding was concerned. And feuding was now seen as a grave threat to the interests of the nobles. As the Rothenberg joint owners explained in 1525 to one of their number who wished to use the castle against a prince, they could not allow it because it would negatively affect not only the Rothenberg, but the nobility as a whole.[54] The first quarter of the sixteenth century witnessed, then, a significant change in the attitude of the nobles to the feud. This change was not primarily the upshot of a moral awakening or a reformation of manners. But in the final analysis it did not matter that the nobles' newly acquired sensitivity about feuding was based not so much on principle as on pragmatic considerations of utility. The cumulative result was the abandonment of the feud.

Much the same can be said of the other chief source of feuding, the princes: until the sixteenth century, their arguments against feuds were mainly specific, directed against particular feuds, not against the phenomenon per se. As far as they were concerned, feuding

---

[52] Carl, *Der Schwäbische Bund*, 481–2.

[53] StAA, Ganerbschaft Rothenberg, no. 2538a, Montag–Mittwoch nach Matthei [24–26 September] 1520; Montag–Mittwoch nach Michaelis [30 September–2 October] 1521; Montag nach Veitstag [22 June] 1523; Montag nach Christi Erhebung [18 May] 1523.

[54] 'hierin bedenken und ansehen, die geschwinden leuffte, die itzt uber den gemeinen adel gericht, so er ... sich der öffnung des schloß gebrauchen würdt, weß allem von adel, nit allein zum Rotenberg, sunder in andern ihren schlossen, leib und güttern, fur mercklich unüberwintlich nachttheil reichen möcht.' Ibid., Montag nach Reminiscere [13 March] 1525.

was not predominantly a matter of legal principle, but of practical politics. This was reflected in their conflicts with Rothenberg co-heirs. The bishop of Bamberg, for instance, was in 1501 in feud with two joint owners: Silvester von Schaumberg and Burgrave Albrecht Stiebar.[55] The bishop informed the Rothenberg members that both Schaumberg and Stiebar were placed under the imperial ban, and demanded that they should not give them any assistance, nor suffer Stiebar as their burgrave.[56] But for all his invocation of the law in order to discredit his noble enemies, the bishop agreed to an offer of the co-heirs to appoint four of their number as arbiters.[57] That the prince-bishop was prepared to negotiate was more than an admission that the impregnable walls of the Rothenberg placed Schaumberg and Stiebar beyond his grasp; by his very protestations against the illegalities committed in its name he effectively conceded the legitimacy of feuding in principle.[58] Princes also gave a more direct recognition to feuding in the early years of the sixteenth century, for they too continued to resort to feuding, or else to take advantage of noblemen's feuds.[59] For all their increasing use of Roman Law, it was less the influence of new legal or moral currents than the political obligations entailed by their common membership in the Swabian League that made it more difficult for the Franconian princes to go on utilising the feud.[60]

Both princes and nobles became integrated into political structures that increasingly worked against feuding. The relationship between

---

[55] StAB, Fehde-Akten, no. 133; Otto Seefried, *Aus dem Stiebar-Archiv: Forschungen zur Familiengeschichte von Bauer, Bürger und Edelmann in Ober- und Mittelfranken* (Nuremberg, 1953), 8–9.

[56] StAB, Fehde-Akten, no. 133, docs. 12, 13.   [57] Ibid., docs. 12–15, 29.

[58] In a letter to the co-heirs the bishop protested that the feuders acted contrary to the Rothenberg *Burgfrieden*: ibid., doc. 14.

[59] Cf. Reinle, 'Fehden und Fehdebekämpfung am Ende des Mittelalters', 367–9.

[60] Carl, *Der Schwäbische Bund*, 481–2.

nobles and princes, in as far as it was structured around the feud, began to dissolve. A potent cause of feuding for many decades, this relationship lost much of its former vigour. It is hard to miss the irony in that. For both the Swabian League and the Rothenberg were to a large measure 'feud communities': the threat of feud and the pledge of mutual help in the event of a feud were constitutive elements of their *raison d'être.*[61] The assumption that feuds were a natural and inevitable feature of social life, and that feuds were to be countered by feuds, was central to their constitutions. Yet in the long run both organisations contributed to a reduction in the incidence of feuding. The paradox is especially noticeable in the case of the Rothenberg and, more generally, the Knightage. Born out of opposition to the perceived encroachments by princes and emperor on the nobles' traditional rights and liberties, they did not lead to collective violence and rebellion (as did, for example, a union of Bavarian nobles in 1488–9).[62] On the contrary, the Rothenberg and the Knightage initiated political processes that brought the feud under tighter control, exercised by the nobles themselves. By politically institutionalising the pre-existing social interdependence among the nobles, they created self-imposed restraints on feuds. This was a cost none of the nobles was happy to pay as an individual, but which as a collective they well understood was a condition of a successful preservation of independent status. In the end, the political tradition of the aristocratic confraternities prevailed over the cultural tradition of aristocratic feuding, as a new, more formal and political model of nobility superseded another, older model. An echo of this transformation can be heard in the words which the

---

[61] For the Swabian League as a 'Fehdegenossenschaft' see Carl, *Der Schwäbische Bund*, 425. See also Obenaus, *Recht und Verfassung der Gesellschaft mit St Jörgenschild in Schwaben*, 46.

[62] Joachim Schneider, *Spätmittelalterlicher deutscher Niederadel: Ein landschaftlicher Vergleich* (Stuttgart, 2003), 520–34.

burgrave of the Rothenberg appended to the minutes of a meeting in 1537:

It was considered necessary that our *Burgfrieden* should be approved by His Imperial Majesty. If this occurred, then we would be able to use [the castle] against princes, lords, cities and others all the more properly ... We trust that it would then be more to the liking of other honest people to join our castle and buy a part [in it]. But for this to happen it is necessary that our *Burgfrieden* be diligently provided for so that it can be revised in accordance with the law; otherwise the approval would be difficult to obtain.[63]

---

[63] 'Zum andern so wurdt fur notwendig angesehen daß unser burgfried durch kay: maiit: bestettigt werden möchte und so es geschehe, so hetten wir unß desselbigen gegen fürsten heren stätten und andern desto stattlicher zugebrauchen ... trosten, eß wär den auch andere redliche leuth desto lieber zu unsern schloß stellen und theil kaufen. Aber ehe dann solches geschehe ist von nöthen daß zuvor unser Burgfriedt mit fleiß versehen damit derselbe den rechten gemeß reformiret werde ohn daß wär die bestettigung schwerlich erlangt werden.' StAA, Ganerbschaft Rothenberg, no. 2538a, Montag nach Misericordia domini [16 April] 1537. See also Seefried, *Aus dem Stiebar-Archiv*, 48.

Noble feuds in Franconia in chronological order, 1440–1570

Note: Manuscript sources are cited in full. Printed sources and secondary works are given in short-title form, with full references in the bibliography.

(1) Oettingen, Count Johann of vs Marschall von Pappenheim, Heinrich and Konrad. 1440–4
Source: Chronicon Elvacense, 48; Pappenheim, *Die frühen Pappen-heimer Marschälle*, 31.

(2) Henneberg, Count Wilhelm II of vs Bickenbach, Dietrich von. 1441
Source: Erck (ed.), *Rapsodiae sive Chronicon Hennebergicum*, 407–8; Schultes, *Diplomatische Geschichte*, II, 107.

(3) Henneberg, Count Wilhelm II of vs Haun, Reinhard von. 1441
Source: Erck (ed.), *Rapsodiae sive Chronicon Hennebergicum*, 407–8.

(4) Rosenberg, Thomas von vs Nuremberg. 1441
Source: Müllner, *Die Annalen*, 349.

(5) Truchseß, Berthold vs Nuremberg. 1441
Source: Müllner, *Die Annalen*, 349.

(6) Muggenthal, Weinmar von vs Nuremberg. 1441
Source: Müllner, *Die Annalen*, 352; *Die Chroniken der deutschen Städte*, vol. x, 160.

(7) Hutten, Ludwig von vs Nuremberg. 1441
Source: GNM, Hs 22 547, fol. 44v; Müllner, *Die Annalen*, 349.

(8) Elm, Wilhelm von vs Nuremberg. 1441
Source: GNM, Hs 22 547, fol. 44v; Müllner, *Die Annalen*, 351.

(9) Waldenfels, Friedrich and Hans von vs Nuremberg. 1441–6
Source: GNM, Hs 22 547, fol. 46r; Müllner, *Die Annalen*, 365–70; *Die Chroniken der deutschen Städte*, vol. x, 161.

(10) Egloffstein, Heraus von, and Hans Modschiedler vs bishop of Bamberg. 1442
Source: StAB, Fehdeakten, no. 501, doc. 1.

(11) Seinsheim, Michael von vs Schweinfurt. 1442
Source: Stein (ed.), *Monumenta Suinfurtensia*, 352.

(12) Henneberg, Count Georg of, and Seinsheim, Hermann von vs Treusch von Buttlar, Konrad d.Ä. and Konrad; Heimbrot, Philipp von; Boineburg, Reinhard and Konrad von; Buttlar, Georg von. 1442?–3
Source: Erck (ed.), *Rapsodiae sive Chronicon Hennebergicum*, 407–8; Mötsch (ed.), *Regesten*, I, 452, no. 935.

(13) Seckendorff, Sigmund von vs Nuremberg. 1443
Source: StAN, Reichsstadt Nürnberg, 35 neue Laden der unteren Losungsstube, v 89/1 2065.

(14) Raueheneck, Friedrich von vs Nuremberg. 1443
Source: Müllner, *Die Annalen*, 363.

(15) Henneberg, Count Heinrich of vs his minor nephews. 1444–9
Source: Spangenberg, *Hennebergische Chronica*, 388–401; Mötsch (ed.), *Regesten*, I, 468–9, nos. 973–5.

(16) Seckendorff, Hans von vs bishop of Bamberg. 1445
Source: Rechter, *Die Seckendorff*, I, 150.

(17) Schlitz genannt von Görtz, Heinrich and Otto von vs bishop of Würzburg. 1445
Source: Luckhard (ed.), *Die Regesten*, 135, no. 489.

(18) Kere, Georg von der vs Nuremberg. 1445
Source: Müllner, *Die Annalen*, 377.

(19) Motschiedler, Hans vs bishop of Würzburg. 1447
Source: Müllner, *Die Annalen*, 389.

(20) Voit von Rieneck, Eitel vs Nuremberg. 1447
Source: Müllner, *Die Annalen*, 392; Amrhein, 'Gotfrid Schenk von Limpurg', 82–4.

(21) Eberstein, Erasmus von vs duke of Mosbach-Neumarkt. 1448
Source: StAN, Fehdeakten, no. 55, doc. of Montag nach unser Frauentag 1448.

(22) Oettingen, Count Ulrich of vs Nördlingen, Dinkelsbühl, Bopfingen. 1448
Source: StAN, Fstm.Ansb., Fehdeakten, no. 56.

(23) Thüngen, Reuß von vs Karsbach, Hans and Endres von. 1448
     Source: Amrhein, 'Gotfrid Schenk von Limpurg', 90–1.

(24) Hutten, Konrad von and Seinsheim-Schwarzenberg, Hermann von
     vs Henneberg, Count Heinrich of. 1448–50
     Source: StAN, Fstm.Ansb., AA-Akten, no. 515, doc. of Dienstag nach
     Johannis Baptiste 1448; ibid., undated doc. [*c.* 1450]

(25) Schaumberg, Veit and Georg von vs Nuremberg. 1449
     Source: Müllner, *Die Annalen*, 407.

(26) Eberstein, Gerlach von vs bishop of Würzburg. 1450
     Source: StAW, Stb, no. 1012, fol. 498r.

(27) Vestenberg, Hans von vs Schneidenwind, Hans. 1450
     Source: StAN, Fstm.Ansb., Fehdeakten, no. 63.

(28) Seckendorff, Burkhard von vs Anon. non-noble. *c.* 1450.
     Source: Rechter, *Die Seckendorff*, II, 153.

(29) Wallenstein, Simon and Eberhard von vs Henneberg, Counts of. 1451
     Source: Mötsch (ed.), *Regesten*, I, 507, no. 1052.

(30) Hohenlohe, Counts Albrecht II and Kraft V of vs Bombach, Asmus
     and Lutz von, and Meysenbach, Wilhelm von. 1451
     Source: Taddey, 'Macht und Recht im späten Mittelalter', *WFr* 61
     (1977), 79–110, at 96.

(31) Wolfstein, Hans and Albrecht von vs bishop of Würzburg. 1451
     Source: StAW, Ldf, no. 9, pp. 484–92; Amrhein, 'Gotfrid Schenk
     von Limpurg', 135–6.

(32) Hohenlohe, Counts Kraft V and Albrecht II of vs Hornberg, Neithard
     and Horneck d.J. von. 1451–2
     Source: Ehmer, 'Horneck von Hornberg', 86.

(33) Bibra, Bartholomäus and Berthold von vs duke of Saxony. 1451–5
     Source: Bibra, *Beiträge zur Familiengeschichte*, 189–99; Wagenhöfer,
     Die Bibra, 290.

(34) Rüdt von Collenberg, Eberhard d.J. vs Windsheim. 1452
     Source: StAN, Reichsstadt Windsheim, Akten, no. 14.

(35) Obernitz, Hans von vs Nuremberg. 1453
     Source: Müllner, *Die Annalen*, 500.

(36) Seinsheim, Engelhard von vs Windsheim. 1454
     Source: StAN, Reichsstadt Windsheim, Akten, no. 13, doc. 41.

(37) Seinsheim-Schwarzenberg, Georg von vs Schwarzach. 1454
     Source: Fugger, *Die Seinsheim*, 145.

(38) Rüdt von Collenberg, Heinrich and Eberhard d.J. vs Nuremberg and other cities. 1455
Source: Müllner, *Die Annalen*, 507–8.

(39) Rotenhan, Lutz von vs Schweinfurt. 1455
Source: Stein (ed.), *Monumenta Suinfurtensia*, 353.

(40) Henneberg, Count Wilhelm of vs Schweinfurt. 1455
Source: Stein (ed.), *Monumenta Suinfurtensia*, 353.

(41) Erlingshofen, Sigmund von vs Erstlingen, Georg von. 1455
Source: StAN, Fstm.Ansb., Fehdeakten, no. 70.

(42) Henneberg, Count Wilhelm III of vs Bibra, Adam, Heinrich, Georg and Karl von. 1455
Source: StAW, ldf, no. 12, p. 650.

(43) Wenkheim, Georg von vs Württemberg, Count Ulrich of 1455–6
Source: StAN, Fstm.Ansb., Fehdeakten, no. 74.

(44) Seinsheim, Ludwig von vs Dottenheim, Philipp von. 1455–6
Source: StAN, Fstm.Ansb., Fehdeakten, no. 73.

(45) Eberstein, Erasmus von vs archbishop of Mainz. 1456
Source: Fries, *Chronik der Bischöfe von Würzburg*, 136.

(46) Muggenthal, Heimeran von vs Hetzelsdorf, Heinz von. 1456
Source: StAN, Fstm.Ansb., Fehdeakten, no. 75.

(47) Lichtenstein, Hans d.Ä. von and Eberstein, Wilhelm von vs archbishop of Mainz and Bickenbach, Konrad von. 1456
Source: StAW, Ldf, no. 12, p. 662.

(48) Eberstein, Erasmus von vs Nuremberg. 1456
Source: Müllner, *Die Annalen*, 512.

(49) Wolmarshausen, Sittich von vs Püttrich, Hans. 1456
Source: StAN, Fstm.Ansb., Fehdeakten, no. 76.

(50) Eberstein, Erasmus von vs Rothenburg. 1457
Source: Eberstein, *Abriß der Urkundlichen Geschichte des reichsritterlichen Geschlechtes Eberstein* (1885–93), 91–2.

(51) Berlichingen, Konrad von and Hohenried, Philipp von vs Kirchensall. 1457
Source: Berlichingen-Rossach, *Geschichte des Ritters Götz von Berlichingen*, 594.

(52) Eberstein, Erasmus von vs Steinau gen. Steinrück, Heinrich von. 1457
Source: Steinau-Steinrück, 'Abriß aus der Geschichte des fränkischen Geschlechtes von Steinau genannt Steinrück', 62.

(53) Rüdt von Collenberg, Heinrich vs Rothenburg and Dinkelsbühl. 1458
     Source: StAN, Fstm.Ansb., Fehdeakten, no. 81.

(54) Hutten, Lorenz von vs bishop of Würzburg. 1458/9–62
     Source: StAW, Ldf, no. 11, p. 44; Fries, *Chronik der Bischöfe von Würzburg*, 144; Battenberg (ed.), *Isenburger Urkunden*, 600, 649, nos. 2343, 2587.

(55) Steinau gen. Steinrück, Jakob, Hans, Konrad, Hans, Otto, Heinrich and Hildebrand von vs abbot of Fulda. 1459
     Source: Schannat (ed.), *Fuldischer Lehn-Hof*, 335, no. 477.

(56) Tettau, Kaspar von vs margrave of Brandenburg. 1459
     Source: StAN, Fstm.Ansb., Gemeinbücher, no. 4, fol. 10v.

(57) Herdegen, Hans vs margrave of Brandenburg. 1459
     Source: StAN, Fstm.Ansb., Gemeinbücher, no. 4, fols. 11r–v.

(58) Kotzau, Hans d.J. von vs Eger. 1459
     Source: Dobeneck, 'Geschichte des ausgestorbenen Geschlechts von Kotzau', 56–7.

(59) Riedesel, Hermann vs Bibra, Adam von. 1459
     Source: Becker, *Die Riedesel zu Eisenbach*, 208.

(60) Bimbach, Heinrich von vs Riedesel, Hermann. 1459
     Source: Becker, *Die Riedesel zu Eisenbach*, 208.

(61) Rotenhan, Hans von vs bishop of Bamberg. 1460
     Source: Rotenhan, 'Streit und Fehde um die Burg Stuffenberg', 76–7.

(62) Schwarzenberg, Sigmund von vs Seinsheim, Philipp von. 1460
     Source: StAN, Fstm.Ansb., Fehdeakten, no. 94.

(63) Fuchs von Preppach, Hans d.J. vs Seinsheim, Neidhard von. *c.* 1460
     Source: StAW, Ldf, no. 12, p. 733.

(64) Stetten, Wilhelm, Hans and Kaspar von vs Wertheim, Count Albrecht of. 1460–1
     Source: StAB, Hofrat Ansbach-Bayreuth, no. 513.

(65) Rotenhan, Lutz von vs bishop of Bamberg. 1460–6
     Source: Bachmann (ed.), *Briefe und Acten*, 72, no. 57; Rotenhan, 'Streit und Fehde um die Burg Stuffenberg'.

(66) Gebsattel, Georg von vs bishop of Würzburg. 1461
     Source: Fries, *Chronik der Bischöfe von Würzburg*, 168.

(67) Riedesel, Hermann vs Bibra, Georg von. 1461
     Source: Becker, *Die Riedesel zu Eisenbach*, 208.

(68) Thüngen, Reuss von vs Schweinfurt. 1462
      Source: Stein (ed.), *Monumenta Suinfurtensia*, 360.

(69) Eyb, Albrecht von vs Ellrichshausen, Georg von. 1462
      Source: Fries, *Chronik der Bischöfe von Würzburg*, 201–2; Herrmann,
      Albrecht von Eyb, 241–53.

(70) Schwarzenberg, Sigmund von vs bishop of Würzburg. 1462
      Source: Fries, *Chronik der Bischöfe von Würzburg*, 195, 200, 201
      n. 627.

(71) Schaumberg [?], Paul von vs bishop of Würzburg. 1462
      Source: Bachmann (ed.), *Briefe und Acten*, 387–8.

(72) Seckendorff, Friedrich von vs non-noble. 1462
      Source: Rechter, *Die Seckendorff*, II, 153.

(73) Riedesel, Hermann vs Henneberg, Count Wilhelm III of. 1462
      Source: Becker, *Die Riedesel zu Eisenbach*, 208, 253.

(74) Absberg, Engelhard von vs Heideck, Konrad of. 1462
      Source: StAN, Fstm.Ansb., AA-Akten, no. 392, doc. of Pfintztag
      nach Petri et Pauli 1462.

(75) Fuchs, Heinz vs Rotenhan, Marx and Jobst von. 1462
      Source: Bachmann (ed.), *Briefe und Acten*, 460, no. 367.

(76) Fuchs von Bimbach, Christoph vs bishop of Bamberg. 1462–6
      Source: Fries, *Chronik der Bischöfe von Würzburg*, 205–23; StAW, Stb,
      no. 717, fols. 257r–v.

(77) Aufseß, Konrad von vs Eger. 1463
      Source: Aufseß, *Geschichte des uradelichen Aufseß'schen Geschlechtes*,
      147.

(78) Seinsheim, Wilhelm and Erkinger von vs Nuremberg. 1463
      Source: Müllner, *Die Annalen*, 551.

(79) Vestenberg, Veit von vs Thüngfeld, Heinz von. 1463
      Source: StAN, Fstm.Ansb., Urfehden, no. 25.

(80) Fuchs von Kannenberg, Melchior vs Nuremberg. 1463
      Source: Müllner, *Die Annalen*, 551.

(81) Seckendorff, Lamprecht von vs bishop of Würzburg. 1463–4
      Source: StAW, Stb, no. 717, fols. 299r, 300v-301r; StAW, Stb, no.
      892, fols. 266v–267r; Fries, *Chronik der Bischöfe von Würzburg*, 207,
      212.

(82) Stettner, Heinz vs Helmstatt, Reinhard von. 1464
      Source: StAN, Fstm.Ansb., Fehdeakten, no. 107.

(83) Aufseß, Konrad von vs bishop of Würzburg. 1464
Source: Fries, *Chronik der Bischöfe von Würzburg*, 212; Auf-
seß, *Geschichte des uradelichen Aufseß'schen Geschlechtes*, 146–63;
Priebatsch (ed.), *Politische Correspondenz*, I, 597–8, no. 734.

(84) Truchseß von Pommersfelden, Hans vs non-nobles. 1464
Source: Müllner, *Die Annalen*, 557.

(85) Fuchs, Heinz vs bishop of Bamberg. 1464–6
Source: Fries, *Chronik der Bischöfe von Würzburg*, 218; StAW, Stb, no.
717, fol. 142v; Rotenhan, *Die Rotenhan*, 149.

(86) Plassenberg, Götz von vs bishop of Bamberg. 1465
Source: StAB, Hofrat Ansbach-Bayreuth, no. 519.

(87) Dottenheim, Georg and Philipp von vs Zobel, Heinrich and bishop
of Würzburg. 1465
Source: StAW, Ldf, no. 15, pp. 556–8.

(88) Rüdt von Collenberg, Heinrich vs league of Swabian cities. 1465
Source: Pietsch (ed.), *Die Urkunden des Archivs der Reichsstadt
Schwäbisch Hall*, 310, U 2503.

(89) Berlichingen, Diether von vs Hohenlohe, Counts Ludwig and Ulrich
of. 1465–7
Source: Berlichingen-Rossach, *Geschichte des Ritters Götz von
Berlichingen*, 572.

(90) Riedesel, Hermann and Georg vs Stein, Siegfried and Hertnidt vom.
1465–71
Source: Becker, *Die Riedesel zu Eisenbach*, 254–62.

(91) Riedesel, Hermann and Georg vs abbot of Fulda. 1465–71
Source: Becker, *Die Riedesel zu Eisenbach*, 254–62.

(92) Rüdt, Heinz von vs bishop of Bamberg. 1465–73
Source: StAB, Hofrat Ansbach-Bayreuth, no. 528; Priebatsch (ed.),
Politische Correspondenz, I, 521, 523, 540, nos. 597, 602, 641.

(93) Eberstein, Erasmus von vs bishop of Bamberg. 1466
Source: StAB, Hofrat Ansbach-Bayreuth, no. 507, doc. 2.

(94) Egloffstein, Georg von vs bishop of Bamberg. 1466
Source: StAB, Hofrat Ansbach-Bayreuth, no. 501.

(95) Wertheim, Count Johann of vs Württemberg, Count Heinrich of
1466
Source: Most, 'Schiedsgericht', 128–32; Rechter, *Die Seckendorff*, III,
54.

(96) Vestenberg, Veit von vs Vestenberg, Hans, Stefan and Konrad. 1466
Source: StAN, Fstm.Ansb., AA-Akten, no. 580, doc. 2.

(97) Rosenberg, Georg von vs Windsheim and Nuremberg. 1467–8
Source: StAN, Reichsstadt Windsheim, Akten, no. 15; Müllner, *Die Annalen*, 574–5.

(98) Henneberg, Counts Otto and Friedrich of vs Wertheim, Count Wilhelm of. 1469
Source: StAN, Fstm.Ansb., AA-Akten, no. 737.

(99) Seinsheim, Michael von vs Henneberg, Count Heinrich of. 1469
Source: Engel, W. (ed.), *Die Rats-Chronik*, 31–2, nos. 96–7.

(100) Rosenberg, Georg von vs Schwäbisch Hall. 1470
Source: Pietsch (ed.), *Die Urkunden des Archivs der Reichsstadt Schwäbisch Hall*, 337, U 2636.

(101) Riedern, Georg von vs Nuremberg. 1470
Source: Roth, *Geschichte des Nuernbergischen Handels*, 243.

(102) Gebsattel, Georg von vs Schweinfurt. 1470
Source: Stein (ed.), *Monumenta Suinfurtensia*, 363.

(103) Rosenberg, Friedrich von vs: Hornberg, N. Horneck von. 1470
Source: StAN, Fstm.Ansb., Fehdeakten, no. 132.

(104) Berlichingen, Engelhard von vs Enslingen, Walther von. 1470
Source: Pietsch (ed.), *Die Urkunden des Archivs der Reichsstadt Schwäbisch Hall*, 337, U 2633.

(105) Schott, Heinz vs Milz, Otto, Engelhard and Dietz von. 1470
Source: StAN, Fstm.Ansb., AA-Akten, no. 737, doc. of Samstag nach Oculi 1470.

(106) Steinrück, Otto and Hildebrand von vs Henneberg, Count Heinrich of. 1470
Source: Spangenberg, *Hennebergische Chronica*, 404.

(107) Zollner, Reinhard vs abbot of Fulda. 1470?
Source: Spangenberg, *Hennebergische Chronica*, 415.

(108) Henneberg, Count Heinrich of vs Lüder, Karl von and Buchenau, Engelhard von. *c.* 1470?
Source: Spangenberg, *Hennebergische Chronica*, 403–4.

(109) Henneberg, Count Otto of vs Hutten, Konrad von. 1470–2
Source: StAN, Fstm.Ansb., AA-Akten, no. 738, doc. 6.

(110) Zollner von der Hallburg, Konrad vs Schweinfurt. 1471
Source: Stein (ed.), *Monumenta Suinfurtensia*, 363.

(111) Riedesel, Hermann and Georg vs archbishop of Mainz. 1471–6
      Source: Becker, *Die Riedesel zu Eisenbach*, 262–7.
(112) Wolfskeel, Wolf vs bishop of Bamberg. 1471(?)–8
      Source: Oesterreicher, *Geschichtliche Darstellung der Burg Neideck*,
      33–6.
(113) Heßberg, Darius von vs bishop of Bamberg and Nuremberg. 1472
      Source: StAN, Fstm.Ansb., Fehdeakten, no. 346; Würdinger, *Kriegs-
      geschichte*, II, 107.
(114) Marschall, Erhard vs Nuremberg. 1472
      Source: *Die Chroniken der deutschen Städte*, vol. X, 332–3.
(115) Reitzenstein, Thomas von vs Sparneck, Fritz von. 1472
      Source: Burkhardt (ed.), *Das funfft merkisch Buech*, 211.
(116) Vestenberg, Veit von vs margrave of Brandenburg. 1472–3
      Source: StAN, Fstm.Ansb., Urfehden, no. 25.
(117) Seckendorff, Hans von vs duke of Bavaria. 1472–3
      Source: 'Hellers Chronik', 130–1; Rechter, *Die Seckendorff*, III, 34–5.
(118) Henneberg, Count Otto of vs Hutten, Frowin von and Thüngen,
      Philipp von. 1472–3
      Source: Stein (ed.), *Monumenta Suinfurtensia*, 364; Spangenberg, *Hen-
      nebergische Chronica*, 277.
(119) Plassenberg, Götz von vs duke of Bavaria. 1473
      Source: Guttenberg, 'Regesten', 225, no. 226.
(120) Vestenberg, Veit von vs Steinrück, Hildebrand von. 1473
      Source: StAW, Adel 1114.
(121) Henneberg, Count Wilhelm III of vs Bibra, Heinrich von. 1473
      Source: StAN, Fstm.Ansb., AA-Akten, no. 728, doc. of Dienstag
      nach Assumptio Marie, doc. of Donnerstag nach Assumptio Marie
      1473.
(122) Schaumberg, Ulrich von and Schäfstal, Moritz von vs bishop of
      Bamberg. 1473
      Source: Würdinger, *Kriegsgeschichte*, II, 107.
(123) Schott, Lutz vs Rosenberg, Georg von. 1473
      Source: StAN, Reichsstadt Nürnberg, 35 neue Laden der unteren
      Losungsstube, V 90/2 2447.
(124) Thüngen, Reuß and Werner von vs Hutten, Lorenz von. 1473–82
      Source: Morsel, *La noblesse contre le prince*, 413–14.
(125) Aufseß, Konrad von vs duke of Austria. 1473–88

Source: StAN, Fstm.Ansb., Fehdeakten, nos. 151, 176; Priebatsch (ed.), *Politische Correspondenz*, I, 597–8, no. 734; Aufseß, *Geschichte des uradelichen Aufseß'schen Geschlechtes*, 146–63.

(126) Wirsberg, Soldan von vs Lichtenstein, Apel von. 1474
Source: 'Hellers Chronik', 132–6.

(127) Dobeneck, Künmuth von vs Mosen, Friedrich von. 1474–5
Source: StAN, Fstm.Ansb., Urfehden, no. 33; Priebatsch (ed.), *Politische Correspondenz*, II, 192–3, no. 167.

(128) Stetten, Kilian and Simon von vs Hohenlohe, Counts Albrecht II and Kraft VI of. 1475–89
Source: Bechstein, *Die Tierberger Fehde*.

(129) Rosenberg, Georg von vs bishop of Würzburg. 1476
Source: StAN, Fstm.Ansb., AA-Akten, no. 738, doc. 14; Priebatsch (ed.), *Politische Correspondenz*, II, 274, no. 260.

(130) Wallenrod, Veit von vs Guttenberg, Heinz von. 1477
Source: StAN, Fstm.Ansb., Fehdeakten, no. 162; StAB, Fehde-Akten, no. 76.

(131) Schaumberg, Hans von vs bishop of Bamberg. 1477–9
Source: Priebatsch (ed.), *Politische Correspondenz*, II, 332, 351, 559, nos. 334, 356, 606.

(132) Wallenrod, Veit von vs bishop of Bamberg. 1477–81
Source: Würdinger, *Kriegsgeschichte*, II, 107; Rupprecht, *Ritterschaftliche Herrschaftswahrung*, 297–9.

(133) Henneberg, Count Otto of vs Rüdigheim, Rudolph von. 1478–9
Source: StAN, Fstm.Ansb., AA-Akten, no. 392, doc. of Freitag nach Assumptionis 1478, doc. of Dienstag nach Mathei 1478; ibid., no. 738, docs. 26–36; StAB, Fehde-Akten, no. 79; Priebatsch (ed.), *Politische Correspondenz*, II, 408, no. 420.

(134) Feilitzsch, Friedrich and Peter von vs margrave of Brandenburg. 1478–82
Source: Priebatsch (ed.), *Politische Correspondenz*, II, 604–8, no. 659; III, 172–4, no. 861; Dobeneck, *Geschichte der Familie von Dobeneck*, 368–72.

(135) Feilitzsch, Friedrich and Peter von vs Lüchau, Konrad von. c. 1478–82.
Source: Priebatsch (ed.), *Politische Correspondenz*, II, 604–8, no. 659; III, 172–4, no. 861; Dobeneck, *Geschichte der Familie von Dobeneck*, 368–72.

(136) Zollner von Rothenstein, Martin vs Greusing, Heinz. 1479
Source: Spielberg, 'Martin Zollner von Rothenstein', 169.

(137) Schaumberg, Konrad von vs Heyden, Georg von. 1479
Source: Priebatsch (ed.), *Politische Correspondenz*, II, 545–6,
no. 586.

(138) Streitberg, Paul von vs king of Bohemia. *c.* 1479
Source: Oesterreicher, *Die Burg Streitberg*, 14; Priebatsch (ed.), *Politische Correspondenz*, II, 606 n. 1, no. 659.

(139) Buchenau, Kaspar d.J. von vs bishop of Würzburg. 1479
Source: Fries, *Chronik der Bischöfe von Würzburg*, 259; Wilmowsky,
'Die Geschichte der Ritterschaft Buchenau', 23–4; Würdinger,
Kriegsgeschichte, II, 103.

(140) Seinsheim, Erkinger von vs Schwarzenberg, Sigmund von. 1479–81
Source: StAN, Fstm.Ansb., Fehdeakten, no. 172.

(141) Schaumberg, Karl von vs duke of Mosbach-Neumarkt. 1479–
84
Source: Priebatsch (ed.), *Politische Correspondenz*, III, 284, 300–1, nos.
986, 1001; Keller (ed.), *Geschichten und Taten*, 58; Rabeler, *Niederadlige Lebensformen*, 139–43.

(142) Henneberg, Count Otto of vs Marschall von Ostheim, Werner.
1480–1
Source: StAN, Fstm.Ansb., AA-Akten, no. 738, docs. 37–9.

(143) Reitzenstein, Sigmund von vs Reitzenstein, Thomas von. 1480–2
Source: Priebatsch (ed.), *Politische Correspondenz*, III, 173, no. 861.

(144) Fuchsstadt, Konrad von vs bishop of Bamberg. 1481
Source: Zeißner, *Rudolf II. von Scherenberg*, 69.

(145) Milz, Otto von vs non-noble. *c.* 1481
Source: StAW, Ms. 1671.

(146) Motschiedler, Georg vs bishop of Würzburg. 1483
Source: Zeißner, 'Dr Kilian von Bibra', 105–6.

(147) Vestenberg, Veit von vs Schwarzenberg, Sigmund von. 1484
Source: StAB, Hofrat Ansbach-Bayreuth, no. 535.

(148) Schlitz gen. von Görtz, Simon VI and Ludwig I von vs Hanau, Count
Philipp of. 1484
Source: Battenberg (ed.), *Schlitzer Urkunden*, 35–6, no. 143.

(149) Vestenberg, Veit von vs Vestenberg, Kaspar, Eukarius and Kunz.
1484–5
Source: StAN, Fstm.Ansb., Ansbacher Historica, no. 210.

(150) Bibra, Anton von vs counts of Henneberg. 1485–7
Source: Wagenhöfer, *Die Bibra*, 308; Rabeler, *Niederadlige Lebensformen*, 143–5.

(151) Schlammersdorf, Georg von vs bishop of Bamberg. 1486
Source: StAB, Fehde-Akten, no. 101.

(152) Bibra, Anton von vs Marschall von Ostheim, Karl. 1486
Source: Bibra, *Beiträge zur Familiengeschichte*, 270.

(153) Rosenberg, Georg, Arnold and Friedrich von vs bishop of Würzburg. 1486–7
Source: StAW, Stb, no. 1012, fol. 445v; Engel (ed.), *Die Rats-Chronik*, 45–6, no. 141; Fries, *Chronik der Bischöfe von Würzburg*, 264–6; Veesenmeyer, 'Nachricht von zwei Rosenbergischen Fehden', 41–56.

(154) Schwarzenberg, Sigmund von vs Thüngen, Sigmund von. 1486–92
Source: StAB, Fehde-Akten, no. 102; Höfler (ed.), 'Fränkische Studien IV.', part 1, 127, no. 113.

(155) Voit von Rieneck, Michael vs bishop of Würzburg. 1487
Source: Wendehorst, *Das Bistum Würzburg*, III, 34.

(156) Randersacker, Peter von vs the Wolfskeels. 1487
Source: StAW, Ldf, no. 15, p. 72.

(157) Schott, Konrad and Georg vs Marschall von der Schney, Konrad. 1487–9
Source: Keller (ed.), *Geschichten und Taten*, 70–1; Rabeler, *Niederadlige Lebensformen*, 145–6; 172–5.

(158) Redwitz, Balthasar von vs bishop of Würzburg and dean of cathedral chapter. 1488
Source: StAB, Hofrat Ansbach-Bayreuth, no. 540.

(159) Henneberg, Count Friedrich of vs the von Bebenburgs. 1488
Source: Luckhard (ed.), *Die Regesten*, 190, no. 728.

(160) Oettingen, Counts Joachim and Wolfgang of vs duke of Bavaria. 1488–90
Source: Stauber, *Herzog Georg von Bayern-Landshut*, 478–83.

(161) Aufseß, Eukarius von vs bishop of Bamberg. 1488–92
Source: Aufseß, *Geschichte des uradelichen Aufseß'schen Geschlechtes*, 183–5.

(162) Guttenberg, Philipp von vs Wallenrod, Veit von. 1488–98
Source: StAN, Fstm.Ansb., AA-Akten, no. 1753.

(163) Henneberg, Count Otto of vs Hutten, Lorenz von. 1489
       Source: StAN, Fstm.Ansb., AA-Akten, no. 738, doc. 43–74.

(164) Henneberg, Count Otto of vs Riedesel, Hermann. 1489
       Source: StAW, Stb, no. 1012, fol. 350v; Becker, *Die Riedesel zu Eisenbach*, 299–300.

(165) Heßberg, Darius von vs Regensburg. 1489
       Source: StAW, G 15471; *Die Chroniken der deutschen Städte*, vol. XI, 551.

(166) Rotenhan, Erasmus von vs Schenk, Götz. 1489
       Source: StAW, Ldf, no. 15, pp. 219–21.

(167) Schaumberg, Karl von vs bishop of Bamberg and abbess of Schlüsselau. 1489–91.
       Source: StAB, Fehde-Akten, no. 133; Kipp, *Silvester von Schaumberg*, 33.

(168) Henneberg, Count Hermann of vs the von Boineburgs. *c.* 1490.
       Source: Erck (ed.), *Rapsodiae sive Chronicon Hennebergicum*, 84.

(169) Wirsberg, Albrecht von and Redwitz, Balthasar von vs bishop of Bamberg. 1491
       Source: StAB, Hofrat Ansbach-Bayreuth, no. 543.

(170) Bibra, Konrad von vs Württemberg, count of. 1492
       Source: Bibra, *Beiträge zur Familiengeschichte*, 114–15.

(171) Stiebar, Albrecht vs bishop of Bamberg. 1492
       Source: Seefried, *Aus dem Stiebar-Archiv*, 8–9; Würdinger, *Kriegsgeschichte*, II, 117; StAB, Fehde-Akten, no. 133.

(172) Hutten, Lorenz, Ludwig, Friedrich and Ulrich von vs Hanau, Count Philipp of. 1492–3
       Source: Battenberg (ed.), *Isenburger Urkunden*, 818, no. 3406.

(173) Brandenstein, Albrecht von vs Giech, Christoph von. 1492–3
       Source: StAB, Hofrat Ansbach-Bayreuth, no. 545.

(174) Zobel, Stefan vs bishop of Würzburg. 1492–5
       Source: StAW, Stb, no. 817, fols. 29r–30r; StAN, Fstm.Ansb., Fehdeakten, no. 209, doc. 1.

(175) Gottsmann, Wolf vs bishop of Bamberg. 1493
       Source: StAN, Fstm.Ansb., AA-Akten, no. 392; Rupprecht, *Ritterschaftliche Herrschaftswahrung*, 136 n. 271.

(176) Absberg, Paul von vs Nuremberg. 1493
       Source: StAN, Fstm.Ansb., Fehdeakten, no. 201.

(177) Adelmann von Adelmannsfelden, Wilhelm and Balthasar vs Nördlingen. 1493–7
Source: Carl, *Der Schwäbische Bund*, 467.

(178) Buchenau, Engelhard von vs abbot of Fulda. 1494
Source: Leinweber, *Das Hochstift Fulda*, 22.

(179) Giech, Christoph von vs bishop of Bamberg. 1494
Source: StAB, Hofrat Ansbach-Bayreuth, no. 545.

(180) Schütz, Karl vs bishop of Bamberg. 1494
Source: StAB, Hofrat Ansbach-Bayreuth, no. 552.

(181) Wertheim, Count Johann of vs archbishop of Mainz. 1494
Source: Chmel (ed.), *Urkunden, Briefe und Actenstücke*, 27–8, nos. 35, 39.

(182) Stein zum Altenstein, Hartung vom vs bishop of Bamberg. 1495
Source: StAB, Hofrat Ansbach-Bayreuth, no. 553.

(183) Aufseß, Eukarius von vs bishop of Würzburg. 1495
Source: Aufseß, *Geschichte des uradelichen Aufseß'schen Geschlechtes*, 186–7; Zeißner, *Rudolf II. von Scherenberg*, 70.

(184) Randersacker, Peter von vs bishop of Würzburg. 1495
Source: StAW, Stb, no. 788, part 3.

(185) Rotenhan, Eberhard von vs bishop of Würzburg. c. 1495
Source: StAW, Stb, no. 1012, fol. 454r; Rotenhan, *Die Rotenhan*, 216.

(186) Birkenfels, Eustachius von vs bishop of Eichstätt. 1496
Source: StAN, Fstm.Ansb., Fehdeakten, no. 214.

(187) Wirsberg, Konrad von vs Guttenberg, Philipp von. 1496
Source: StAN, Fstm.Ansb., AA-Akten, nos. 1753, 1831.

(188) Abenberg, Hans von vs Zwinger, Martin and Christoph. 1497–8
Source: StAN, Fstm.Ansb., Fehdeakten, no. 222.

(189) Streitberg, Eberhard von vs Streitberg, Peter von. 1497–8.
Source: Oesterreicher, *Die Burg Streitberg*, 46.

(190) Guttenberg, Philipp and Moritz von vs margrave of Brandenburg. 1497–1502
Source: Rupprecht, *Ritterschaftliche Herrschaftswahrung*, 72–99.

(191) Rechenberg, Ernst von vs Bibra, Lorenz von. 1498–9
Source: StAB, Hofrat Ansbach-Bayreuth, no. 557; StAN, Kaiserliches Landgericht Burggraftums Nuremberg, no. 211.

(192) Vestenberg, Veit von vs Crailsheim, Marx and Georg von. 1498–1500

Source: StAN, Fstm.Ansb., Fehdeakten, no. 226; StAN, Akten des 7farbigen Alphabets, no. 35, doc. 49.

(193) Schott, Konrad vs Nuremberg. 1499
Source: StAN, Bb, no. 45, passim.

(194) Giech, Christoph von vs Nuremberg. 1499
Source: StAN, Bb, no. 45, passim.

(195) Fuchs, Philipp vs Fuchs, Thomas. 1499
Source: StAW, Ldf, no. 19, p. 100.

(196) Lüchau, Jobst von vs bishop of Bamberg. 1500
Source: StAB, Fehde-Akten, no. 152.

(197) Reitzenstein, Hans von vs bishop of Bamberg. 1500
Source: StAB, Fehde-Akten, no. 152, doc. 25; ibid., no. 166; Würdinger, *Kriegsgeschichte*, II, 118.

(198) Rosenberg, Georg von and Thüngen, Sigmund von vs Dinkelsbühl. 1500
Source: Klüpfel (ed.), *Urkunden*, 429.

(199) Selbitz, Hans von vs Henneberg, Count Hermann VIII of. c. 1500
Source: StAN, Fstm.Ansb., AA-Akten, no. 515.

(200) Crailsheim, Marx and Georg von vs margrave of Brandenburg. 1500
Source: StAN, Fstm.Ansb., AA-Akten, no. 1733.

(201) Schaumberg, Karl von vs Staffelstein. 1500
Source: Kipp, *Silvester von Schaumberg*, 13, 14–15 n. 2.

(202) Stiebar, Ewald vs bishop of Bamberg. 1500
Source: StAB, Fehde-Akten, no. 152, doc. 25; StAB, Fehde-Akten, no. 133.

(203) Bernheim, Klaus von vs bishop of Bamberg. 1500–1
Source: StAN, Fstm.Ansb., Fehdeakten, no. 233; StAB, Fehde-Akten, no. 152, doc. 25.

(204) Vestenberg, Veit von vs Crailsheim, Wilhelm von. 1501
Source: StAN, Fstm.Ansb., AA-Akten, no. 392, doc. of Samstag nach St Oswald 1501.

(205) Henneberg, Count Wilhelm IV of vs Henneberg, Count Hermann of. 1501
Source: StAN, Fstm.Ansb., AA-Akten, no. 728, doc. of Freitag nach Francisci 1501.

(206) Eusenheim gen. Heuslein, Georg von vs bishop of Würzburg. 1501
Source: StAW, Stb, no. 788, part 3.

(207) Seinsheim, Hans von vs bishop of Würzburg. 1501–2
       Source: StAN, Fstm.Ansb., Fehdeakten, nos. 240–1; StAB, Hofrat
       Ansbach-Bayreuth, no. 561.

(208) Gebsattel, Konrad von vs bishop of Würzburg. 1501–2
       Source: StAN, AA-Akten, no. 392, doc. of Samstag nach dem Sonn-
       tag Quasimodo Geniti 1502; StAB, Hofrat Ansbach-Bayreuth, no.
       561.

(209) Gottsmann, N. vs Egloffstein, Martin and Georg von. 1501–2
       Source: Auer (ed.), 'Die undatierten Fredriciana'.

(210) Schaumberg, Silvester von vs bishop of Bamberg. 1501–3
       Source: StAB, Fehde-Akten, no. 133.

(211) Bebenburg, Wilhelm von vs Spies, Konrad. 1502
       Source: Herolt, *Chronica*, 122–3.

(212) Lüchau, Jobst von vs Nuremberg. 1502
       Source: StAN, Bb, no. 48, fols. 179r–180r.

(213) Schaumberg, Karl von vs Truchseß, Leopold. 1502
       Source: StAB, Fehde-Akten, no. 133.

(214) Wemding, Reinwold von vs Axter, Wilhelm. 1502
       Source: StAN, Fstm.Ansb., Fehdeakten, no. 236.

(215) Zollner, Hans vs Bere, Hans. 1502
       Source: StAW, Ldf 19, pp. 137–8, 144–6.

(216) Zufraß, Erasmus vs bishop of Würzburg. 1502–3
       Source: StAW, Stb, no. 788, part 3; ibid., Ldf, no. 19, pp. 165–6,
       311–12.

(217) Absberg, Paul von vs bishop of Eichstätt. 1503
       Source: Schlecht (ed.), 'Die Kleinen Annalen des Kilian Leib', 43;
       Wilhelm, 'Die Edeln von und zum Absberg', 122.

(218) Süzel, Melchior vs bishop of Würzburg. 1503
       Source: StAA, Ganerbschaft Rothenberg, no. 2538a, under anno 1503;
       StAW, Stb, no. 788, part 3.

(219) Stein, Christoph vom vs bishop of Würzburg. 1503–4
       Source: StAW, Stb, no. 788, part 3; StAA, Ganerbschaft Rothenberg,
       no. 2538a, under anno 1504.

(220) Brandenstein, Eberhard von vs duke of Saxony. 1503/6
       Source: StAA, Ganerbschaft Rothenberg, no. 2538a, under anno 1503
       and 1506.

(221) Wertheim, Count Erasmus of vs bishop of Würzburg. 1505

Source: Aschbach (ed.), *Wertheimisches Urkundenbuch*, no. 205;
Aschbach, *Geschichte der Grafen von Wertheim*, 285.

(222) Berlichingen, Götz von vs the Waldstromer von Reichelsdorf. 1505
Source: Ulmschneider (ed.), *Götz von Berlichingen*, 81–2.

(223) Gottsmann, Wolf vs bishop of Bamberg. 1507
Source: StAA, Ganerbschaft Rothenberg, no. 2538a, under anno 1507.

(224) Schaumberg, Adam von vs Reitzenstein, Thomas von. 1507
Source: StAN, Fstm.Ansb., Fehdeakten, no. 245.

(225) Zeyern, Georg von vs Reitzenstein, Hans von. 1508
Source: StAB, Fehde-Akten, no. 166.

(226) Stiebar, Sebastian von vs Teutonic Order. 1508–9
Source: StAA, Ganerbschaft Rothenberg, no. 2538a, under anno 1508,
1509.

(227) Berlichingen, Götz von vs Cologne. 1508–10
Source: Ulmschneider (ed.), *Götz von Berlichingen*, 83–4.

(228) Seckendorff, Sebastian von vs Nuremberg. 1508–12
Source: StAN, Bb, 65, fol. 21r; Rechter, *Die Seckendorff*, II, 71.

(229) Aufseß, Eukarius von vs bishop of Bamberg. 1509
Source: Aufseß, *Geschichte des uradelichen Aufseß'schen Geschlechtes*,
187–8.

(230) Eyb, Ludwig von vs Arnold, Kunz. 1510
Source: Rabeler, *Niederadlige Lebensformen*, 317–18.

(231) Gnottstadt, Konrad von vs bishop of Würzburg. 1510
Source: StAW, Stb, no. 788, part 3.

(232) Eyb, Kaspar von vs Theininger, Peter. 1510
Source: StAN, Fstm.Ansb., Fehdeakten, no. 254.

(233) Seckendorff, Balthasar von vs Rabenstein, Hans von. 1510
Source: Rechter, *Die Seckendorff*, II, 55.

(234) Bibra, Friedrich von vs Truchseß von Wetzhausen, Johann and Zollner, Johann. 1510
Source: Wagenhöfer, *Die Bibra*, 403.

(235) Thüngen, Eustachius von vs bishop of Bamberg. *c.* 1510–11
Source: Ulmschneider (ed.), *Götz von Berlichingen*, 88–90.

(236) Buchenau, Georg von vs bishop of Würzburg. 1510–12
Source: StAW, Stb, no. 788, part 3, passim.

(237) Brandenstein, Ernst von vs Henneberg, Count Wilhelm IV of. 1510–
12
Source: Spangenberg, *Hennebergische Chronica*, 462–5.

(238) Schenk von Limpurg, Gottfried vs Thüngen, Eustachius von. 1511
Source: Herolt, *Chronica*, 121–2.

(239) Herbilstadt, Wolf von vs Henneberg, Count Wilhelm IV of. 1512
Source: Spangenberg, *Hennebergische Chronica*, 465.

(240) Feilitzsch, Wolf von vs Sparneck, Sebastian von. 1512
Source: StAB, Hofrat Ansbach-Bayreuth, no. 563.

(241) Lüder, Weigand von vs bishop of Würzburg. 1512
Source: StAW, Stb, no. 788, part 3.

(242) Berlichingen, Götz von vs Nuremberg. 1512–14
Source: Ulmschneider (ed.), *Götz von Berlichingen*, 91–8.

(243) Vestenberg, Matern von vs Bishop of Würzburg. 1512–15
Source: StAA, Ganerbschaft Rothenberg, no. 2538a, under anno
1512–15.

(244) Zobel, Stefan vs Zobel, Klaus. 1514
Source: Bossert, 'Urkunden des Klosters Frauenthal', 84.

(245) Marschall von Pappenheim, Georg vs Dachs, Peter. 1514–15
Source: StAN, Fstm.Ansb., Fehdeakten, no. 262.

(246) Beulwitz, Ernst von vs Entzenberg, Otto von. 1515
Source: StAN, Fstm.Ansb., Fehdeakten, no. 263.

(247) Berlichingen, Götz von vs Mainz. 1515–16
Source: Ulmschneider (ed.), *Götz von Berlichingen*, 106–14.

(248) Eberstein, Mangold von vs Nuremberg. 1516–22
Source: Eberstein (ed.), *'Dem Landfrieden ist nicht zu trauen'*.

(249) Wolfskeel, Wende von vs Rothenburg ob der Tauber. 1517
Source: StAN, Fstm.Ansb., Fehdeakten, no. 274.

(250) Aufseß, Eukarius von vs bishop of Bamberg. 1518
Source: Aufseß, *Geschichte des uradelichen Aufseß'schen Geschlechtes*,
188–9, 192–3.

(251) Helb, Philipp von vs bishop of Bamberg. 1519
Source: StAA, Ganerbschaft Rothenberg, no. 2538a, under anno 1519.

(252) Helb, Philipp von vs bishop of Würzburg. 1519
Source: StAA, Ganerbschaft Rothenberg, no. 2538a, under anno 1519.

(253) Absberg, Hans Georg von vs Schwarzenberg, Johann von. 1519
Source: StAN, Fstm.Ansb., Fehdeakten, no. 69, doc. 10–11.

(254) Vellberg, Wolf von, and Crailsheim, Wilhelm, Sebastian and Kaspar
von vs Vellberg, Wilhelm von. 1519
Source: StAN, Fstm.Ansb., Fehdeakten, no. 277.

(255) Redwitz, Ernst von vs Bishop of Eichstätt. 1519–25

Source: StAA, Ganerbschaft Rothenberg, no. 2538a, under anno
1519–25.

(256) Absberg, Hans Thomas von vs Oettingen, Counts Joachim and Wolf-
gang of. 1520
Source: Baader (ed.), *Verhandlungen über Thomas von Absberg*, 1–2;
Ritzmann, '"Plackerey in teutschen Landen"', 131–2.

(257) Schenk von Arberg, Karl von vs bishop of Eichstätt. *c.* 1520.
Source: Schlecht (ed.), 'Die Kleinen Annalen des Kilian Leib', 65.

(258) Hutten, Frowin, Lorenz and Hans von vs Eberstein, Philipp von.
1520s
Source: Decker, 'Klientel und Konkurrenz', 43.

(259) Guttenberg, Achaz von vs Gera, Heinrich d.Ä. von. 1520–1
Source: Bischoff, *Genealogie*, 151, no. 615.

(260) Gottsmann, Albrecht vs Nuremberg. 1521
Source: StAA, Ganerbschaft Rothenberg, no. 2538a, under anno
1521.

(261) Sparneck, Wolf von vs Sparneck, Sebastian von and Lüchau, Heinz
von. 1523
Source: Baader (ed.), *Verhandlungen über Thomas von Absberg*, 60.

(262) Heßberg, Karl von vs non-noble. 1524
Source: StAN, Fstm.Ansb., AA-Akten, no. 392, doc. 105.

(263) Rain, Georg von vs margrave of Brandenburg. 1524–9
Source: StAN, Fstm.Ansb., Fehdeakten, no. 290.

(264) Rain, Georg von and Rain, Götz von vs Seckendorff, Hans von.
1524–9
Source: StAN, Fstm.Ansb., Fehdeakten, no. 290.

(265) Rain, Georg von vs Seckendorff, Kilian von. 1524–9
Source: StAN, Fstm.Ansb., Fehdeakten, no. 290.

(266) Thüngen, Adam von vs Rothenburg ob der Tauber. 1525–6
Source: Baumann (ed.), *Quellen zur Geschichte des Bauernkriegs*, 570,
576–80, 610–15.

(267) Streitberg, Rochus and Balthasar von vs Streitberg, Gabriel von. 1530
Source: Looshorn, *Die Geschichte des Bisthums Bamberg*, 789–91;
Grötsch, 'Eine blutige Ritterfehde'.

(268) Feilitzsch, Hans von vs Machwitz, Sigmund von. 1531
Source: StAB, Hofrat Ansbach-Bayreuth, no. 574.

(269) Hutten, Ludwig von vs Schwarzenberg, Friedrich von. 1531–4

Source: British Library, C.38.k.16.; *Unser Friderichen Freyherren von Schwartzenberg und zu Hohenlandsperg . . . warhafftiger bericht und gegenschrifft / auff Ludwigs der sich von Hutten und einen ritter nennt ausschreiben . . .* (1533).

(270) Guttenberg, Hektor von vs Guttenberg, Achaz von. 1536
Source: Rupprecht, *Ritterschaftliche Herrschaftswahrung*, 186.

(271) Rosenberg, Albrecht von vs Nuremberg. 1539–55
Source: StAN, Bb, no. 134, fols. 3v–5r; 39v–42v; Frey, 'Die Fehde der Herren von Rosenberg'.

(272) Grün, Hans d.Ä. von der vs Grün, Hans d.J. von der. 1540
Source: StAB, Hofrat Ansbach-Bayreuth, no. 578.

(273) Seckendorff, Hans Arnold von vs Eyb, Hans Christoph von. 1542
Source: Rechter, *Die Seckendorff*, II, 215.

(274) Schwarzenberg, Friedrich von vs Absberg, Hans Christoph von. 1544
Source: Kolb (ed.), *Widmans Chronica*, 290.

(275) Egloffstein, Hans von vs bishop of Bamberg. 1545
Source: StAB, Hofrat Ansbach-Bayreuth, no. 579.

(276) Wildenstein, Moritz von vs Reitzenstein, Balthasar, Christoph, Hans-Sixt and Georg-Ernst von. 1549
Source: StAB, Fehde-Akten, no. 221.

(277) Marschall von Pappenheim, Alexander vs Marschall von Pappenheim, Wolf. 1553
Source: StAN, Herrschaft Pappenheim, Akten, no. 2797.

(278) Grumbach, Wilhelm von vs bishop of Würzburg. 1563–7
Source: Press, 'Wilhelm von Grumbach'.

Select bibliography

MANUSCRIPT SOURCES

STAATSARCHIV AMBERG

Ganerbschaft Rothenberg (Rep. A I 20) 2538a.

STAATSARCHIV BAMBERG

B 28   Bamberger Landtagsakten: 1.
C 3   Hofrat Ansbach-Bayreuth: 6, 501, 507, 513, 519, 528, 535, 540, 543,
        545, 553, 557, 561, 563, 565, 574, 575, 578, 579, 1563.
J 8   Fehde-Akten: 76, 79, 101, 102, 133, 152, 166, 221, 501.

Neuverzeichnete Akten: 70142, 70143.

GEHEIMES STAATSARCHIV PREUSSISCHER KULTURBESITZ, BERLIN

Brandenburg-Preußisches Hausarchiv

Rep 27 E. 1. 6
Rep. 44. 1

BIBLIOTHEK DES GERMANISCHEN NATIONALMUSEUMS, NÜRNBERG

Hs 22 547.

STAATSARCHIV NÜRNBERG

Fürstentum Ansbach

AA-Akten: 392, 515, 580, 728, 737, 738, 768, 1402, 1733, 1753, 1831.
Ansbacher Historica: 1, 210.
Ansbacher Landtagsakten: 8.
Brandenburger Literalien: 643
Differenzen mit Benachbarten, Bayerische Bücher: 8.
Fehdeakten: 55, 56, 63, 70, 73, 74, 75, 76, 81, 84, 94, 107, 132, 143, 151, 162,
    172, 176, 201, 209, 214, 222, 226, 227, 233, 236, 240, 241, 245, 254, 262,
    263, 274, 277, 290, 346.
Geheimregistratur, Bamberger Zugang: 39.
Gemeinbücher: 4.
Generalrepertorium Bamberger Abg. 1996: 237 I.
Herrschaftliche Bücher: 5, 35.
Kaiserliches Landgericht Burggraftums Nürnberg: 211.
Urfehden: 25, 33.

Herrschaft Pappenheim

Akten: 2797.

Reichsstadt Nürnberg

Akten des siebenfarbigen Alphabets: 32.
Briefbücher des Inneren Rates: 45, 48, 65, 134.
35 neue Laden der unteren Losungsstube, v 89/1 2065.

Reichsstadt Windsheim

Akten: 13, 14, 15.

STAATSARCHIV WÜRZBURG

Adel: 1114.
Misc. 1029.
Libri diversarum formarum: 9, 12, 15.
Standbücher: 717, 788, 892, 948, 1012.

PRINTED SOURCES

Aschbach, Joseph (ed.), *Wertheimisches Urkundenbuch*, 2nd part of his *Geschichte der Grafen von Wertheim von den ältesten Zeiten bis ʒu ihrem Erlöschen in Mannsstamme im Jahre 1556* (Frankfurt am Main, 1843).

Auer, Leopold (ed.), 'Die undatierten Fredriciana des Haus-, Hof- und Staatsarchivs', *Mitteilungen des österreichischen Staatsarchivs* 27 (1974), 405–30.

Baader, Joseph (ed.), *Verhandlungen über Thomas von Absberg und seine Fehden gegen den Schwäbischen Bund 1519 bis 1530* (Tübingen, 1873).

Bachmann, Adolf (ed.), *Briefe und Acten ʒur österreichisch-deutschen Geschichte im Zeitalter Kaiser Friedrich III.* (Vienna, 1885).

Battenberg, Friedrich (ed.), *Isenburger Urkunden: Regesten ʒu Urkundenbeständen und Kopiaren der fürstlichen Archive in Birstein und Büdingen 947–1500*, vol. II (Darmstadt, 1976).

(ed.), *Schlitʒer Urkunden: Regesten ʒum Urkundenarchiv der Grafen von Schlitʒ gen. von Görtʒ (Abt. B 8) 1285–1939*, 2 vols. (Darmstadt, 1979).

Baumann, Franz Ludwig (ed.), *Quellen ʒur Geschichte des Bauernkriegs aus Rotenburg an der Tauber* (Tübingen, 1878).

Birk, Ernst, *Urkunden-Ausʒüge ʒur Geschichte Kaiser Friedrich des III. in den Jahren 1452–1467 aus bisher unbenütʒten Quellen* (Vienna, 1853).

Böcking, Eduard (ed.), *Ulrichi Hutteni, equitis Germani, Opera quae reperiri potuerent omnia*, 5 vols. (Leipzig, 1859–61).

Bossert, G., 'Urkunden des Klosters Frauenthal', *Württembergische Vierteljahrshefte für Landesgeschichte* 13 (1890), 80–90.

Burkhardt, Carl August Hugo (ed.), *Das funfft merkisch Buech des Churfuersten Albrecht Achilles* (Jena, 1857).

(ed.), *Correcturen und Zusätʒe ʒu Quellenschriften für hohenʒollerische Geschichte*, vol. I, *Das kaiserliche Buch des Markgrafen Albrecht Achilles herausgegeben von Constantin Höfler* (Jena, 1861).

Chmel, Joseph (ed.), *Materialien ʒur österreichischen Geschichte*, vol. II (Vienna, 1838).

(ed.), *Regesta Chronologico-Diplomatica Friderici IV. Romanorum Regis (Imperatoris III.)*, part 1, *Vom Jahre 1440 bis März 1452* (Vienna, 1838).

(ed.), *Urkunden, Briefe und Actenstücke ʒur Geschichte Maximilian's I. und seiner Zeit* (Stuttgart, 1845).

Chronicon Elvacense, in *Die Ellwanger und Neresheimer Geschichtsquellen*, ed. J. A. Giefel, in *Württembergische Vierteljahrshefte für Landesgeschichte* 11 (1888), 33–55.

Das Wappenbuch Conrads von Grünenberg, Ritters und Bürgers zu Constanz. Bayerische Staatsbibliothek, Munich, Cgm 145.

Decker-Hauff, Hansmartin (ed.), *Die Chronik der Grafen von Zimmern*, vol. 11 (Sigmaringen, 1967).

Die Chroniken der deutschen Städte vom 14. bis ins 16. Jahrhundert, vols. X, XI (Leipzig, 1872–4).

Ebendorfer, Thomas, *Chronica Austriae*, ed. Alphons Lhotsky (Berlin and Zurich, 1967).

Eberstein, Louis Ferdinand von (ed.), '*Dem Landfrieden ist nicht zu trauen': Fehde Mangold's von Eberstein zum Brandenstein gegen die Reichsstadt Nürnberg 1516–1522. Charakterbild der rechtlichen und wirtschaftlichen Zustände im deutschen Reiche unmittelbar vor dem grossen Bauernkriege* (Nordhausen, 1868).

Eibl, Elfie-Marita (ed.), *Die Urkunden und Briefe aus den Archiven und Bibliotheken des Freistaates Sachsen*, Regesten Kaiser Friedrichs III. (1440–1493) nach Archiven und Bibliotheken geordnet, ed. Heinrich Koller und Paul-Joachim Heinig, part 11 (Vienna, 1998).

Eigenhändiger Aufzeichnung des Siegmund von Gebsattel über die Turniere von 1484–1487, in *Anzeiger für Kunde der deutschen Vorzeit*, n.s. 1, no. 4 (1853), coll. 67–9.

Engel, W. (ed.), *Die Rats-Chronik der Stadt Würzburg (*XV*. und* XVI*. Jahrhundert)* (Würzburg, 1950).

Erck, Christoph Albrecht (ed.), *Rapsodiae sive Chronicon Hennebergicum Weyland M. Sebastian Glasers, Hennebergischen Cantzlers vom Jahr 1078. bis 1559. Welches noch niemahlen im Druck erschienen, sondern nur in einigen Bibliothecis priuatis latitiret, zur Erläuterung der spangenberg-hennebergischen Chronic* (Meiningen, 1755).

Fries, Lorenz, *Chronik der Bischöfe von Würzburg 742–1495*, vol. IV, *Von Sigmund von Sachsen bis Rudolf II. von Scherenberg (1440–1495)*, ed. Ulrike Grosch, Christoph Bauer, Harald Tausch and Thomas Heiler (Würzburg, 2002).

Gollwitzer, Heinz (ed.), *Deutsche Reichstagsakten, mittlere Reihe*, vol. VI, *Reichstage von Lindau, Worms und Freiburg 1496–1498* (Göttingen, 1979).

Gradl, Heinrich, 'Die Bamberger Turnierordnung von 1478', *Bericht des Historischen Vereins Bamberg* 45 (1883), 87–97.

Gumppenberg, Ludwig Adalbert von (ed.), 'Nachrichten über die Turniere zu Würzburg und Bamberg in den Jahren 1479 und 1486', *AU* 19, no. 2 (1867), 164–210.

Guttenberg, Franz Carl von (ed.), 'Regesten des Geschlechts von Blassenburg und dessen Nachkommen', *AO* 23, no. 2 (1907), 113–233.

'Hellers Chronic der Stadt Bayreuth', part 1, *AO* 1, no. 1 (1838), 102–47.

Herolt, Johann, *Chronica zeit- unnd Jarbuch von der Statt Hall ursprung und was sich darinnen verloffen unnd wasz fur Schlösser umb Hall gestanden*, ed. Christian Kolb (Stuttgart, 1894).

Höfler, Constantin (ed.), *Das kaiserliche Buch des Markgrafen Albrecht Achilles: Vorkurfürstliche Periode 1440–1470* (Bayreuth, 1850).

(ed.), 'Fränkische Studien IV', parts 1–3, *Archiv für Kunde österreichischer Geschichts-Quellen* 7 (1851), 1–146; 8 (1852), 235–322; 11 (1853), 1–56.

Hutten, Ulrich von, 'Die Anschauenden', in *Ulrich von Hutten: Deutsche Schriften*, ed. Peter Ukena (Munich, 1970), 136–61.

Die Räuber, in *Gespräche von Ulrich von Hutten*, ed. and trans. David Friedrich Strauß (Leipzig, 1860), 315–89.

Keller, Adalbert von (ed.), *Die Geschichten und Taten Wilwolts von Schaumburg* (Stuttgart, 1859).

Klüpfel, Karl (ed.), *Urkunden zur Geschichte des Schwäbischen Bundes (1488–1533)*, vol. 1 (Stuttgart, 1846).

Kolb, Christian (ed.), *Widmans Chronica* (Stuttgart, 1904).

Luckhard, Fritz (ed.), *Die Regesten der Herren von Ebersberg genannt Weyhers in der Röhn (1170–1518)* (Fulda, 1963).

Lünig, Johann Christian, *Des Teutschen Reichs-Archiv partis specialis continuatio III*, part 2 (Leipzig, 1713).

Menzel, Karl (ed.), *Regesten zur Geschichte Friedrich's I. des Siegreichen, Kurfürsten von der Pfalz*, in *Quellen und Erörtungen zur bayerischen Geschichte*, vol. II (Munich, 1862), 209–499.

Mötsch, Johannes (ed.), *Regesten des Archivs der Grafen von Henneberg-Römhild*, 2 vols. (Cologne, 2006).

Müllner, Johannes, *Die Annalen der Reichsstadt Nürnberg von 1623*, ed. Gerhard Hirschmann, vol. II (Nuremberg, 1984)

Piccolomini, Aeneas Silvius de, *Österreichische Geschichte*, trans. Jürgen Sarnowsky (Darmstadt, 2005).

Pietsch, Friedrich (ed.), *Die Urkunden des Archivs der Reichsstadt Schwäbisch Hall*, vol. II (Stuttgart, 1972).

Priebatsch, Felix (ed.), *Politische Correspondenz des Kurfürsten Albrecht Achilles*, 3 vols. (Leipzig, 1894–8).

Rabeler, Sven (ed.), *Das Familienbuch Michels von Ehenheim (um 1462/63–1518): Ein niederadliges Selbstzeugnis des späten Mittelalters. Edition, Kommentar, Untersuchung* (Frankfurt am Main, 2007).

Schannat, Johann Friedrich (ed.), *Fuldischer Lehn-Hof sive de clientela fuldensi beneficiaria nobili et equestri tractatus* (Frankfurt am Main, 1726).

Schlecht, Joseph (ed.), 'Die Kleinen Annalen des Kilian Leib, Priors zu Rebdorf. Nach dem Codex Münch im bischöfl. Ordinariats-Archiv zu Eichstätt', *Sammelblatt des Historischen Vereins Eichstätt* 2 (1887 [1888]), 39–68.

Schwarzenberg, Friedrich von, *Unser Friderichen Freyherren von Schwartzenberg und zu Hohenlandsperg diser zeit Wirtembergischen Obervogts zu Schorndorf / warhafftiger bericht und gegenschrifft / auff Ludwigs der sich von Hutten und einen ritter nennt ausschreiben zum andern mal im druck ausgangen / im angang / mittel / ende / und durchaus erlogen (sovil er des wider und zusein vermeint) dann er sich auch sonst abermals in vil stucken selbst zum höchsten und mer verletzt / dann verantwort hat* (1533).

Schwarzenberg, Johann von, *Ain Lied mit vorgehender anzaygung / wider das mordlaster des raubens* (1513).

Das Büchlein vom Zutrinken, ed. Willy Scheel (Halle, 1900).

Shiedsspruch Kurfürst Philipp des Aufrichtigen von der Pfalz in der Irrung zwischen Erasmus Graf von Wertheim und Ritter Georg von Rosenberg (1502). Bayerische Staatsbibliothek Munich, Ded. 350 c.

Spangenberg, Cyriacus, *Hennebergische Chronica: Der uralten löblichen Grafen und Fürsten zu Henneberg, Genealogia, Stamm-Baum und Historia, ihrer Ankunfft, Lob und denckwürdigen Tathen, Geschichten und Sachen wahre und gründliche Beschreibung* (Meiningen, 1755).

Speierische Chronik, in *Quellensammlung der badischen Landesgeschichte*, ed. Franz Joseph Mone, vol. I (Karlsruhe, 1848), 367–520.

Stamm, Heide (ed.), *Das Turnierbuch des Ludwig von Eyb (cgm 961). Edition und Untersuchung mit einem Anhang: Die Turnierchronik des Jörg Rugen (Textabdruck)* (Stuttgart, 1986).

Stehlin, K. (ed.), 'Ein spanischer Bericht über ein Turnier in Schaffhausen im Jahr 1436', *Basler Zeitschrift für Geschichte und Altertumskunde* 14 (1915), 145–75.

Stein, Friedrich (ed.), *Monumenta Suinfurtensia historica inde ab anno DCCXCI usque ad annum MDC: Denkmäler der Schweinfurter Geschichte bis zum Ende des 16. Jahrhundert* (Schweinfurt, 1875).

Thumser, Matthias (ed.), *Ludwig von Eyb der Ältere (1417–1502): Schriften. Denkwürdigkeiten, Gültbuch, Briefe an Kurfürst Albrecht Achilles 1473/74, Mein Buch* (Neustadt a.d. Aisch, 2002).

Trillitzsch, Winfried, 'Der Brief Ulrich von Huttens an Willibald Pirckheimer', in *Ulrich von Hutten: Ritter, Humanist, Publizist. Katalog zur Ausstellung des Landes Hessen anläßlich des 500. Geburtstag*, ed. Peter Laub (Kassel, 1988), 211–29.

Ulmschneider, Helgard (ed.), *Götz von Berlichingen. Mein Fehd und Handlung* (Sigmaringen, 1981).

Verhandlungen zwischen der Stadt Nürnberg und der fränkischen Ritterschaft wegen Christoph von Giech und Contz Schott (Nuremberg, 1500).

Wolkan, Rudolf (ed.), *Der Briefwechsel des Eneas Silvius Piccolomini*, part 3, *Briefe als Bischof von Siena*, vol. 1 (Vienna, 1918).

Wrede, Adolf (ed.), *Deutsche Reichstagsakten, jüngere Reihe*, vol. III (Gotha, 1901).

Zeumer, Karl, *Die Goldene Bulle Kaiser Karls IV.*, part 2, *Text der Goldenen Bulle und Urkunden zu ihrer Geschichte und Erläuterung* (Weimar, 1908).

SECONDARY LITERATURE

Algazi, Gadi, 'The Social Use of Private War: Some Late Medieval Views Reviewed', *Tel Aviver Jahrbuch für deutsche Geschichte* 22 (1993), 253–73.

'"Sie würden hinten nach so gail": Vom sozialen Gebrauch der Fehde im späten Mittelalter', in *Physische Gewalt: Studien zur Geschichte der Neuzeit*, ed. Thomas Lindenberger and Alf Lüdtke (Frankfurt am Main, 1995), 39–77.

Herrengewalt und Gewalt der Herren im späten Mittelalter: Herrschaft, Gegenseitigkeit und Sprachgebrauch (Frankfurt am Main, 1996).

'Otto Brunner – "Konkrete Ordnung" und Sprache der Zeit', in *Geschichte als Legitimationswissenschaft, 1918–1945*, ed. Peter Schöttler, 2nd edn (Frankfurt am Main, 1998), 166–203.

Amrhein, August, 'Gotfrid Schenk von Limpurg: Bischof von Würzburg und Herzog zu Franken 1442–1455', part 3, *AU* 53 (1911), 1–153.

Andermann, Kurt, 'Der Überfall im württembergischen Geleit bei Markgröningen im Jahre 1459 – ein klassischer Fall von Straßenraub?' in *Aus südwestdeutscher Geschichte. Festschrift für Hans-Martin Maurer. Dem Archivar und Historiker zum 65. Geburtstag*, ed. Wolfgang Schmierer, Günter Cordes, Rudolf Kieß and Gerhard Taddey (Stuttgart, 1994), 273–86.

'Raubritter – Raubfürsten – Raubbürger? Zur Kritik eines untauglichen Begriffs', in *'Raubritter' oder 'Rechtsschaffene vom Adel'? Aspekte von Politik, Friede und Recht im späten Mittelalter*, ed. Kurt Andermann (Sigmaringen, 1997), 9–29.

Andermann, Ulrich, *Ritterliche Gewalt und bürgerliche Selbsbehauptung: Untersuchungen zur Kriminalisierung und Bekämpfung des spätmittelalterlichen Raubrittertums am Beispiel norddeutscher Hansestädte* (Frankfurt am Main, 1991).

Arnold, Thomas, *The Renaissance at War* (London, 2001).

Aufseß, Otto von, *Geschichte des uradelichen Aufseß'schen Geschlechtes in Franken* (Berlin, 1889).

Bachmann, Matthias, *Lehenhöfe von Grafen und Herren im ausgehenden Mittelalter: Das Beispiel Rieneck, Wertheim und Castell* (Cologne, 2000).

Baum, Hans-Peter, 'Soziale Schichtung im mainfränkischen Niederadel um 1400', *ZHF* 13 (1986), 129–48.

'Der Lehenhof des Hochstifts Würzburg im Spätmittelalter (1303–1519): Eine rechts- und sozialgeschichtliche Studie', 3 vols. (*Habilitationsschrift*, University of Würzburg, 1990).

Bayer, Victor, *Die Historia Friderici III. Imperatoris des Enea Silvio de' Piccolomini: Eine kritische Studie zur Geschichte Kaiser Friedrichs III.* (Prague, 1872).

Bechstein, Eberhard, *Die Tierberger Fehde zwischen den Grafen von Hohenlohe und den Herren von Stetten (1475 bis 1495): Ein Streit zwischen Rittern, Grafen, Fürsten und dem Kaiser am Vorabend der Reichsreform* (Cologne, 2004).

Becker, Eduard Edwin, *Die Riedesel zu Eisenbach: Geschichte des Geschlechts der Riedesel Freiherrn zu Eisenbach*, vol. 1, *Vom ersten Auftreten des Namens bis zum Tod Hermanns III. Riedesel 1500* (Offenbach, 1923).

Berlichingen-Rossach, F. W. Graf von, *Geschichte des Ritters Götz von Berlichingen mit der eisernen Hand und seiner Familie* (Leipzig, 1861).

Betzig, Laura, 'Medieval Monogamy', *Journal of Family History* 20, no. 2 (1995), 181–216.

Bibra, Wilhelm von, *Beiträge zur Familiengeschichte der Reichsfreiherrn von Bibra*, vol. II (Munich, 1882).

Bischoff, Johannes, *Genealogie der Ministerialen von Blassenberg und Freiherren von (und zu) Guttenberg 1148–1970* (Würzburg, 1971).

Bittmann, Markus, *Kreditwirtschaft und Finanzierungsmethoden: Studien zu den Verhältnissen des Adels im westlichen Bodenseeraum* (Stuttgart, 1991).

Boockmann, Hartmut, 'Ritterliche Abenteuer – adlige Erziehung', in his *Fürsten, Bürger, Edelleute: Lebensbilder aus dem späten Mittelalter* (Munich, 1994).

Boone, James L., 'Paternal Investment and Elite Family Structure in Pre-industrial States: A Case Study of Late Medieval – Early Modern Portuguese Genealogies', *American Anthropologist* 88 (1986), 859–78.

Brown, Keith M., *Bloodfeud in Scotland: Violence, Justice and Politics in an Early Modern Society* (Edinburgh, 1986).

Brunner, Otto, 'Beiträge zur Geschichte des Fehdewesens im spätmittelalterlichen Oesterreich', *Jahrbuch für Landeskunde von Niederösterreich* 22 (1929), 431–507.

'Moderner Verfassungsbegriff und mittelalterliche Verfassungsgeschichte', *Mitteilungen des österreichischen Instituts für Geschichtsforschung. Erg.-Band* 14 (1939), 513–28.

'Land' and Lordship: Structures of Governance in Medieval Austria, trans. Howard Kaminsky and James Van Horn Melton (Philadelphia, 1992).

Büchert Netterstrøm, Jeppe, and Bjørn Poulsen (eds.), *Feud in Medieval and Early Modern Europe* (Aarhus, 2007).

Bürger, Sven-Uwe, 'Burg Amlishagen – Anmerkungen zur Besitzgeschichte', *Württembergisch Franken* 76 (1992), 39–60.

Buss, David M., *The Evolution of Desire: Strategies of Human Mating* (New York, 1994).

Camerer, Colin F., *Behavioral Game Theory: Experiments in Strategic Interaction* (Princeton, 2003).

Carl, Horst, *Der Schwäbische Bund, 1488–1534: Landfrieden und Genossenschaft im Übergang vom Spätmittelalter zur Reformation* (Leinfelden-Echterdingen, 2000).

Carroll, Stuart, 'The Peace in the Feud in Sixteenth-Century France', *Past and Present* 178 (2003), 74–115.

Blood and Violence in Early Modern France (Oxford, 2006).

Decker, Klaus Peter, 'Klientel und Konkurrenz: Die ritterschaftliche Familie von Hutten und die Grafen von Hanau und von Ysenburg', *Hessisches Jahrbuch für Landesgeschichte* 38 (1988), 23–48.

Dobeneck, Alban von, 'Geschichte des ausgestorbenen Geschlechtes der von Sparneck', part 1, *AO* 22, no. 3 (1905), 1–65.

Geschichte der Familie von Dobeneck (Schöneberg-Berlin, 1906).

'Die Geschichte des ausgestorbenen Geschlechts von Kotzau', *AO* 24, no. 1 (1909), 1–111.

Duby, Georges, 'Youth in Aristocratic Society: Northwestern France in the Twelfth Century', in *The Chivalrous Society*, trans. Cynthia Postan (Berkeley, 1977), 112–22.

Eberstein, L. F. von, *Abriß der Urkundlichen Geschichte des reichsritterlichen Geschlechtes Eberstein vom Eberstein auf der Rhön* (Dresden, 1885–93).

Ehmer, Hermann, 'Horneck von Hornberg: Raubritter oder Opfer fürstlicher Politik', in *'Raubritter' oder 'Rechtsschaffene vom Adel'? Aspekte von Politik, Friede und Recht im späten Mittelalter*, ed. Kurt Andermann (Sigmaringen, 1997), 65–88.

Fehn-Claus, Janine, 'Erste Ansätze einer Typologie der Fehdegründe', in *Der Krieg im Mittelalter und in der Frühen Neuzeit: Gründe, Begründungen, Bilder, Bräuche, Recht*, ed. Horst Brunner (Wiesbaden 1999), 93–138.

Fehr, Ernst, Urs Fischbacher and Simon Gächter, 'Strong Reciprocity, Human Cooperation, and the Enforcement of Social Norms', *Human Nature* 13, no. 1 (2002), 1–25.

Fellner, Robert, *Die fränkische Ritterschaft von 1495–1524* (Berlin, 1905).

Fischer, Mattias G., *Reichsreform und 'Ewiger Landfrieden': Über die Entwicklung des Fehderechts im 15. Jahrhundert bis zum absoluten Fehdeverbot von 1495* (Aalen, 2007).

Frank, Robert H., *Passions within Reason* (New York, 1988).

Frey, Joseph, 'Die Fehde der Herren von Rosenberg auf Boxberg mit dem Schwäbischen Bund und ihre Nachwirkungen (1523–1555)', PhD thesis, University of Tübingen, 1924.

Fritz, Thomas, *Ulrich der Vielgeliebte (1441–1480): Ein Württemberger im Herbst des Mittelalters. Zur Geschichte der württembergischen Politik im Spannungsfeld zwischen Hausmacht, Region und Reich* (Leinfelden-Echterdingen, 1999).

Fugger, Eberhard Graf von, *Die Seinsheim und ihre Zeit: Eine Familien- und Kulturgeschichte von 1155 bis 1890* (Munich, 1893).

Gambetta, Diego, *The Sicilian Mafia: The Business of Private Protection* (Cambridge, Mass., 1993).

'Can We Make Sense of Suicide Missions?' in *Making Sense of Suicide Missions*, ed. Diego Gambetta (Oxford, 2006), 259–99.

Giersch, Robert, Andreas Schlunk and Berthold von Haller, *Burgen und Herrensitze in der Nürnberger Landschaft* (Lauf, 2006).

Görner, Regina, *Raubritter: Untersuchungen zur Lage des spätmittelalterlichen Niederadels, besonders im südlichen Westfalen* (Münster in Westfalen, 1987).

Graf, Klaus, 'Gewalt und Adel in Südwestdeutschland: Überlegungen zur spätmittelalterlichen Fehde', *Online-Reprint eines Beitrags auf dem Bielefelder Kolloquium 'Gewalt' am 29.11.1998*; www.histsem. uni-freiburg.de/mertens/graf/gewalt.htm (2000).

Grötsch, A., 'Eine blutige Ritterfehde aus dem 16. Jahrhundert (Familie Streitberg)', *Die Oberpfalz* 16 (1922), 119–20.

Guerreau, Alain, 'L'honneur blessé (note critique)', *Annales E.S.C* 48, no. 1 (1993), 227–33.

Gutkas, Karl, *Geschichte Niederösterreichs* (Vienna, 1984).

Guttenberg, Erich von, *Das Bistum Bamberg*, part 1 (Berlin, 1937).

Haidt, Jonathan, and Craig Joseph, 'Intuitive Ethics: How Innately Prepared Intuitions Generate Culturally Variable Virtues', *Daedalus* (Fall 2004), 55–66.

Heinig, Paul-Joachim, *Kaiser Friedrich III. (1440–1493): Hof, Regierung und Politik*, 3 vols. (Cologne, 1997).

Herlihy, David, 'Some Psychological and Social Roots of Violence in the Tuscan Cities', in *Violence and Civil Disorder in Italian Cities 1200–1500*, ed. Lauro Martines (Berkeley, 1972), 129–54.

Herrmann, M., *Albrecht von Eyb und die Frühzeit des deutschen Humanismus* (Berlin, 1893).

Herzfeld, M., 'Honour and Shame: Problems in the Comparative Analysis of Moral Systems', *Man*, n.s., 15 (1980), 339–51.

Hill, J., 'Prestige and Reproductive Success in Man', *Ethology and Sociobiology* 5 (1984), 77–95.

Höfler, Constantin, 'Betrachtungen über das deutsche Städtewesen im XV. und XVI. Jahrhunderte', *Archiv für Kunde österreichischer Geschichts-Quellen* 11 (1853), 177–229.

Jackson, William H., 'Tournaments and the German Chivalric *renovatio*: Tournament Discipline and the Myth of Origins', in *Chivalry in the Renaissance*, ed. Sydney Anglo (Woodbridge, 1990), 77–91.

Jendorff, Alexander, and Steffen Krieb, 'Adel im Konflikt: Beobachtungen zu den Austragungsformen der Fehde im Spätmittelalter', *ZHF* 30 (2003), 179–206.

Jouanna, Arlette, 'Recherches sur la notion d'honneur au XVIème siècle', *Revue d'histoire moderne et contemporaine* 15 (1968), 597–623.

Kamann, Johann, *Die Fehde des Götz von Berlichingen mit der Reichsstadt Nürnberg und dem Hochstifte Bamberg 1512–1514* (Nuremberg, 1893).

Kaminsky, Howard, 'The Noble Feud in the Later Middle Ages', *Past and Present* 177 (2002), 55–83.

Kaplan, Hillard, and Kim Hill, 'Hunting Ability and Reproductive Success among Male Ache Foragers: Preliminary Results', *Current Anthropology* 26, no. 1 (1985), 131–3.

Keen, Maurice, *Chivalry* (New Haven, 1984).

Kipp, Friedrich, *Silvester von Schaumberg, der Freund Luthers: Ein Lebensbild aus der Reformationszeit* (Leipzig, 1911).

Kleinschmidt, Harald, 'Disziplinierung zum Kampf: Neue Forschungen zum Wandel militärischer Verhaltensweisen im 15. und 16. Jahrhundert', *Blätter für deutsche Landesgeschichte* 132 (1996), 173–200.

Kortüm, Hans-Henning, '"Wissenschaft im Doppelpaß"? Carl Schmitt, Otto Brunner und die Konstruktion der Fehde', *HZ* 282 (2006), 585–617.

Leinweber, J., *Das Hochstift Fulda vor der Reformation* (Fulda, 1972).

Lentz, Matthias, *Konflikt, Ehre, Ordnung: Untersuchungen zu den Schmähbriefen und Schandbildern des späten Mittelalters und der frühen Neuzeit (ca. 1350 bis 1600); Mit einem illustrierten Katalog der Überlieferung* (Hanover, 2004).

Looshorn, Johann, *Die Geschichte des Bisthums Bamberg*, vol. IV, *Das Bisthum Bamberg von 1400–1556* (Munich, 1900).

Merz, Johannes, *Fürst und Herrschaft: Der Herzog von Franken und seine Nachbarn 1470–1519* (Munich, 2000).

Merzbacher, Friedrich, 'Johann Freiherr zu Schwarzenberg', *Fränkische Lebensbilder* 4 (1971), 173–85.

Miller, Geoffrey, *The Mating Mind: How Sexual Choice Shaped the Evolution of Human Nature* (New York, 2000).

Molho, Anthony, *Marriage Alliance in Late Medieval Florence* (Cambridge, Mass., 1994).

Morsel, Joseph, 'Le tournoi, mode d'éducation politique en Allemagne à la fin du Moyen Âge', in *Education, apprentissages, initiation au Moyen Âge: Actes du premier colloque international de Montpellier*, vol. II (Montpellier, 1993), 309–31.

'"Das sy sich mitt der besstenn gewarsamig schicken, das sy durch die widerwertigenn Franckenn nit nidergeworffen werdenn": Überlegungen zum sozialen Sinn der Fehdepraxis am Beispiel des spätmittelalterlichen Franken', in *Strukturen der Gesellschaft im Mittelalter: Interdisziplinäre Mediävistik in Würzburg*, ed. Dieter Rödel and Joachim Schneider (Wiesbaden, 1996), 140–67.

La noblesse contre le prince: L'espace sociale des Thüngen à la fin du Moyen Âge (Franconie, vers 1250–1525) (Sigmaringen, 2000).

Most, Ingeborg, 'Schiedsgericht, rechtliches Rechtsgebot, ordentliches Gericht, Kammergericht: Zur Technik fürstlicher Politik im 15. Jahrhundert', in *Aus Reichstagen des 15. und 16. Jahrhunderts* (Göttingen, 1958), 116–53.

Muir, Edward, *Mad Blood Stirring: Vendetta and Factions in Friuli during the Renaissance* (Baltimore, 1993).

Müller, Uwe, *Die ständische Vertretung in den fränkischen Markgraftümern in der ersten Hälfte des 16. Jahrhunderts* (Neustadt a.d. Aisch, 1984).

Neumaier, Helmut, *'Das wir kein anderes Haupt oder von Gott eingesetzte zeitliche Obrigkeit haben'*: Ort Odenwald der fränkischen Reichsritterschaft von den Anfängen bis zum Dreißigjährigen Krieg (Stuttgart, 2005).

Neuschel, Kristen B., *Word of Honor: Interpreting Noble Culture in Sixteenth-Century France* (Ithaca, 1989).

Noflatscher, Heinz, *Räte und Herrscher: Politische Eliten an den Habsburgerhöfen der österrreichischen Länder, 1480–1530* (Mainz, 1999).

Nye, R. A., 'Honor Codes in Modern France: A Historical Anthropology', *Ethnologia Europae* 21 (1991).

Obenaus, Herbert, *Recht und Verfassung der Gesellschaft mit St Jörgenschild in Schwaben: Untersuchungen über Adel, Einung, Schiedsgericht und Fehde im fünfzehnten Jahrhundert* (Göttingen, 1961).

Oesterreicher, Paul, *Die Burg Streitberg* (Bamberg, 1819).

Geschichtliche Darstellung der Burg Neideck (Bamberg, 1824).

Pappenheim, Haupt Graf zu, *Die frühen Pappenheimer Marschälle. Zweiter Teil der Hausgeschichte vom* XV. *bis zum* XVIII. *Jahrhundert* (Munich-Solln, 1951).

Paravicini, Werner, *Die ritterlich-höfische Kultur des Mittelalters* (Munich, 1994).

Patschovsky, Alexander, 'Fehde im Recht: Eine Problemskizze', in *Recht und Reich im Zeitalter der Reformation*, ed. Christine Roll (Frankfurt am Main, 1996), 145–78.

Peristiany, J. G. (ed.), *Honour and Shame: The Values of Mediterranean Society* (London, 1965).

Press, Volker, 'Wilhelm von Grumbach und die deutsche Adelskrise der 1560er Jahre', *Blätter für deutsche Landesgeschichte* 113 (1977), 396–431.

Kaiser Karl V., König Ferdinand und die Entstehung der Reichsritterschaft, 2nd edn (Wiesbaden, 1980).

Rabeler, Sven, *Niederadlige Lebensformen im späten Mittelalter: Wilwolt von Schaumberg (um 1450–1510) und Ludwig von Eyb d.J. (1450–1521)* (Würzburg, 2006).

Ranft, Andreas, 'Turniere der vier Lande: Genossenschaftlicher Hof und Selbstbehauptung des niederen Adels', *Zeitschrift für die Geschichte des Oberrheins* 142 (1994), 83–102.

Adelsgesellschaften: Gruppenbildung und Genossenschaft im spätmittelalterlichen Reich (Sigmaringen, 1994).

'Einer von Adel: Zu adligem Selbstverständnis und Krisenbewußtsein im 15. Jahrhundert', *HZ* 263 (1996), 317–343.

Rechter, Gerhard, *Die Seckendorff: Quellen und Studien zur Genealogie und Besitzgeschichte*, 3 vols. (Neustadt a.d. Aisch, 1987–97).

Reinle, Christine, *Ulrich Riederer (ca. 1406–1462): Gelehrter Rat im Dienste Kaiser Friedrichs III.* (Mannheim, 1993).

Bauernfehden: Studien zur Fehdeführung Nichtadliger im spätmittelalterlichen römisch-deutschen Reich, besonders in den bayerischen Herzogtümern (Stuttgart, 2003).

'Fehden im Spannungsfeld von Landesherrschaft, Adel und bäuerlicher Bevölkerung', in *Tradition und Erinnerung in Adelsherrschaft und bäuerlicher Gesellschaft*, ed. Werner Rösener (Göttingen, 2003), 173–94.

'Fehden und Fehdebekämpfung am Ende des Mittelalters: Überlegungen zum Auseinandertreten von "Frieden" und "Recht" in der politischen

Praxis zu Beginn des 16. Jahrhunderts am Beispiel der Absberg-Fehde', *ZHF* 30 (2003), 355–88.

'Bauerngewalt und Macht der Herren: Bauernfehden zwischen Gewohnheitsrecht und Verbot', in *Gewalt im Mittelalter: Realitäten-Imaginationen*, ed. Manuel Braun (Munich, 2005), 105–22.

'Umkämpfter Friede: Politischer Gestaltungswille und geistlicher Normenhorizont bei der Fehdebekämpfung im deutschen Spätmittelalter', in *Rechtsveränderung im politischen und sozialen Kontext mittelalterlicher Rechtsvielfalt*, ed. Stefan Esders and Christine Reinle (Münster, 2005), 147–74.

'Fehdefürung und Fehdebekämpfung am Ende des Mittelalters', in *Der Altenburger Prinzenraub 1455: Strukturen und Mentalitäten eines spätmittelalterlichen Konflikts*, ed. Joachim Emig, Wolfgang Enke, Guntram Martin, Uwe Schirmer and Andre Thieme (Beucha, 2007), 83–124.

'"Fehde" und gewaltsame Selbsthilfe in England und im römisch-deutschen Reich', in *Akten des 36. Deutschen Rechtshistorikertages*, ed. Rolf Lieberwirth and Heiner Lück (Zurich, 2008), 99–132.

Ridley, Matt, *The Red Queen: Sex and the Evolution of Human Nature* (Harmondsworth, 1993).

The Origins of Virtue (Harmondsworth, 1996).

Ritzmann, Peter, '"Plackerey in teutschen Landen": Untersuchungen zur Fehdetätigkeit des fränkischen Adels im frühen 16. Jahrhundert und ihrer Bekämpfung durch den Schwäbischen Bund und die Reichsstadt Nürnberg, insbesondere am Beispiel des Hans Thomas von Absberg und seiner Auseinandersetzung mit den Grafen von Oettingen (1520–31)', PhD thesis, University of Munich, 1993.

Rotenhan, Gottfried von, *Die Rotenhan: Genealogie einer fränkischen Familie von 1229 bis zum Dreißigjährigen Krieg* (Neustadt a.d. Aisch, 1985).

'Streit und Fehde um die Burg Stuffenberg bei Baunach 1460/66', *Bericht des Historischen Vereins Bamberg* 129 (1993), 75–90.

Roth, Johann Ferdinand, *Geschichte des Nuernbergischen Handels*, vol. 1 (Leipzig, 1800).

Ruff, Julius R., *Violence in Early Modern Europe, 1500–1800* (Cambridge, 2001).

Rupprecht, Klaus, *Ritterschaftliche Herrschaftswahrung in Franken: Die Geschichte der von Guttenberg im Spätmittelalter und zu Beginn der Frühen Neuzeit* (Neustadt a.d. Aisch, 1994).

'Vom Landfriedensbündnis zur Adelseinung: Genossenschaftliche Organisationsformen im spätmittelaterlichen Franken', in *Franken im Mittelalter: Francia orientalis, Franconia, Land zu Franken: Raum und Geschichte*, ed. Johannes Merz and Robert Schuh (Munich, 2004), 101–19.

Sablonier, Roger, *Adel im Wandel: Eine Untersuchung zur sozialen Situation des ostschweizerischen Adels um 1300* (Göttingen, 1979).

Sanderson, Stephen K., *The Evolution of Human Sociality: A Darwinian Conflict Perspective* (Lanham, Md, 2001).

Schaumberg, Oskar von, *Neuaufstellungen der Stammtafeln des uradelig fränkischen Geschlechts von Schaumberg* (Bamberg, 1953).

Schieber, Martin, '"Auf das sie also die Milch Gottes Worts mit Nutz und Freuden mugen drincken": Die Ganerbschaft Rothenberg als lutherisches Territorium 1529–1629', in *Frömmigkeit, Theologie, Frömmigkeitstheologie: Contribution to European Church History: Festschrift für Berndt Hamm zum 60. Geburtstag*, ed. Gudrun Litz (Leiden and Boston, 2005), 483–96.

Schirmer, Uwe, 'Kunz von Kaufungen und der Prinzenraub zu Altenburg (1455): Strukturen eines mittelalterlichen Konflikts', *ZHF* 32 (2005), 369–405.

Schmid, Peter, *Der Gemeine Pfennig von 1495: Vorgeschichte und Entstehung, verfassungsgeschichtliche, politische und finanzielle Bedeutung* (Göttingen, 1989).

Schmitt, Richard, *Frankenberg: Besitz- und Wirtschaftsgeschichte einer reichsritterschaftlichen Herrschaft in Franken, 1528–1806 (1848)* (Ansbach, 1986).

Schmitt, Sigrid, 'Schutz und Schirm oder Gewalt und Unterdrückung? Überlegungen zu Gadi Algazis Dissertation "Herrengewalt und Gewalt der Herren in späten Mittelalter"', *Vierteljahrschrift für Sozial- und Wirtschaftsgeschichte* 89 (2002), 72–8.

Schneider, Joachim, 'Legitime Selbstbehauptung oder Verbrechen: Soziale und politische Konflikte in der spätmittelalterlichen Chronistik am Beispiel der Nürnberger Strafjustiz und des Süddeutschen Fürstenkriegs von 1458–1463', in *Schriftlichkeit und Lebenspraxis im Mittelalter: Erfassen, Bewahren, Verändern*, ed. Hagen Keller, Christel Meier and Thomas Scharff (Munich, 1999), 219–41.

Spätmittelalterlicher deutscher Niederadel: Ein landschaftlicher Vergleich (Stuttgart, 2003).

'Die Wetterauer Ganerbenverbände im Zusammenhang landschaftlicher Adelseinungen und Hoforden: Zu einer vergleichenden Landesgeschichte des Reiches im späten Mittelalter', *ZHF* 31 (2004), 529–49.

Schubert, Ernst, *Die Landstände des Hochstifts Würzburg* (Würzburg, 1967).

Schultes, Johann Adolph, *Diplomatische Geschichte des Gräflichen Hauses Henneberg*, 2 parts (Hildburghausen, 1788–91).

Schütz, Martin, 'Die Ganerbschaft Rothenberg in ihrer politischen, juristischen und wirtschaftlichen Bedeutung', PhD thesis, University of Erlangen, 1924.

Schwarzenberg, Karl Fürst zu, *Geschichte des reichsständischen Hauses Schwarzenberg* (Neustadt a.d. Aisch, 1963).

Schweier, Thomas, *Feudalismus in den Artusepopöen Hartmanns von Aue? Kritik der Schriften Otto Brunners im Rahmen sozialgeschichtlicher Interpretationen* (Würzburg, 2004).

Seabright, Paul, *The Company of Strangers: A Natural History of Economic Life* (Princeton, 2004).

Seefried, Otto, *Aus dem Stiebar-Archiv: Forschungen zur Familiengeschichte von Bauer, Bürger und Edelmann in Ober- und Mittelfranken* (Nuremberg, 1953).

Seyboth, Reinhard, *Die Markgraftümer Ansbach und Kulmbach unter der Regierung Markgraf Friedrichs des Älteren (1486–1515)* (Göttingen, 1985).

'"Raubritter" und Landesherren: Zum Problem territorialer Friedenswahrung im späten Mittelalter am Beispiel der Markgrafen von Ansbach-Kulmbach', in *'Raubritter' oder 'Rechtsschaffene vom Adel'? Aspekte von Politik, Friede und Recht im späten Mittelalter*, ed. Kurt Andermann (Sigmaringen, 1997), 115–31.

Simmel, Georg, *Soziologie: Untersuchungen über die Formen der Vergesellschaftung* (Leipzig, 1908).

Spielberg, Werner, 'Martin Zollner von Rothenstein und seine Sippe', parts 1 and 2, *Familiengeschichtliche Blätter* 15 (1917), 129–36; 167–80.

Spieß, Karl-Heinz, *Familie und Verwandtschaft im deutschen Hochadel des Spätmittelalters: 13. bis Anfang des 16. Jahrhunderts* (Stuttgart, 1993).

'Aufstieg in den Adel und Kriterien der Adelszugehörigkeit im Spätmittelalter', in *Zwischen Nicht-Adel und Adel*, ed. Kurt Andermann and Peter Johanek (Stuttgart, 2001), 1–26.

Sprandel, Rolf, 'Die territorialen Ämter des Fürstentums Würzburg im Spätmittelalter', *JffL* 37 (1977), 45–64.

'Das Raubrittertum und die Entstehung des öffentlichen Strafrechts', *Saeculum* 57 (2006), 61–76.

Stälin, Christoph Friedrich von, *Wirtembergische Geschichte*, part 3: *Schwaben und Südfranken: Schluß des Mittelalters, 1296–1496* (Stuttgart, 1856).

Stauber, Reinhard, *Herzog Georg von Bayern-Landshut und seine Reichspolitik: Möglichkeiten und Grenzen reichsfürstlicher Politik im wittelsbachisch-habsburgischen Spannungsfeld zwischen 1470 und 1505* (Kallmünz, 1993).

Steinau-Steinrück, Richard von, 'Abriß aus der Geschichte des fränkischen Geschlechtes von Steinau genannt Steinrück in bezug auf seine Zugehörigkeit zu dem Hochstifte Würzburg und im besonderen auf seine Besitzungen daselbst', *AU* 49 (1907), 1–134.

Steinhofer, Johann Ulrich, *Neue Wirtembergische Chronik*, vol. II (Stuttgart, 1746).

Taddey, Gerhard, 'Macht und Recht im späten Mittelalter: Die Auseinandersetzungen zwischen Hohenlohe und Hessen um die Grafschaften Ziegenhain und Nidda', *Württembergisch Franken* 61 (1977), 79–110.

Tilly, Charles, 'War Making and State Making as Organized Crime', in *Bringing the State Back In*, ed. Peter B. Evans, Dietrich Rueschemeyer and Theda Skocpol (Cambridge, 1985), 169–91.

Trivers, Robert, 'The Evolution of Reciprocal Altruism', *Quarterly Review of Biology* 46 (1971), 35–57.

Turke, Paul W., and L. L. Betzig, 'Those Who Can Do: Wealth, Status, and Reproductive Success on Ifaluk', *Ethology and Sociobiology* 6 (1985), 79–87.

Ulmschneider, Helgard, *Götz von Berlichingen: Ein adeliges Leben der deutschen Renaissance* (Sigmaringen, 1974).

Ulrichs, Cord, *Vom Lehnhof zur Reichsritterschaft: Strukturen des fränkischen Niederadels am Übergang vom späten Mittelalter zur frühen Neuzeit* (Stuttgart, 1997).

Veesenmeyer, Georg, 'Nachricht von zwei Rosenbergischen Fehden: (1) Jörgen, Adolphs und Friedrichs von Rosenberg mit dem Bistume Würzburg, 1486; (2) Jörgen von Rosenberg mit Asmus, Grafen von Wertheim, 1501–1502', *Verhandlungen des Vereins für Kunst und Alterthum in Ulm und Oberschwaben* 12 (1860), 41–56.

Vogel, Thomas, *Fehderecht und Fehdepraxis im Spätmittelalter am Beispiel der Reichsstadt Nürnberg (1404–1438)* (Frankfurt am Main, 1998).

Volckart, Oliver, 'The Economics of Feuding in Late Medieval Germany', *Explorations in Economic History* 41 (2004), 282–99.

Wagenhöfer, Werner, *Die Bibra: Studien und Materialien zur Genealogie und zur Besitzgeschichte einer fränkischen Niederadelsfamilie im Spätmittelalter* (Neustadt a.d. Aisch, 1998).

Weiss, Dieter, 'Franken am Ausgang des späten Mittelalters', in *Handbuch der Bayerischen Geschichte*, vol. III, part 1, *Geschichte Frankens bis zum Ausgang des 18. Jahrhundert*, ed. Andreas Kraus (Munich, 1997), 427–50.

Wendehorst, Alfred, *Das Bistum Würzburg*, vols. II and III (Berlin, 1969–78).

Wendehorst, Alfred, and Gerhard Rechter, 'Ein Geldverleiher im spätmittelalterlichen Franken: Philipp von Seckendorff-Gutend', in *Hochfinanz, Wirtschaftsräume, Innovationen: Festschrift für Wolfgang von Stromer*, ed. Uwe Bestmann, Franz Irsigler and Jürgen Schneider, vol. I (Trier, 1987), 487–529.

Wilhelm, H., 'Die Edeln von und zum Absberg: Ein Beitrag zur fränkischen Geschichte', *Alt-Gunzenhausen* 8 (1931), 3–197.

Wilmowsky, Hubertus von, 'Die Geschichte der Ritterschaft Buchenau von ihren Anfängen bis zum Wiener Kongreß', *Fuldaer Geschichtsblätter* 40 (1964), 1–47.

Wilson, Margo, and Martin Daly, 'Competitiveness, Risk Taking, and Violence: The Young Male Syndrome', *Ethology and Sociobiology* 6 (1985), 59–73.

Wright, Robert, *The Moral Animal: Evolutionary Psychology and Everyday Life* (New York, 1994).

Würdinger, Joseph, *Kriegsgeschichte von Bayern, Franken, Pfalz und Schwaben von 1347 bis 1506*, 2 vols. (Munich, 1868).

Zeißner, Sebastian, 'Dr Kilian von Bibra: Dompropst von Würzburg (ca. 1426–1494)', *Mainfränkisches Jahrbuch für Geschichte und Kunst* 2 (1950), 78–121.

Rudolf II. von Scherenberg: Fürstbischof von Würzburg 1466–1495, 2nd edn (Würzburg, 1952).

Zmora, Hillay, 'Adelige Ehre und ritterliche Fehde: Franken im Spätmittelalter', in *Verletzte Ehre: Ehrkonflikte in Gesellschaften des*

Mittelalters und der Frühen Neuzeit, ed. Klaus Schreiner and Gerd Schwerhoff (Cologne, 1995), 92–109.

State and Nobility in Early Modern Germany: The Knightly Feud in Franconia, 1440–1567 (Cambridge, 1997).

'The Princely State and the Noble Family: Conflict and Co-operation in the Margraviates Ansbach-Kulmbach in the Fifteenth and Sixteenth Century', *The Historical Journal* 49, no. 1 (2006) 1–21.

'The Formation of the Imperial Knighthood in Franconia: A Comparative European Perspective', in *The Holy Roman Empire, 1495–1806*, ed. R. J. W. Evans, Michael Schaich and Peter H. Wilson (Oxford, 2011), 283–302.

Index